The Cultural Transition

The Cultural Transition

Human experience and social transformation in the Third World and Japan

---

Edited by Merry I. White and Susan Pollak

ROUTLEDGE & KEGAN PAUL

Boston, London and Henley

First published in 1986
by Routledge & Kegan Paul plc

9 Park Street, Boston, Mass. 02108, USA

14 Leicester Square, London WC2H 7PH, England and

Broadway House, Newtown Road,
Henley on Thames, Oxon RG9 1EN, England

Set in Times, 10 on 12pt
by Inforum Ltd of Portsmouth
and printed in Great Britain
by T.J. Press (Padstow) Ltd,
Padstow, Cornwall.

Library of Congress Cataloging in Publication Data

The Cultural transition.

Includes index.
1. Social change—Cross-cultural studies—Addresses,
essays, lectures. 2. Social role—Cross-cultural
studies—Addresses, essays, lectures. 3. Ethnopsychology
—Addresses, essays, lectures. 4. Educational anthropology—Addresses, essays, lectures. I. White, Merry I.
II. Pollak, Susan.
GN358.C85   1985   303.4'8   85–2182

ISBN 0-7102-0572-4

CONTENTS

v

Contents

Notes on contributors

Alfred Collins received his B.A. from the University of Chicago, and an M.A. and two Ph.D.'s from the University of Texas at Austin, where he went after Chicago to work with Gardner Lindzey. He holds doctorate degrees in Indian Studies and Clinical Psychology. He is a psychoanalyst-in-training through the Chicago C. G. Jung Institute. His publications range from physiological psychology, to a reconsideration of the Rig-Vedic 'Hymn of Creation,' to several Jungian pieces on films and popular music.

Veena Das is professor of Sociology at the University of Delhi, where she has taught since 1969. She has also taught for brief periods at the University of Chicago and at Harvard. Her publications include *Structure and Cognition* and *Aspects of Hindu Caste and Ritual*, Oxford University Press, which was the winner of the Ghurye Award for 1977.

Prakash Desai is a psychiatrist, Chief of the Psychiatry Service at the Veterans Administration West Side Medical Center in Chicago. He has practised and taught in Chicago since 1964, having received his M.D. from M.S. University in Baroda, India in 1962. His many publications include *The Indian mind and the western science of Psychiatry* and 'Indian immigrants in America: some cultural aspects of psychological adaptation' in Saran and Eames (eds) *New Ethnics, Asian Indians in the US* (Praeger, 1980).

Notes on contributors

Sumiko Iwao is a professor of Social Psychology at Keio University in Japan. She is best known for her studies on the effects of television violence on children in Japan and the United States. She is also the author of numerous cross-cultural studies, and has lectured widely in the US, Europe and Australia.

Sudhir Kakar is a psychoanalyst, associated with the Center for the Study of Developing Societies, Delhi. He is the author of *Shamans, Mystics and Doctors* (Knopf, 1982) and *The Inner World* (Oxford University Press, 1980).

Richard Katz is currently Associate Professor at the Harvard Graduate School of Education. His research focuses on healing as a generic phenomenon underlying processes of education, therapy and development; the education of healers; the development of models of community in which valued resources are shared and expanding. His primary field-work has been in the Kalahari Desert with the !Kung San, and in the Fiji Islands with indigenous Fijians. His most recent book is *Boiling Energy: Community Healing Among the Kalahari !Kung* (Harvard Press, 1982).

B.K. Ramanujam is a psychiatrist practicing in New York City. He has published on subjects ranging from mental retardation to the changing role of the Indian family.

Lamin Sanneh is a professor of comparative religion at the Harvard Divinity School. He was educated in the Gambia and Britain, and received his Ph.D. from The School of Oriental and African Studies at the University of London. His publications include *The Jakhanke*, International African Institute, 1979, and *West African Christianity, The Religious Impact* (Hurst, 1983).

Julia Shiang is the originator and former Director of The Learning Cooperative, Inc., a non-profit parent–teacher communication project in New Haven, Connecticut. She received her Master's Degree from Bank Street College of Education and her doctorate from Harvard University. Her current work centers on the impact of cultural values on the parent–child relationship, with a special focus on the concerns of the Chinese-American elderly and their adult children. She is a psychotherapist at the Clifford Beers Child Guidance Clinic in New Haven, Connecticut.

Jennifer E. Spratt is a doctoral candidate in cross-cultural human development at the Graduate School of Education at the University of Pennsylvania. She received her undergraduate degree in African History at Yale University in 1978, and served as a Peace Corps volunteer in Morocco from 1978 to 1980.

Lois Taniuchi is a doctoral candidate in Human Development at the Harvard Graduate School of Education. She is presently completing her dissertation on the Suzuki Method of Musical Training.

Carlos E. Vasco is a Jesuit priest and an Associate Professor of Mathematics at the Graduate School of the National University of Colombia. His publications range from papers on logic and science education to a book on the history of Renaissance algebra and a five-volume series on the application of General Systems theory to educational change.

Daniel A. Wagner is an Associate Professor at the Graduate School of Education and Director of the Literacy Research Center at the University of Pennsylvania. Dr Wagner has recently edited *Child Development and International Development: Research-policy Interfaces* (Jossey-Bass, 1983), and with Harold Stevenson, *Cultural Perspectives on Child Development* (Freeman, 1982).

Merry I. White served as Director of the Project on Human Potential. She is a Lecturer at the Harvard Graduate School of Education and Administrator of the East Asian Studies Program at Harvard. A specialist on modern Japanese society, she is co-author with Robert A. LeVine of *Human Conditions: The Cultural Basis of Educational Development* (Routledge & Kegan Paul, 1985).

Susan Pollak was a principal researcher at the Van Leer Project, producing a major survey of pre-modern schooling as well as philosophical essays on the concept of the person. She is currently a clinical intern at the Harvard University Health Services. Her published work includes reviews in *Psychology Today* as well as scholarly articles.

ACKNOWLEDGMENTS

This collection has been achieved through the efforts and contributions of many people. We would like to acknowledge first the support we have received from the Bernard van Leer Foundation, in creating the Project on Human Potential at the Harvard Graduate School of Education. The Foundation's vision and confidence made this venture possible, and we would particularly like to thank Mr Oscar van Leer and Dr Willem Welling for their encouragement and support.

Our colleagues on the Project have, through their constant encouragement and contributions, made this volume a reality. Prof. Robert A. LeVine, as director of cross-cultural research for the Project, provided us with a framework, as well as with enthusiastic intellectual stimulus. Gerald Lesser, Howard Gardner, and Israel Scheffler, in our many Project discussions, probed and queried and acted as most sympathetic gadflies. Professors Paul Ylvisaker and Francis Keppel helped oversee our efforts over the term of the Project. Leonie Gordon helped organize meetings and prepared many reports on our cross-cultural workshops: her syntheses were very useful in preparing an overview for this book. Our friends and staff members who have seen the book through from draft to draft are the very backbone of the operation. We'd like to thank especially Dorothy Appel, Margaret Herzig, Laura Stephens-Swannie, Damaris Chapin and Nan Kortz.

Finally, but with deepest appreciation, we would like to thank the authors of the essays in this volume, and their associates whose work does not appear here but which formed such a significant part

Acknowledgments

of our Project. To our colleagues in West Africa, the People's Republic of China, India, Egypt, Mexico and Japan, we owe the deepest debt of gratitude and hope that they will see this book as only the beginning of our collaboration and friendship.

MERRY I. WHITE
SUSAN POLLAK

Cambridge, Mass., October 1984

NOTE ON THE PROJECT ON HUMAN POTENTIAL

The Bernard van Leer Foundation of The Hague, Netherlands is an international non profit-making institution dedicated to the cause of disadvantaged children and youth. It supports innovative projects that develop community approaches to early childhood education and child care, in order to help disadvantaged children to realize their potential.

In 1979, the Foundation asked the Harvard Graduate School of Education to assess the state of scientific knowledge concerning human potential and its realization. Proceeding from this general directive, a group of scholars at Harvard has over the past several years been engaged in research exploring the nature and realization of human potential. Activities sponsored by the Project on Human Potential have included reviews of relevant literature in history, philosophy, and the natural and social sciences, a series of international workshops on conceptions of human development in diverse cultural traditions, and the commissioning of papers and books.

The principal investigators of the Project represent a variety of fields and interests. Gerald S. Lesser, who chaired the Project's steering committee, is an educator and developmental psychologist, a principal architect in the creation of educational television programs for children. Howard Gardner is a psychologist who has studied the development of symbolic skills in normal and gifted children, and the impairment of such skills in brain-damaged adults. Israel Scheffler is a philosopher who has worked in the areas of philosophy of education, philosophy of science, and philosophy of language. Robert LeVine, a social anthropologist, has worked in sub-saharan Africa and Mexico, studying family life, child care and psychological development. Merry White is a sociologist and Japan specialist who has studied education, formal organizations and the roles of women in the Third World and Japan. This wide range of interests and disciplines enabled the Project to take a multi-faceted approach to issues of human potential.

The first volume published under the aegis of the Project was Howard Gardner's *Frames of Mind* (Basic Books, 1983), a study of human intellectual potentials which drew not only on psychological research but also on the biological sciences and on findings about the development and use of knowledge in different cultures.

Israel Scheffler's *Of Human Potential* (RKP, 1985) was the second book of the Project to appear, and it offers a treatment of philosophical aspects of the concept of potential. Sketching the background of the concept and placing it in the context of a general theory of human nature, this treatment then proposes three analytical reconstructions of the concept and offers systematic reflections on policy and the education of policy makers.

Human Conditions: The Cultural Basis of Educational Development, by Robert A. LeVine and Merry I. White, will be published in 1986 by Routledge & Kegan Paul. Emphasizing the crucial role of cultural factors in the progress of human development, the book offers new models for development based on the social anthropology of the life span and the social history of family and school.

To provide background for the study of diversity in development, the Project established teams of consultants in Egypt, India, Japan, Mexico, the People's Republic of China, and West Africa. The present volume, *The Cultural Transition*, edited by Merry I. White and Susan Pollak, presents papers by these consultants and associates. Representatives of international development agencies were also engaged as consultants and advisors over the five-year period of the Project. Through such international dialogue and research, the Project has sought to create a new multidisciplinary environment for understanding human potential.

The Hague, Netherlands, August 1985

INTRODUCTION

Transitions imply movement from one state or condition to another state or condition, but also imply an intermediate waystation. In considering what has variously been called modernization, development, or in less deterministic language, social transformation, in the context of human lives, the 'transition,' in our view, never ends, and yet there are many possible visions of the termini. There are, of course, more universal goals for development planners, targets for those who hope to raise the level of literacy, health and production while improving general social welfare. And the political and economic environments in which these planners operate have very often imbued these goals with the urgency of their ideologies or cost/benefit analyses. What has been left out of the planning and the goal-setting is the factor which, paradoxically, must be considered before planning can be effective and yet which, if taken seriously, ultimately prevents the success of the more universalistic goals and targets, which keeps social transformation in permanent transition: that is, *culture*. While developers categorize nations as 'poor' or 'advanced,' while they develop paradigms and seize upon models which will improve the potential for success in less developed societies, attention is seldom given to the whole range of less easily categorized and less translatable human conditions and the local explanations and belief system organizing them into cultural experiences which might enrich and complicate policymakers' perceptions.

Not to see folk healing as an obstacle to the dissemination of western medical care, or the modern school as the only means for

1

socializing children to appropriate lives requires a major departure from conventional development thinking. Culture might be 'controlled' through typologies, or placated through superficial attention in the visitation of alien programs on the less developed. More frequently, however, the poor or non-modern are seen as a 'treatment category.' But poverty is not a culture and 'less developed' characterizes no people on earth in a useful way.

The project which produced this collection, as well as several other volumes, was established in part to consider what role culture has to play in successful human development planning. The Bernard van Leer Foundation in the Hague came to Harvard University in 1978 to establish a study of human potential which would provide background in the social and behavioral sciences for the work of international agencies in child development and education. The Project on Human Potential, based at the Harvard Graduate School of Education from September 1979 to September 1984, brought together scholars from the fields of anthropology, sociology, developmental psychology, and philosophy as principal investigators in a broad survey of learning and human development. The project also established teams of counterpart scholars and practitioners in several countries and regions: Japan, India, West Africa, Egypt, Mexico, and the People's Republic of China.

Out of meetings and workshops held in these places and elsewhere came the essays contained in this volume, which represent the wide range of topics considered but which unfortunately, because of lack of space, do not include the full wealth of detail and analysis which was provided by all participants. Many of the other papers written for the Project are available through ERIC (Educational Resources Information Center – Department of Education Washington) and a full list of these may be found in an Appendix.

These papers and the conversations and formal discussions which both contributed to and benefited from their creation also provide a kind of text resource for the conceptualization of the cultural perspective on educational development which informs another volume in the Project's series, *Human Conditions: The Cultural Basis of Educational Development*, co-authored by Robert A. LeVine and Merry I. White (Routledge & Kegan Paul, 1986). This book treats human development from an anthropological perspective, as the product of cultural influences and motivations, and establishes a model for considering the meaning of learning over the life course in traditional agrarian societies as well as modern industrialized nations. The papers in *The Cultural Transition* provide exemplary material which supports the premises of our *cultural* perspective on development.

The essays in this volume fall into three categories: those dealing with indigenous psychologies of the person and contexts, such as religious conversion, influencing personal change; those treating the social organization and local interpretation of learning; and those focused on cultural definitions of the meaning of life strategies and stages, the goals of familial relationships and personal achievement. As in the Project which provided the frame for these essays, there is little of the human experience that is not relevant to the question of cultural contexts for considering human potential, and the breadth and depth of these works conveys a slice of the concerns which may be addressed in a culturally-sensitive approach to human development.

The first group of essays, under the heading 'Psychologies of the person and cultural contexts for personal change,' includes several different perspectives on culture and transformations in healing and religious contexts. These essays make the point, explicitly and implicitly, that health and illness are subject to a broad range of definition as well as a variety of interpretations, attributions, and treatments. The setting within which a personal change is effected is highly culture-specific, and ranges from a totally internal process in the individual with very little reference to other people or settings, to a community-wide environment where every aspect of the society and its cosmology is involved. Kakar's paper stresses the relationship between the human and the natural world, rather than the process of healing as an individual passage. Katz's paper continues this theme, but stresses the fact that, among the !Kung and the Fijians, health is connectedness in a synergistic community. Ramanujam uses clinical case material to demonstrate that healing in Indian society is brought about through the concrete familial nexus. The broader questions of personal meaning and transformation, this time in an African context, are treated in Sanneh's discussion of local and borrowed religious traditions.

The second group of essays, titled 'Social organization and environments for learning,' includes selected descriptions of cultural definitions and settings for the educational process. As in the first section of the book, these papers consider indigenous meanings of a significant aspect of personal development. Spratt and Wagner's treament of the modern Islamic school and the relationship between teacher and student traces the continuing significance of the Qu'ran in the cognitive and moral development of the child in modern times. Taniuchi's description of Suzuki violin training in Japan emphasizes the cultural and phsychological environment for the early inculcation of highly complex skills in children, and notes that mothers' and teachers' goals and methods focus on understanding and engagement, on process rather than product. Vasco's study of math learning in Colombia concludes that the teaching and learning of mathematics is culturally determined and that children have their own mathematical conceptual systems as well which need to be understood by teachers.

The three papers in the last section, 'Cultural perspectives on the life course,' treat conceptions of the person within cultural models for the life course and for the fulfillment of personal and social potentials. Shiang's paper on intergenerational relationships in Chinese families notes the reciprocities involved in the expression of affection and commitment and analyzes the Chinese term 'heart' which characterizes such relationships. Das describes death and mourning in the Punjab, and treats the question as to whether grief represents integration or separation in the families suffering bereavement. Iwao's paper looks at the lives of Japanese women who have been successful in the contemporary business world, and notes their use of affiliative skills in gaining their goals. She concludes that personal success need not, as in American culture, be associated with an individual's separation from ongoing personal relationships but, on the contrary, that in Japan, interpersonal continuity is the goal of personal achievement.

Attention to cultural interpretations in the context of improving human living conditions and educational goals focuses on two very different perspectives on culture. For those concerned with the search for appropriate 'universals' by which to mobilize services and institutions (and paradigms and theories) for the improvement of people's welfare, the examples of diversity in meaning of such basic aspects of life as the definition of childhood itself, the proper relationship of parent and child, the organization of learning and its relevance to stages in a person's life, the understanding of the relationship between the supernatural and the person, all cannot help but bring greater sensitivity to the search for meanings which span cultures. For those who, on the other hand, see cultures as providing infinite divergence and, ultimately, a barrier to successful formulation of transferable models and policies, the essays in this book provide a commonality of purpose in creating a culture-sensitive discourse on human conditions and reveal underlying resonances which are shared by all people: more particularly, that learning is a crucial and central aspect of all people's lives. What we have learned most tellingly from our work with our colleagues represented here is that western models have failed to provide satisfactory institutions and what the Japanese call *ikigai*, or a purpose in living, for most of the non-western world to which they have been exported, and that this is due to two very important factors. One lies in the fact that the transfer has been effected without much contextual understanding of the culture to which it has been sent, and the second is that western, particularly American, cultural conceptions which deeply color our exports are, of the world's cultural models, perhaps particularly inappropriate as export products.

When viewed from the perspective of most non-western perceptions of the person and society, ours appear to be most unlike and most extreme. If a continuum were to be established of cultural conceptions of the significance of human relationships, for example, our ideologies and institutions would place us at the remote end, very far from those of most of the world where the relational nexus is given high social value and institutional priority. It is not clear, however, that westerners are ultimately satisfied with the ideologies and social systems which advocate the unattached portability of the self in a context of theoretically infinite individual potential. Our psychologies and philosophies of human development are diverse and eclectic, and there is no consensus as to what will achieve the realization of our potential. We too seek lasting bonds with others, nurturant support and the agreement with our kin and workmates that what we are and do is relevant and good. But this seeking is conducted in a cultural and institutional vacuum, with only evanescent reassurances that there is an agreed-upon, meaningful life to be led. Most of us, however, do not consider the cultural abyss, but continue to live in a personally-constructed meaning, perhaps several times in a lifetime destroyed and reconstructed. This, whether it is supported by the idealization of 'rugged individualism' or by trendier conceptions of 'keeping one's options

5

open', does not tend to satisfy the underlying quest for cultural meaning in our lives, and to export this even implicitly in development programs is to create confusion and dislocation. The western 'case' is not represented explicitly in this volume, but in each essay there is an implicit comparison to be made with the systems of belief and institutions and ways of living which in the colonial past and development present were and are being adopted in very different settings.

These essays also deal implicitly or explicitly with development paradigms. Paradigms, however balanced with alternatives or successively superseded by new models, cannot capture the multitude of experiences and meanings and cannot create the conditions for successful programs for human development. The message, if there is one, is that human conditions are diversely experienced, represented, codified and transmitted and that understanding the *active value* of this diversity is the most important premise for development.

PART I

PSYCHOLOGIES OF THE PERSON AND CULTURAL CONTEXTS FOR PERSONAL CHANGE

In this age of alternative therapies, transpersonal psychologies, and holistic healing, the diversity of options for personal transformation makes a reexamination of cultural beliefs concerning healing of great interest. While in the past, healing has been inseparably tied to religion and to a wide cluster of cultural norms, this is no longer the case as the scientific doctor, not the community priest or shaman, becomes responsible for physical and mental health and healing itself is conceptually compartmentalized. As Freud pointed out in his lectures on psychoanalysis, cultural norms and ideals, like the cracks which reveal the structure of a crystal, are often seen most clearly through abnormal behavior. Thus, in this part, culture is viewed through the lens of illness, and the relationship between healing and illness is explored. The changing role of the healer is also a focal point of this part – is the healer inside or outside the society? Does he or she embody the power that heals, or does the healer function as an intermediary, a vessel through which power flows? And finally, the question of the cultural transfer of healing theories and therapies is explored – can one culture's norms and definitions of health and sickness be exported successfully to another culture? Or do the very ideals of health and illness differ so radically that transport becomes impossible?

I

PSYCHOTHERAPY AND CULTURE: HEALING IN THE INDIAN TRADITION

Sudhir Kakar

ABSTRACT

Sudhir Kakar's essay, 'Psychotherapy and culture: healing in the Indian tradition' begins with two premises – the universality of concerns that underlie emotional illness, and the relativity of all therapeutic endeavors. Kakar believes that all psychotherapies reflect the themes and goals of the culture, and that one cannot understand a particular form of therapy unless one also grasps the Schwerpunkt *of that culture. He explores these issues through the case study of an Indian woman and her search for healing in an indigenous form of therapy. Kakar believes that the essential question behind Indian psychotherapy is 'What is the relationship between the human and the natural?' stressing the relationship rather than the individual. He concludes that while eastern and western forms of healing have both individual and collective elements, each focuses on different parts of the healing mechanism.*

For the past few years I have been absorbed in the study of various Indian traditions for the healing of emotional disorder.[1] In my encounters with the patients and healers of these traditions – shamans, gurus, psychiatrists of indigenous medicine – I have been greatly impressed by two issues: one, the universality of human concerns that underlie emotional illness and two, the relativity of all psychotherapeutic endeavours, eastern or western. It became increasingly evident for me that Indian patients – whether Hindu,

Muslim or tribal – are engaged in the same struggles as their counterparts elsewhere in the world as they attempt to find a balance between the rewards and pressures of an external world and the desires and fantasies of an internal world haunted by ghosts of sexual and aggressive wishes, by envy, and by reproachful voices from the past. In the west these concerns are more liable to be expressed in scientific abstractions and analytic truths, in psychological systems that rearrange reality in some artificial pattern, testifying to the continuing hold of the philosophy of enlightenment on the modern western mind. In India, these concerns are expressed more in the language of religious experience, myths and poetical images of a people whose values are nearer to those of counter-enlightenment.[2]

The Indian God is less a mathematician than a poet, who (in Wendy O'Flaherty's felicitous image) not only plays dice with the world but also cheats.

It also became clearer to me how every psychotherapy follows the unique 'centre for gravity' of its culture and manifests the culture's major theme in its practice and its goals; the character and value of a psychotherapy is only understandable if one grasps the *Schwerpunkt* of the culture from which it derives. In this sense every psychotherapy is an ethnopsychotherapy and the evolutionist view, also going back to the enlightenment, that psychotherapeutic systems of other cultures are at incipient and less adequate stages in the development of a universal psychiatric understanding, seems untenable. I would like to explore and illustrate these two issues through the case history of an Indian patient and the indigenous therapy she received.

Asha was a twenty-six-year-old woman from a lower-middle class family in Delhi who had become possessed by two spirits. A thin, attractive woman with sharply chiselled features and a dusky complexion, Asha had a slight, girlish figure that made her look younger than her age. She had suffered from periodic headaches ever since she could remember, though her acute distress began two and a half years ago when a number of baffling symptoms made their first appearance. Among these were violent stomach aches that would convulse her with pain and leave her weak and drained of energy. Periodically, she had the sensation of ants crawling over her body, a sensation that would gradually concentrate on her head and produce such discomfort that she could not even bear to touch her head. There were bouts of gluttony and fits of rage in which she would break objects and physically lash out at anyone who happened to be near her. 'Once I even slapped my father during such a rage,' Asha said. 'Can you imagine a daughter hitting her father, especially a father who I have loved more than anyone else in this world?'

Treatment with drugs (her uncle was a western-style medical doctor) and consultations with an exorcist did not make any appreciable difference to her condition, but what really moved Asha to come to the healing temple of Balaji (where I met her) was her discovery, six months after her father's death, that her skin had suddenly turned dark. This caused her intense mental anguish, since she has always prided herself on her fair complexion. Asha now felt that she had become very unattractive and toyed with the idea of suicide.

The temple of Balaji to which Asha came, accompanied by her mother and her uncle, lies 250 miles south of Delhi and is famous all over northern India for curing illnesses that result from spirit possession. The therapy takes place through a series of temple rituals that seem to be patterned after judicial procedures. The first step is called the 'application' in which the patient makes an offering of rice worth one and a quarter rupees and gives two sweets to an attendant every morning and evening before the start of the temple service. During these services, a priest touches the sweets to a part of the god Balaji's idol and then gives them back to the patient to eat. It is believed that with the eating of the sweets the power of Balaji – the Lord of the Spirits – goes into the patient and forces the possessing spirit to make its appearance in the god's court – the dramatic high point of the healing rituals. If the application is unsuccessful and the spirit does not appear, then the patient can successively make a 'petition' in which the 'court costs' are seventeen and a quarter rupees worth of foodstuffs, and a 'major petition' in which the costs are raised to twenty one and a quarter rupees. Meanwhile, the family members have also been active. Many of them are chanting specific mantras that are designed to summon and involve the concerned gods in the healing process. Others are found in the temple halls, chanting mantras over spoonfuls of water that they keep transferring from one pot to another. These mantras supposedly impart divine energy to the water, which is later drunk by the patient, presumably to the further dismay of the possessing

11

spirit. It is quite understandable that the possessing spirit is rarely able to withstand the concerted onslaught of so many 'divine energies.' In secular language we would say that the application and petition rituals incorporate the awesome authority of the gods in their demand that the patient go into the trancelike state of 'appearance.' The demand is reinforced by the expectations of the priests and family members and is encouraged by the contagious effect of observing other patients having their 'appearance' in the midst of approving groups.

The start of an 'appearance' is marked by well defined signs of which the rhythmic swaying of the upper half of the body and the violent sideways shaking of the head are the surest evidence of the spirit having presented itself in the god's court. In many patients, the spirit begins by challenging the god. The people around the patient try to provoke the spirit by shouting slogans in praise of the god. Excited, the spirit often becomes angry and abusive, hurling obscenities at the god and mocking the piety of the onlookers. The torrent of aggressive abuse, especially when it is issuing out of the otherwise demure mouths of frail young girls and women, leaves little doubt that we are witnessing a convulsive release of pent-up aggression and a rare rebellion against the norms and mores of a conservative Hindu society of which its gods are the most obvious representatives. Temporarily, some of the patients even opt out of the Hindu fold by their spirit claiming that it is a Muslim grandee who is as powerful as Balaji and would never admit defeat. The excitement crescendoes as the community now brings its full weight to bear upon the rebellious and wayward spirit, begging the god to give it a thrashing. Indeed the patient begins to hit herself, which simultaneously increases the volume of her spirit's protesting screams. After some time, the patient, patently tired, stops beating herself and the spirit admits defeat. There is obvious relief among the onlookers at the reestablishment of the normal cosmic order and the patient's acceptance of old values and old authorities. The ritual now goes into its next phase of 'statement' where the spirit identifies itself and states its wishes. The spirit then promises to leave the patient alone and to throw itself at the mercy of Balaji's court. Sometimes the god might send a reformed, benign spirit to protect the patient against the onslaught of other malignant spirits; the coming of the benign spirit is signaled by a short trancelike state in which the patient repeatedly prostrates herself before the idol.

12

After coming to Balaji, the appearance of Asha's spirits was immediate. She had barely finished eating the two sweets when she fell down on the floor and revealed that she was possessed by two spirits. The first spirit, who caused the stomach aches, stated that it was sent by Asha's brother's wife. Its name was Masan, it said, a ghost that inhabits cemeteries and cremation grounds and whose 'speciality' is the eating of unborn babies in the womb. The second spirit admitted its responsibility for the sensation of crawling ants and for Asha's rages, and further revealed that it had been sent by the elder brother of Asha's fiancé.

Though Asha was anything but secretive and talked animatedly about her life and her problems, the talk was mostly diffused and scattered. She flitted from one experience to another, from the present to the past and back to the present again so that a chronological piecing together of her life history became a difficult task. Dramatic impressions and nostalgic memories, described with elaborate gestures and in a theatrical voice, succeeded each other with bewildering rapidity, making it difficult to sift facts from impressions, reality from fantasy.

As the youngest child in the family and the only daughter after a succession of five boys, Asha had always been her father's favourite. The memories of her childhood were pervaded by images of a father–daughter closeness and of their delight in each other that had excluded other members of the family from their charmed circle. The first thing the father did on coming home from the office every evening was to ask for his beloved daughter and play with her till it was time for dinner. Even when she was twenty, Asha remembers that her father inevitably brought her sweets in the evening, and then, lifting the now not-so-little girl upon his shoulders, he would romp around the house, often exclaiming, 'O my darling daughter, what would I do when you get married and leave this house! My life would be ever so empty!'

The only discordant note in the 'idyllic' father–daughter relationship occurred when Asha was fifteen. She fell in love with a young college student who had been engaged as her tutor. When her father came to know of their budding romance, he was furious and packed Asha off to her aunt in a nearby town. There she was so closely watched that she could neither write nor receive letters. For one year the girl pined away in virtual imprisonment and came back to Delhi only when her father fell sick and refused to be nursed by anyone except his favourite daughter. Asha devotedly nursed him back to health and the subject of the young tutor was never mentioned by either one of them; in fact, the episode seemed to have brought the father and daughter even closer.

The sequence of events that led to Asha's possession by the two spirits seems to have been as follows. Three years ago, Asha's favourite brother had got married, and according to Asha, under the influence of his wife he became quite indifferent to his sister. Asha felt very unhappy at her brother's 'betrayal' but continued to perform all her sisterly duties. Once, when she had gone to her brother's house for a short stay – her sister-in-law was pregnant – Asha found some of her own clothes in her sister-in-law's closet, which made her very upset at her 'thieving' sister-in-law. Her stomach aches started shortly afterward.

It was during this time that a young man from the neighborhood began to take a pronounced romantic interest in Asha. Every day the man dropped in at the clinic where Asha helped her uncle in his work and would talk to her for hours. Asha was uninterested in her ardent suitor, she claims, but this did not faze the young man in the least. In their long and frequent conversations the man openly declared his love for the girl. When Asha's father came to know of the young man's pursuit of his daughter, he was, once again, furious. Accompanied by two of his sons, her father went to the man's house to remonstrate with his family. The man's mother persuaded Asha's father and her brothers that Asha should be married into their family and it was decided (it was not clear how and by whom) that Asha would marry not her suitor but his younger brother instead. Asha felt very unhappy at this arrangement but her father fell sick and she could not give vent to her feelings as that might have worsened his cardiac condition. Once again she devotedly nursed her father through his illness.

The elder brother of her fiancé had now become bolder and even more insistent in his sexual advances toward the girl. He seemed unmoved by Asha's repeated plea that since she would soon become the wife of his younger brother he should, like a good Hindu, begin to look upon her as his daughter. It was during this period that Asha was attacked by her second spirit for the first time. She had gone to her mother-in-law's house for a visit but found that everyone was out except her lovelorn admirer. He had asked her to come up to his room and Asha had fainted. The rages, the sensation of crawling ants, and the headaches began soon afterward.

From a psychoanalytic perspective, apart from its Indian stage and Punjabi lower middle-class setting, Asha's case seems to be a part of the same genre that is often encountered in the early psychoanalytic literature on young women who fell ill while caring for an older, sick relative. Torn between her duty and her love for her father and her own unacknowledged sexual wishes towards another man, Asha's conflict is similar to that of many girls in the European bourgeois society of the late nineteenth century – that of Freud's patient Elisabeth von R., for instance.[3] With her need for intense closeness to her father, Asha seems to have had little choice but to deny the hostile component of her feelings toward him – as she must have denied her rage during her first, abortive love affair with her tutor. Given the present stressful circumstances – her father's illness, her engagement and the man's importunate demands – Asha's defense of denying her aggressive and sexual wishes was no longer sufficient but needed to be supplemented by having these wishes split off from consciousness and attributed to the machinations of a spirit. Naturally, the spirit was 'sent' by the lovelorn swain who is unconsciously held to be responsible for the conflicting emotions that constantly threaten to overwhelm her. Asha's other spirit – the embryo-eater Masan – too represents a similar symbiosis of destructive and sexual wishes. Her stomach aches, I would speculate, are an expression of her unconscious pregnancy fantasy, created by means of an identification with the 'fortunate rival,' the sister-in-law. The ghost killer of unborn babies then symbolizes the idea, 'It is not I who would like to destroy my sister-in-law's unborn baby but she who wants to kill my (fantasized) baby.' Asha's bouts of gluttony would seem to reinforce this interpretation. As many creative writers have also known, neurotic greed is the reflection not of the need for food but of wishes that can never be assuaged by eating. For instance, in his novel, *Two Women*, Balzac in his description of a pregnant woman's passion for rotten oranges intuitively recognizes the cannibalistic nature of her wishes directed against the child in her body.

We can, of course, go beyond the purely individual understanding of Asha's case to its social setting. Where Asha and other Indian hysterical personalities differ from their European counterparts, for instance, is in the display of a rich, dramatic and concrete imagery of the spirits. This kind of visual imagery is diffuse, if not completely absent, in the recorded cases of *la grande hystérie* in the west. The rich mythological world peopled by many gods, goddesses and other supernatural beings in which the Indian child grows up as well as his early experiences of multiple caretakers, all contribute to the imagery of possessing spirits. Moreover, the wide prevalence of hysterical personality among Indian women and their use of this particular cultural myth of possessing spirits, are also reflections of certain social conditions prevailing in the society. In other words, there is no individual anxiety that does not also reflect a latent concern common to the group, a fact that Erik Erikson pointed out long ago but which we clinicians often tend to underplay in our pursuit of the uniquely individual in case history.[4] In a village community where the young bride is expected to be completely subservient and not even think angry thoughts about her husband's family and especially about her 'lord and master,' possession by spirits who behave otherwise seems to be one way for a young girl to express and yet not acknowledge the resentment against the powerlessness of her condition. Anger against 'superior' family members seems to be particularly difficult to express. Even 'she hates me,' as in the case of Asha and her sister-in-law, is not easy to acknowledge. One has to be terribly ill and possessed by all manners of spirits to be able to express, 'I hate him (or her).'

What can we say about the psychotherapy carried out at the temple of the Lord of the Spirits? As an analyst, I am of course inclined to first perceive its individualistic elements, to focus on the ways temple healing deals with the cut-off parts of the self. We can see that as far as these cut-off parts are concerned, the therapy proceeds along two separate lines. First, the individual's tolerance of the possessing spirit is sought to be increased by lessening the spirit's fearsomeness. Patients (and their families) exchange detailed case histories within and outside the temple premises. If two patients encounter each other in the street, then 'How is your "distress" doing?' is both an acceptable greeting and a mode of inquiry about the other's well-being. The possible response to such an inquiry – 'There is no change,' 'It is turning out well' – are very much like the matter-of-fact exchanges between two graduate students in physics on the progress of their experiment. Thus, possession illness and the presence of spirits are accepted in a plain, uncomplicated way. In the boarding houses, after their gates are closed for the night, patients and their families spontaneously form into small groups to discuss each other's distress well into the night. In such group sessions, the most intimate details of the individual's distress are revealed, speculations on the probable origins of the spirit are advanced and the possible outcomes of a particular healing ritual are debated. Besides lessening any residual feelings of shame, the public sharing of the illness certainly makes the malignant spirits lose their private terrors. Indeed, the patients begin to address their possessing spirits – the *bhuta* – derisively with the diminutive 'bhutra.' What one's *bhurtra* did on a particular day during the healing ritual in the temple is related to others in an indulgent manner, as if the spirit were a naughty child whose antics had to be suffered patiently.

In addition, the spirit's potentially benign nature – the *bhuta* being replaced by the protective *duta*, the god's 'messenger' – is pointed out and it is re-emphasized that according to the Indian theory, malignant spirits are only unfortunate ancestral spirits who have yet to enter their destined abode and thus deserve compassion rather than anxious reactions. In psychoanalytic terms, the unconscious content of the psyche is considered neither fixed and immutable nor malignant and threatening (as in the notion of the psychoanalytic 'id'), but as fundamentally capable of a benign transformation. We must also remember that the spirits are only defendants in Balaji's court and not outside the pale of society; the Lord of the Spirits, after all, is as much a defense lawyer who must look after the spirits' interest as a judge who must punish them.

Second, the appearance ritual attempts to transform the patient's belief into a conviction that her bad traits and impulses are not within but without – that they are not her own but belong to the spirit. The fact that fifteen out of twenty-eight patients whose case histories I collected were possessed by a Muslim spirit indicates the extent of this projection in the sense that the Muslim seems to be *the* symbolic representation of the alien in the Hindu unconscious. Possession by a Muslim spirit reflects the patient's desperate efforts to convince herself and others that her hunger for forbidden foods, tumultuous sexuality and uncontrollable rage belong to the Muslim destroyer of taboos and are farthest away from her 'good' Hindu self.

We have, however, seen that in the judicial metaphor of the temple's healing, the therapeutic task, is not primarily the reintegration of the cut-off parts of the self, (as in Western psychotherapy),

17

but rather the ending of the patient's alienation from his social and cosmic order – the reintegration of the individual with his community. This requires a polyphonic social drama that attempts a ritual restoration of the dialogue not only within the patient but within the family structure. Much of this work of reintegration takes place outside the healing rituals.According to the temple rules, a patient can stay in a boarding house only if she is escorted by at least one caretaker. In practice there are often three to four family members who accompany the 'sick' person on her pilgrimage that may last for as much as six months. Many rituals that need to be carried out in the temple require the active participation of these family members. By accompanying a patient from morning till late in the evening through the various healing rituals and living in an environment where possession illness is the central theme of community life, the distinction between a 'sick' and a 'normal' member of the family is gradually eroded. There were many cases where a person who had come to Balaji with a possessed relative soon discovered that he too was in distress from a spirit and in need of healing. Another bridge between the 'normal' and the 'sick' is through the concept of spirit transfer. According to this belief, if a close relative of the patient prays to Balaji that he is ready to take on the distress, then the spirit often leaves the patient and possesses the supplicant. By participating in the rituals together with the patient, engaging in dialogues with the possessing spirit and especially in having the spirit transferred onto themselves, the family members also seem to be accepting their share of the blame for the patient's problems.

We see, therefore, that the assumptions underlying the temple healing (and generally of other Indian traditions) are quite different from their modern western counterparts. The assumptions of western psychotherapy are also those of individualism. They are epitomized in psychoanalysis, perhaps the most individualistic of all psychotherapies, as 'its almost limitless respect for the individual, faith that understanding is better than illusion, insistence that our psyches harbour darker secrets than we care to confess, refusal to promise too much, and a sense of the complexity, tragedy and wonder of human life.'[5] The underlying values of the traditional temple healing on the other hand, stress that faith and surrender to a power beyond the individual are better than individual effort and struggle, that the source of human strengths lies in a harmonious integration with one's group, in the individual's affirmation of the community's values and its given order, in his obedience to the community's gods and in his cherishing of its traditions. As I have mentioned at the beginning of this essay, the differences in the therapeutic assumptions and thus in the therapeutic practices, reflect the major thrusts of the two cultures, i.e. they reflect the different questions the cultures ask of the universe which then shape the answers accordingly. Stated in an oversimplified manner, the Indian question is not 'What is human nature?' but rather 'What is the relationship between the human and the natural?' In other words, the Indian question stresses *relationship* rather than *individuality* and both the question and the answer are reflected in many aspects of Indian culture. I will illustrate this cultural *Schwerpunkt* with two examples that are extremely difficult – Hindu medicine and classical poetry.

The traditional Ayurvedic medicine of India is based on the identity of body and nature and postulates that there is no break in the life processes which characterize both the animate and the inanimate world. A nineteenth-century Bengali text on the body unequivocally states its relationship to the cosmos:

> In this universe a great wheel of transformative power (maya-chakra) is spinning ceaselessly. The small individual wheel of transformative power in the bodies of living things are connected with that wheel. Just as, when some great steam-driven wheel turns like the prime mover, then all of the components of the machinery move together in co-ordination and smoothly accomplish their tasks, similarly the small wheels of transformative power that turn through their connection with the great wheel, within the bodies of individual living things, help accomplish such bodily activities as regulating the flow of blood in the body, digesting food, inhaling and exhaling, and moving back and forth.[6]

The Indian body image stresses an unremitting interchange taking place with the environment simultaneously accompanied by a ceaseless change within the body. As Francis Zimmermann writes, 'There is no map nor topography of the body but only an *economy*, that is to say fluids going in or coming out, residing in some *asrya* (recipient) or flowing through some *srotas* (channels).'[7] It is the imagery from the vegetable kingdom, such as the plant's drawing

19

nourishment through the roots, the rising of the sap, and the milky exudation of resinous trees that provides models for the body image in Ayurveda.

In contrast to the Indian image of the body in constant interchange with the environment and in ceaseless transformation, the western image is more of a clearly etched body, sharply differentiated from the rest of the objects in the universe. This vision of the body as a safe stronghold with a limited number of drawbridges that maintain a tenuous contact with the outside world has its own particular cultural consequences. It seems to me that in western discourse, both scientific and literary, there is considerable preoccupation with what is going on *within* the fortress of the individual body. Preeminently, one seeks to explain behavioral processes through psychologies that derive from biology, to the relative exclusion of the natural and the metanatural environment. Let me give an illustration.

For many years, research on child development has focused on what is happening within the child as he grows up. There has been much interesting work on the 'unfolding' of a child's capacities and the construction of a number of sophisticated tests and benchmarks of intellectual and cognitive development. In contrast, the work done on a systematic conception and differentiation of the environment in which the child's development takes place is minimal. At most, the environment has been conceived of in nutritional and human terms – for instance in finding out the effects of maternal deprivation on the child. The natural aspects of the environment – the quality of air, the quantity of sunlight, the presence of birds and animals, the plants and the trees – are *a priori* viewed, when they are considered at all, as irrelevant to intellectual and emotional development. Given the western image of the body, it is understandable that the more 'far-out' Indian beliefs on the effects of the natural world on the human body and psyche, for example, the effects of planetary constellations, earth's magnetic fields, seasonal and daily rhythms, precious stones and metals – are summarily consigned to the realm of fantasy, where they are of interest solely to a 'lunatic fringe' of western society.

Coming to a very different area of human experience, poetry, Daniel Ingalls has observed that where Sanskrit poetry proves most alien to the prevailing spirit of western verse is in its impersonality, its lack of reference to specific individuals in favour of types.[8]

Whatever the shortcomings of this kind of poetry, it is ideally suited to bring out the finest effects of suggestion. By a long process of typifying, each variety of love, each scene of nature, each function of the gods has received a conventional manner of presentation.

> By a single brushstroke, a single word taken from one of these conventional portrayals or descriptions, the whole scene is evoked. It thus becomes far easier than it is under the modern Western ideal of individualism to move back and forth among the fields of nature, humanity, and the gods, and by suggestion to reveal a given mood as embracing the universe.[9]

To give an example (from classical Tamil poetry): the flower *mullai* is associated with a particular feeling of love (patient waiting), a particular landscape (forest), particular gods, food, animals, trees, birds, musical style and so on.[10] (It is intriguing to speculate that the effectiveness of a traditional, standard ritual of healing, as at the Balaji temple, may derive from the same sources that give classsical Indian poetry its impact. Similar to the aesthetic associations evoked by a fixed poetic symbol, each element of the ritual, in its impersonality and through a long process of typification, has come to evoke a range of healing associations.)

I must emphasize here that I am not setting up an irreconcilable dichotomy between Indian and western cultures and psychotherapies. I do not go so far as McKim Marriott who contrasts a western *individual* (indivisible), having a nature that is enduring, closed and has an internally homogenous structure, with an antithetical Indian *dividual* i.e. divisible, who is open, more or less fluid, only temporarily in integration, deriving his personal nature interpersonally, whose affects, needs and motives are relational and whose distresses are solely disorders of relationships.[11] From our case of temple healing (and from the study of other Indian psychotherapies) we know that the psychotherapy must also offer the patient an opportunity for 'airing' his individual conflict and some kind of resolution on the personal plane. A successful traditional healing ritual is not merely an operation (as Lévi-Strauss maintains) where the patient receives a social myth from his collective tradition that reintegrates his alienating experience of sickness within a meaningful whole.[12] (By 'myths' I do not mean false statements about reality but myths as embodiments of a vision of the world.) The therapy must also attend to the individual elements of the patient's sickness.

Conversely, an effective individual resolutions of psychic conflict in most western psychotherapists will, in some measure, also incorporate the collective myth shared by the patient, the therapist and the community of which they both form a part. Normally, this collective myth, based on the western tradition of which individual autonomy and individual worth, knowableness of reality and the possibility of real choice are some aspects, remains relatively unarticulated. Nevertheless, as the elaboration of the individual myth proceeds (and this is especially noticeable in psychoanalytic practice across cultures), the collective myth often becomes audible, as a theme here and just a faint echo there, providing the patient with an opportunity to relate and reintegrate his illness with a larger meaningful whole. Instead of a dichotomy between western and Indian psychotherapies I would then suggest that both operate with collective and individual aspects, though each choose to focus on one part of the dual healing mechanism while it underplays the other.

NOTES

1 See my *Shamans, Mystics and Doctors* (New York: Alfred Knopf, 1982).
2 For the values of the philosophers of counter-enlightenment see Isaiah Berlin, *Against the Current: Essays in the History of Ideas* (Oxford: Oxford University Press, 1981), pp.1 – 24.
3 Sigmund Freud, 'Studies on Hysteria' (1895) in, *The Standard Edition of the Complete Psychological works of Sigmund Freud* (ed. J. Strachey) vol.2 (London: Hogarth Press, 1958), Chapter 2.
4 Erik M. Erikson, *Childhood and Society* (New York: W. W. Norton, 1954), p. 36.
5 Kenneth Keniston quoted in Virginia Adams, 'Freud's Work Thrives as a Theory, Not Therapy,' in *The New York Times, August 14, 1979.*
6 Krsna-dhan Cattopadyaya, *The Doctrine of the Body* (1878), Adati Nath Sarkar (tr.), Ralph Nicholas (ed.), Department of Anthropology, University of Chicago, unpubd MS, p. 31.
7 Francis Zimmermann, 'Remarks on the Conception of the Body in Ayurvedic Medicine,' paper presented at the ACLS – SSRC Seminar on the Person and Interpersonal Relations in South Asia, University of Chicago, 1979, p. 7.
8 Daniel M.M. Ingalls, *An Anthology of Sanskrit Court Poetry* (Cambridge, Mass: Harvard University Press, 1965), p. 22ff.
9 ibid. p. 27.

10 See A.K. Ramanujan, *The Interior Landscape* (Bloomington: Indiana University Press, 1975), pp. 103–8.

11 McKim Marriot, 'The Open Hindu Person and Interpersonal Fluidity' unpub. paper read at the session on 'The Indian Self' at the meetings of the Association for Asian Studies, Washington D.C., March 1980.

12 See Claude Lévi-Strauss, 'The Effectiveness of Symbols,' in *Structural Anthropology* (New York: Basic Books, 1963), pp. 167–85.

II

SOURCE AND INFLUENCE: A COMPARATIVE APPROACH TO AFRICAN RELIGION AND CULTURE

Lamin Sanneh

ABSTRACT

In 'Source and Influence: A Comparative Approach to African Religion and Culture,' Lamin Sanneh develops a distinction between 'in-coming sources' and 'indigenous influences' to analyze Christian mission and Islamic traditions in Africa. Sanneh treats two different contexts of indigenization in West Africa in terms of strategies and adaptations exhibiting the flexibility and resourcefulness of African societies and the 'transforming power' of local tradition.

INTRODUCTION

The science of comparative studies in general has suffered from the absence of a consistent and coherent theory of how *source* and *influence* might be related. In much of the material on the subject we are presented with an uncritical notion that *source* implies *influence*, that evidence of borrowing is incriminating proof of superficiality, with the original carrying the force of *influence*.

I shall consider mainly the situation in Muslim and Christian Africa and try to distinguish between incoming *sources* and indigenous *influence*. The reform tradition in African Islam and the missionary factor in African Christianity will be reassessed in terms of the distinction I am introducing.

This paper sets out to show that *source* and *influence* are two separate issues, even if they are sometimes closely intertwined. We shall attempt to prove that *source* does not necessarily imply *influence* nor are similarities evidence of incompleteness.

DEFINITION

Webster's New World Dictionary gives as one of its definitions of *influence* the power of persons or things to affect others. It says that the word, etymologically meaning 'a flowing in,' was originally applied to the supposed flowing of an ethereal fluid or power from the stars, thought to affect the character and actions of people. *Influence* was later extended to mean *authority* or *power* to command acceptance, belief, obedience based on strength of character, expertness of knowledge or even political or social position. In the world of art and literature *influence* retained much of its etymological defintion, though in religious studies it is the secondary meaning that has come to predominate. For our purposes this secondary meaning of the word should suffice, with the additional idea of a modification of what is thus *influenced*.

On the word *source* Webster says it originally meant a spring or fountain as the starting point of a stream, with the secondary meaning of that from which something comes or develops, a place of origin. In a separate entry it says that *source* material means original or primary *sources* of information on any given subject or study. I employ the word here to mean material or an idea whose provenance is other than the context in which it occurs.

In the conventional way of treating the matter, we have normally ascribed to *source* both the notion of *influence* and the consequences following from that. Yet it is clear from the Dictionary definition that *influence* is the force that shapes the *source* material. It is a 'flowing in' which modifies the fresh material in conformity with the nature of *influence*. The *source* material affects this process only as fuel affects combustion.

APPLYING THE THEORY

When we apply this understanding to culture and religion a new situation arises. Shakespeare's dependence on historical *sources* is one example where *source* is in radical subordination to the *influence* of the dramatist. The cumulative volume of such *sources* does not add up to *influence*. The reverse might be nearer the mark. The *influence* of the dramatist helped to put fresh vitality into a piece of the past that would otherwise remain inaccessible. As such Hamlet, the Henrys and the Richards are more real as *dramatic personae* than as historical characters. It is the reconstructed material that helps us in understanding past themes and thus creating an interest in the *sources*. Shakespeare's *dependence* on *source* material must now be understood in the light of the independent determination to which he subjects what he borrows, not as evidence of an incomplete genius.

In the religious sphere a similar phenomenon can be observed. The Gospel writers borrowed the idea of the Suffering Servant from the Prophet of Second Isaiah and infused it with the *influence* of the corresponding figure in the New Testament. The result is that, whatever the historical genesis of the phrase, it was made to assume the dimensions of the Easter Passion.

To return to the field of literature for the last time, one example may be cited to show that *influence*, as in the ethereal analogy, may operate in a hidden though no less real way. A powerful literary figure may leave traces of his *influence* all over the field without the usual typographical conventions. One such figure is T.S. Eliot. His *influence* on literary English is enormous, though most of us may not – and need not – be aware of it. But a careful examination of modern prose will show the extent to which his towering shadow has continued to fall over us. By contrast, we might think of a *source* being a powerful *influence* on us from the prominence with which it occurs in our consciousness. Yet on closer attention we would find that it was no such thing. Such is the case with the King James Bible, otherwise known as the Authorized Version. The familiar phrases lifted from it are used merely to embellish an idea. They signal their intrusion on our consciousness by the abrupt manner of their introduction or by the stilted pace we are forced to keep. It is all there for effect. Such phrases are no evidence of *influence* whatsoever, as school essays strewn with clumps of Shakespeare or Milton prove.

The next and more substantial way in which I propose to apply the distinction of *source* and *influence* is to the question of religious transformation and the process of indigenization. The materials I shall be considering come from Christianity and Islam in their

interaction with African societies. This should suggest the comparative use to which the theory can be put.

TOWARDS A COMPARATIVE VIEW OF RELIGION AND CULTURE IN AFRICA

We possess a rich body of material on the introduction of Islam and
Christianity into African societies. Consequently we have valuable
details on the origins and adaptation of the two religions in Africa.
Such a situation affords an excellent opportunity to study how
Islamic and Christian materials were reassembled in the African
setting, and what light this might shed on the notion of *source* and
influence.

It is self-evident that Christianity and Islam in their different ways
were transplant religions in Africa. For the most part Africa constituted a congenial host environment for the new communities of
Christians and Muslims. The question we have to ask is why these
religions were successfully assimilated in Africa. In view of the
thousand or so years that Islam has been in Black Africa, it is
surprising that the answer to this question of successful assimilation
has not been consistent with the indigenous factor. Islam is normally credited with possessing an inherent flexibility which has made it
spontaneously appealing, while Christianity for its part is depicted
as an imperialist religion maintained by the forces of alien subjuga-
tion. In our terminology such descriptions assume that the two
religions constitute the *influence* under which African communities
had to comport themselves. The only difference is that we are
supposed to applaud Muslim gains and deplore Christian ones. But
the effect is the same: developments in Africa are by virtue of
external *influence*, which propagates the notion that the continent is
the arena for the battles of ancient rivalry, with a paternalist
attitude towards local culture to boot.

Yet it would be more logical to aver that the transplant varieties
of Islam and Christianity depended on the host African environment for whatever indigenous vitality they came to possess. It was
the local response that created the all-important stimulus by which
the new religions were accommodated. That stimulus determined
the local destiny of the two religions.

What is the nature of this stimulus? It is easy to identify. The long tradition of crossing ethnic frontiers and fostering the existence of minority communities without suppressing their distinctive cultures endowed African societies with the institutional capacity to welcome Muslim and Christian agents in their midst. Thus it was that Christians and Muslims and others found themselves surrounded by ready-made channels of contact and interchange.

Some scholars describe these early forms of religious minority life as being in 'quarantine,' meaning by that a form of social isolation that helped to preserve the essential features of the transplant culture. It aptly describes the notion of 'enclavement.' If we transpose that term to the local one of *zongo* [literally, halting place, transition camp] for example, it would become clear that religious 'quarantine' is an indigenous category allowing foreign materials to be accommodated without comprehensive surrender by either side. Thus the paradox of minimal cross-cultural exchange making for 'quarantine' confirms the Eliot-type *influence* of the host community. (It is instructive to ponder how increasing westernization and Islamization of parts of modern Africa have challenged the tradition of pluralism as an obstacle to a unitary society and religious conformity.)

Once this step is taken of foreign religious communities being implanted in African societies, the stage is set for the next most critical phase. This has to do with the attitude of the two religions to the local culture. Let me return to an earlier point about the alleged spontaneity of Islamic conversions and the supposedly helpless hostages of Christian imperialism. Religious rivalry makes such characterizations easy and attractive. But they make us overlook the indigenous factor. It may seem reasonable to enquire into how Christianity or Islam changed Africa, but it is much more consistent and critical to ask what effects Africa had on the two religions. This, I said, is the next most critical phase in the history of religious transformation.

THE VERNACULAR CULTURE: SOURCE OR INFLUENCE?

The issue of the vernacular languages is the key to the process of the transformation of Christianity and Islam. It is also relevant to the question of what effective religious agency is. Previous attempts to answer the question about the changes brought into being by Islam or Christianity assume that the vernacular culture acts only as *source*, with the active stimulus of the two religions as the determining *influence*. It also assumes that missionaries and the Arabic heritage of Islam are the effective agents of religious transmission. By changing the question around and inquiring into the leavening effect of Africa on the two religions, we reverse those two assumptions. The vernacular culture is the *influence* acting upon incoming materials, with local people as the agents of the all-important process of indigenization. It changes Christianity, for example, from being a foreign religion to one with the potential to be locally assimilated. This has radical implications for the role of missionaries in the development of the most crucial cultural resources, namely, the indigenous languages. The notion that the historical transmission of Christianity was to achieve the statistical expansion of the religion, rigidly upheld by Mission Boards, was abandoned on the ground in Africa as missionaries embarked on vernacular translation. The repercussions of their endeavours went far beyond whatever triumphalist theologies motivated their action.

Some levels of Christian missionary propaganda did adopt a rather truculent attitude towards the local culture and the people they came to convert. But everyone concerned surrendered to the logic that mission was futile and theologically invalid without the vernacular Scriptures, or at any rate without transposing Christian teachings into local categories. The effect was to produce the scientific documentation of local languages, the writing of grammars, primers and dictionaries, and the methodological gathering of ethnographic data.

Again it is easy to impugn missionary motive, but the radical effects of their work is indisputable. The local culture, given access to Christian materials via familiar channels, acquired a written sanction and a broadening of the religious imagination. By adopting the local names for the Supreme Being and the terms for Spirit, sacrifice, salvation, the Sabbath, prophets and other equally significant concepts, Christian missionaries conceded that they had been anticipated and that the standard of religious evaluation was the indigenous language and culture. Missionaries made a much more radical shift in adapting their message to the local context than Africans did in embracing the new religion. In other ways, too, missionaries acquired 'native habits,' with some of them setting out to resist the encroachment of westernism on indigenous values. Colonial officials, determined to demonstrate the cultural inferiority of the African, found their policies being undermined by missionary efforts. To meet this challenge, some missionaries were co-opted while many others came under greater restriction. In the religious sphere, African languages were erected into the indispensable structure for the meaningful assimilation of Christianity, with European languages reduced to secondary importance. Notions and cults of the Supreme Being in traditional religions were perpetuated with the availability of fresh Christian materials. Vernacular translation achieved the triumph of local enterprise. The adoption of existing religious terms had the effect of legitimizing the wider environment, including kinship ties and social roles. It was on the basis of such a religious and cultural re-awakening that the seeds of African nationalism were sown, as the Prophet Movements in modern Africa show.

It is true, as I have said, that the motive for embarking on the development of the vernacular languages was often the triumphalist one of statistical gain. Yet no one can deny that the universal effect of accomplishments in this area was the reinforcement of local culture, no less authentic for being unintended. Africans were quick to realize as a consequence that the language of the missionary was a foreign instrument unsuitable for the expression of the religion in their communities. One African leader declared: 'With a foreign tongue you can never reveal the real mysteries.'[1]. Some missionaries, brought to a painful realization of their marginal role in the vernacular adaptation of Christianity, looked to a possible future when Africans would extend recognition to them. One of them wrote about this, conscious that time was against the missionary. 'Our aim,' he said, 'is of course an African National Church with which eventually the [Missionary] Church must merge, with the particular gifts and blessings that have been bestowed upon her. But will we get the time to reach our first goal (of a strong, self-supporting and self-propagating [Missionary] Zulu Church, before the development overtakes us and the Natives' own National Church builds its walls higher and higher, attracting the masses . . .'[2]. Such materials suggest that the missionary, having embarked on creating a vernacular Bible, was now left belatedly struggling against the unforseen consequences of his own action. The wish to retain control over the religion was in profound conflict with its vernacular destiny.

This wish and the notion of Christianity as an imperialist religion may be helpful in examining the history of Mission Boards, Home Committees and their financial and political alliances, but they are woefully inadequate in accounting for the local dimension of the cause. Here the picture is radically different. The vernacular Scriptures began a process which it was not in the power of the missionary to resist. The point may be underscored by the occasional instance of African resistance to missionary sponsorship of the vernacular languages on the grounds that it prevented local people from acquiring foreign expertise and the rewards that brought with it. But notice the irony of the missionary being cast in the role of oppressor for promoting local languages!

In much of the discussion on missionary imperialism and a foreign Christianity a certain unflattering notion of traditional African culture was propagated, namely, that external forces decided the destiny of the continent by predetermined standards. Such external *influence*, it was assumed, came to act on African materials by producing basic alterations in values and behaviour. It is hard to reconcile this with the vernacular projects of mission, an issue that becomes sharpened with the comparative example of Islam.

When we confront Islamized Africa with the same question of indigenization, a wholly different situation arises. In spite of the apparently spontaneous appeal of the religion, Islam takes a radically different view of the vernacular culture. In embracing the religion Africans have had to develop different strategies towards it while ultimately leaving themselves open to the outside *influence* that an untranslatable Arabic Qu'ran implies. Therefore the dogma of the intrinsic untranslatability of the Qu'ran poses a serious obstacle to the force of indigenization. The flexible strategies developed towards the religion stem from the resourcefulness of African societies. To arrogate this principle to Islam is to belittle local enterprise and ignore Islam's doctrinal emphasis. The empirical situation is that Africans have adopted Islam and expressed it in conformity with pre-existing standards of perception and interpretation. Islam, no less than Christianity, has had to make 'submissive' gestures towards its local hosts. The real difference between the two religions is not so much what their contrasting perception of indigenization is or is not, as in their pattern of accommodating to the local culture. The religious formularies of Christian and Muslim

31

agents did not appear in unmodified forms. Their gains were at a price: the adoption of existing institutions of accommodation implied in *enclavement*.

The contrasting local images of the two religions tell us more about how Africa moulded them than about how they for their turn changed Africa. This theme can be expounded with striking consistency. By embarking on a vernacular course, Christianity allowed itself to be fundamentally transposed into local categories. The reaction of Muslim representatives to this phenomenon was two-faced. On the one hand the facilities of the *zongo* were accepted as a welcome opportunity to introduce the religion. On the other hand, the *zongo* was seen as an obstacle to the religious goal of total political control. It was in the *zongos* that the Islamic puritan tradition was nurtured. In other words, it was the African *influence* of pluralism which enabled Muslims to carve themselves a niche in non-Muslim societies. The result was that Muslims were able to acquire sufficient knowledge of the Arabic heritage of the religion, without any travel exposure in Arab lands, a knowledge they wished to use as a counter-indigenous instrument. The *influence* represented by the vernacular culture is at first accepted as a point of entry until, with growing awareness of the uncompromising 'foreign' nature of Islam, an anti-African ideology develops to repudiate the legitimacy of earlier gains.

Another way of comparing Christianity and Islam in terms of their attitude to indigenization is to examine their view of revitalizing the local culture. Muslim reformers strove to strip the faith of all local accretions. Their standards of value and their procedures for determining the operation of the religious code were located in foreign sources. It became a matter of pride, with enormous political implications, that local Muslims could identify with non-African values emanating from Middle Eastern *sources*. Religious revitalization meant for them the adoption of foreign standards and the borrowing of Arab attire and other cultural symbols.

In the contrasting example of African Christianity, religious revitalization meant the search for greater identity with local culture. Zulu Prophets in South Africa are possessed by the spirit (*Umoya*) of ancient divination and are appropriately metamorphosed into the gods of their affinity (*modimo*). They emerge from their seances ornately festooned in skin and feathers in imitation of King Shaka, the great nineteenth-century military hero, and proclaiming their message of salvation. They are deeply devoted to the Bible. At first, however, this devotion is concentrated on the ceremonial and divinatory resources of the Zulu Scriptures: the elaborate ritual garments of Aaron, the luminous proportions of Zion and its temple, and the sacrificial and purification code of Deuteronomy and Leviticus, all of which is saturated with the water of Biblical faith and healing. London, New York, Paris, Stockholm and other western cities are effectively superseded by the spiritual cities of Jerusalem, Salem, Bethel, Ninevah, Jericho and their counterparts.

It should, of course, be appreciated that African Christian renewal runs the whole gamut, from 'nativistic' and Hebraic movements to iconoclastic ones. But they are all united by the indispensability of the African medium for the religious enterprise. It is this medium which the missionary has done much to restore and strengthen. The anti-African ideology of Muslim militants is in unambiguous contrast to this heritage of missionary labour. It is an intriguing scenario in which to try to resolve exactly what the foreign identity of the missionary was in the light of the major Muslim agents of religious reform.

Critics who stress the foreign nature of Christianity in contrast to Islam's presumed indigenous potential have to contend with a glaring anomaly in one specific example. In Akan culture, exposed to the west and Christianity since the fifteenth century, the prominence of certain central cultural institutions, such as traditional religions, marriage and property customs and laws, mortuary ceremonies, music and art and craft is striking. In the contrasting instance of the Hausa, who were introduced to Islam in a sustained way from at least a corresponding epoch, the indigenous heritage is much less intact. The adoption of a militant Islam in the early nineteenth century had obviously had a profound effect. Nevertheless, the process began much earlier. Islamic *sources*, over a period of centuries, developed into a major *influence* from the reinvocation of the Arabic prescriptions of the faith. In the Akan case in Ghana Christian *sources*, long released into the local stream of the vernacular languages, have failed to acquire a corresponding corroding effect on the culture and produce results attributable to the force of influence. It is easy to see how the factor of the vernacular culture acted to inhibit the development of a foreign sanction for Akan religious and social traditions.

We do not need to go outside Hausa materials to understand how in the pre-*jihad* period Hausa society must have been extremely complex. People practiced an inclusive understanding of religion. The fluidity of the religious life was not necessarily due to religious ignorance among local people, as the *mujahidin* ('militant reformers') charged. It grew out of a tradition of pluralism which allowed different spheres of life to co-exist amicably. When Islam first arrived in such a pluralist world it was appropriately 'influenced' and given a niche in the culture. The orthodox motivations of the *mujahidin* are unquestioned, but if we judge their efforts at wholesale reform as less than a complete success, part of the reason must be the tenacity of local *influence* which continued to cling to Muslim institutions. More than a century after the fires of reform had consumed the old structures of accommodation, pockets of the older dispensation continued to exist. Furthermore, even in the *jihad* sector traces of the *zongo* tradition flourished, with orthodox practice existing alongside patronage of traditional religion. Baba of Karo, a Hausa woman of this century, in her transcribed memoirs, had this to say about the parallelism between Islam and *bori*, a spirit-possession cult:

> The work of the *malams* (Muslim scholars) is one thing, the work of *bori* experts is another, each has his own kind of work and they must not be mixed up. There is the work of *malams*, of *bori*, of magicians, of witches; they are all different but at heart everyone loves the spirits.[3]

Such examples of religious parallelism need not be explained as evidence of waning ardour. Even when the *mujahidin* were busy heaping coals of fire on the heads of their antagonists, the old spirits were roaming free. The Scottish traveller, Hugh Clapperton, went in 1824 to the headquarters of the *jihad* movement, Sokoto in Hausaland, attracted there no doubt by his own Calvinistic scruples, and met the spiritual heir to the founder of the movement. Clapperton was more than a little disconcerted to encounter the force of the pre-*jihad* religious tradition. He wrote in his journals:

> I was unluckily taken for a *fighi*, or teacher, and was pestered, at all hours of the day, to write out prayers by the people. . . .
> Today my washerwoman positively insisted on being paid with a charm, in writing, that would entice people to buy earthen-ware

off her; and no persuasions of mine could either induce her to accept money for her services, or make her believe the request was beyond human power.[4]

Clearly Islam had not done with making 'submissive' gestures towards the *influence* of its host environment. Clapperton's chagrin was complete when the Sultan himself, Muhammad Bello (d. 1837), disarmed him with a knowledgeable interest in dreams and matters of the occult.

The point to be made from all this evidence is that the reform Muslim legacy had not fundamentally altered the structures of the older heritage of pluralism. With the benefit of historical hindsight we might say that the *mujahidin* were shooting at a moving target. The result was an inevitable misalignment between African *influence* and the Islamic materials being constituted into a *counter-influence*. In the Christian example, as we have seen, the vernacular Scriptures pointed towards contrasting inevitable congruence.

However, the issue of the vernacular translation is not always a straightforward one. The recognition of its importance by Christian missions sometimes made them err on the side of indecent haste. The result then was a wooden translation that failed to reproduce the dignity and richness of the original. In the Niger Delta of Nigeria, for example, the use of the Ibo language was the established practice in all Christian work in the formative years between the establishment of missions and the second decade of the twentieth century. But there were few workers, and a certain reliance on non-Ibo African agents became inevitable. Their command of Ibo was poor, which they tried to remedy with zeal. The upshot was a pidgin Ibo calld Union Ibo. One writer, commenting on the invention of this missionary language, writes thus:

> In parts of Ikwerreland (in the Niger Delta) . . . the people have their own language which they use in every other concern except in Christian worship. Even in village churches with no foreigner, and in fact in private family worship too, the people pray in the foreign Ibo language, because that is what they have been taught to do. In recent years, however, especially since the dawn of a new awareness of ethnic nationalism particularly by the creation of the Rivers State of Nigeria, attempts are made to abolish the use of Union Ibo and to substitute with the Ikwerre dialect of Ibo.[5]

This situation, easy to duplicate, and to caricature, arises because the vernacular culture is accepted as the irreplaceable carriage for Christianity. In the Muslim example no amount of vernacular purity would be enough to quieten the qualms of the *mujahidin*.

The profile of Union Ibo as an artificial concoction is easily identifiable in other African languages. The Wolof language, spoken in the Republic of Senegal in West Africa, for example, shows extensive traces of contact with French as well as with Arabic, yet such semantic *sources* do not add up to the force of *influence* as far as the grammatical structure of Wolof is concerned. Mandinka, to take another example, the language of the founders of the medieval empire of Mali in West Africa, shows evidence of early contact with Portuguese in the era of Christopher Columbus. Arabic linguistic materials also occur widely in the language. (Mansa Musa, the emperor of Mali, went on pilgrimage to Mecca in 1325, passing through Cairo where the learned citizenry commented on his commendable grasp of Arabic though royal protocol obliged him to refuse to use it in his dealings with the people). The final linguistic example is the Swahili language. Its proximity to Arabic is well attested, with a growing trickle of English words. However, Swahili is judged by experts to have retained some of the purest forms of the original Bantu language of which it remains a part. In all these examples evidence of foreign *source* material does not constitute *influence* in our sense of the term.

The historical study of religion has often focused on *source* criticism as a means of establishing the original *influence*. Thus *Quellenkritik* assumed an ascendancy in that branch of studies concerned with tracing earlier *influences* with which scholars might reconstruct the issue of 'origins.' Thus the Pagan *influence* on Christian origins, the Judaic *influence* on Christianity, the Jewish foundations of Islam, the Canaanite traditions in Hebrew religion, the Gnostic stream in the Gospels, and the Roman *influence* on Christian institutions and similar subjects became of consuming interest to scholars. Through the method of assuming *source* as evidence of *influence* an extreme position was adopted whereby *influence* was inferred from historical antecedent and subordination from similarity. The later material was consequently overthrown. But the older *source* was not spared either. Each strand of the earlier material was subject to the same stripping and made a carrier of still earlier 'influences.' It knocked the stuffing out of all of them,

too. The net result was an arid methodology. And what use is
Hamlet without the Prince?

The question may be asked about how a major *influence* arises in
the first place and how we might understand the process of the
transformation of one culture by another. These are large issues.
But at the minimum we might say that if borrowing takes place at
all, it is on the basis of an original mutual attraction. Christian
missionary concern with the vernacular languages, for example,
coalesced with the spirit of local enterprise to produce the requisite
atmosphere for effective transmission. Second, depending on the
level of such mutual attraction, indigenous criteria act on the
incoming materials by domesticating them. The emphasis in African Christianity on certain themes in the Old Testament, for
example, stems from their congruity with pre-existing subjects, as
we have seen. Thus the adoption of Scriptural categories was not a
result of missionary *influence*, much of which was starkly Pauline in
its emphasis on guilt and individualism. The suppression of such
missionary concerns by locals is the other aspect of the same
phenomenon of the power of indigenous *influence*. Third, once
assimilated, the new material may act both to judge and justify the
earlier materials. For example, knowledge of the vernacular Scriptures may lead to a call for a return to the past or a striving for its
realization in the present. Some scholars have called this a 'retrac-
tile' movement demanding 'shrinkage' of the cumulative accretions
of history. Or, such knowledge may embolden leaders to call for a
radical programme of change. Depending on the success of a
representative figure to combine the role of conveyor of new
materials and preceptor of old values, a fresh synthesis may develop
to which the name *influence* may apply. It would be the stream in
which the merging of new *sources* and the older materials takes
place, with the indigenous environment determining the climate
and course of the new development. A major *influence* may thus
arise by a radical confrontation of new forces and the older values.
The contact and the ensuing encounter may lead to a new permuta-
tion, though the entire process is grounded in indigenous principles
of perception.

The study of the primary context of the relationship between
source and *influence* should form a necessary consideration in a
comparative science of religion and culture. Given the continuing
interaction between different societies and cultures and the

emergence of new fields of human experience, the student of religion and society is faced with a major challenge of distinguishing between *source* and *influence* in a critical and consistent fashion.

Given the fact that historians accept without quibble the human enterprise as a dynamic process, it should present little difficulty to accept the fact that human experience is similarly set in the context of movement and change. A certain basic openness to new materials is a concomitant of this process. Borrowing, and the transformation triggered as a consequence, reflects the movements that occur in human experience, and is proof of inner vitality, not decay.

My final observation is best made with the help of a passage from the travels of Sir Richard Burton. In it the reader is given a remarkable example of what African culture can do to foreign cultural materials, including the reluctance to abandon notions of western forms and ideas of cultural propriety. The pleasing medium of the English of Sir Richard more than compensates for the sense of discomfiture suffered by him and his colleagues. Sir Richard had been on a mission to the King of Dahomey in West Africa between 1861 and 1864. He describes one occasion when he was summoned to meet the King at court:

The King had repeatedly fixed a day for me to dance before him, and had deferred the operation probably with the delicate motive of allowing me time to prepare myself for so great an event. Now, however, the hour had come. I collected my party in front of the semicircle of caboceers, gave time to the band, and performed a Hindostani *pas seul*, which elicited violent applause, especially from the King. My companion then danced a Dahoman dance with Governor Mark as fugleman, and his *disinvoltura* charmed the people. It was then the Reverend's turn to perform. He posted himself opposite the throne, placed upon another stool his instrument, a large flutina or concertina, and having preliminarily explained the 'God-palaver,' bravely intoned his favourite hymns. They were, Matthias (words by the excellent Dr. Watts and singularly out of place in Agbome), Arnold's *Job*, with a refrain (making 'more' to rhyme with 'endure'), and Martin Luther's 'Old Hundredth' (opening with 'All people that on earth do dwell'). How is it that the Wesleyan mind cannot forego its fondness for this Ennian literature? The people stared and chuckled a little. . .

The Reverend being in his pulpit, so to speak, gave his listeners a good half hour of edification. When the instrument was mute the King proposed a modification. The Reverend was to play and sing, while Mr. Cruikshank and I must dance as before on both sides. It was almost too ridiculous, but we complied. . . . My second *pas seul* which ended the affair, was greeted with firing guns and presenting arms by all my company. . . . It required some strength of mind to prevent holding oneself a manner of prodigy; the people evidently thought the power of dancing, of using a sword, of learning enough to understand them in a month, of writing down everything seen so as to recall it to their memories, and of sketching objects so that even they could recognize them, to be an avatar of intellect.[6]

Burton, like other foreign materials before and after him was required to acquit himself by the standards of local value. In spite of protestations, he obviously had more talent on that score than he suspected, and the people were quick to compliment him. 'Our dancing,' he writes, 'had so excited the multitude that we had hardly dined before an eruption of friends by the score, all wishing to learn "white man's fashion," crowded the house. . . '[7]. The demand to perform came from the value the traditional culture placed on certain skills. The judgement as to the success of the outcome was similarly reserved in the host culture. Finally, the value that continued to be ascribed to dancing would determine and 'influence' the attitude to what Burton and his types might bring into the society. Burton was learning what numerous missionaries had discovered, the transforming power of local tradition on foreign materials.

NOTES

1 Bengt Sundkler: *Zulu Zion and Some Swazi Zionists*, Oxford, 1976, p.88.
2 ibid., p.250.
3 Mary F. Smith: *Baba of Karo*, London; Faber & Faber, 1954, p.222.
4 E.W. Borill, ed.: *Missions to the Niger*, vol. IV: *The Bornu Mission 1822–25*, London: Hakluyt Society Series II, vol. *CXXX*, 1966, pp.669–70.

5 Godwin Tasie: *Christian Missionary Enterprise in the Niger Delta*, Leiden: E.J. Brill, 1978, p.200n.
6 Sir Richard Burton: *A Mission to Gelele, King of Dahome*, London: Routledge & Kegan Paul, 1966, p.273.
7 ibid., p.274.

III
HEALING AND TRANSFORMATION: PERSPECTIVES ON DEVELOPMENT, EDUCATION AND COMMUNITY[1]

Richard Katz

ABSTRACT

Katz's chapter, 'Healing and Transformation: Perspectives on Development, Education and Community,' treats healing as a community ritual and describes the environments of healing among the !Kung of the Kalahari Desert and among the Fijians. In these cases, healing is seen as a process moving participants toward connectedness and balance within their community. In the explicit definition and evocation of crisis and abnormality, healing also serves to focus definitions of a society's realities and norms concerning health, balance and normalcy. Both as process and as source of definition, then, the 'healing transition' is an important key to a society's dominant issues in human potential.

I INTRODUCTION

Among the !Kung hunter-gatherers of the Kalahari Desert and the farming fishing people of the outer Fiji Islands, healing is a central community ritual with significance far beyond effecting a cure. In this article I present field data on healing in these two cultures. The data support a definition of healing as 'a process of transitioning toward meaning, balance, connectedness and wholeness' (Katz, 1982b).

The data also suggest that the study of psychological healing provides special insights into processes of psychological development, education, and community, offering a transformational model.[2] An enhanced state of consciousness, experienced most intensely by the healer, but also shared by the community, is at the core of !Kung and Fijian healing. That enhanced state brings on a sense of connectedness between a spiritual healing power, the healers, and their community. Continual transitioning is the developmental pattern, as the relationship to power is in dynamic flux. The enhanced consciousness establishes the possibility of healing but does not remove healers from the context of daily life. Access to this healing power becomes significant only with its application within the daily life of the community. The healer serves as a vehicle to channel healing to the community, without accumulating power for personal use. The transformational model involves the experience of both accessing the enhanced state of consciousness and applying it within the community.

Individuals and communities which seek healing are often in the midst of crises, confusion, or a search for fulfillment (Katz, 1982b). In their vulnerability and openness to change, they reveal their fears and hopes. These fears and hopes are the context for the healing transition; their resolution or fulfillment, the aim of that transition.[3] Not only is healing a source of insight about human nature; it is also a vehicle for actualizing human potential (Bourguignon, 1973, 1979; Durkheim, 1915; Katz, 1982b; Lévi-Strauss, 1963; LeVine, 1979; Van Gennep, 1960). Focusing as it does on vulnerability, healing deals with a critical link in the actualization of that potential, and thus with paradigmatic issues in community and individual development.

Healing also involves central tasks of psychological development, such as defining reality and making meaning; it is not merely confined to curing sick people. Focusing as it does upon the more intense disruptions and integrations in that reality-definition and meaning-making, healing can thus be studied as a paradigmatic developmental process. Among the !Kung and the Fijians, the process of becoming a healer exemplifies the process of healing itself; the key to both is an experience of transformation which benefits the community. As healers intersect with situations of crisis and opportunity in their efforts to construct reality and work on the dynamics of cultural balance, their education and development become inseparable processes. Thus healing can offer a paradigm for education.

The !Kung and Fijian data in particular provide further support for considering healing in this paradigmatic fashion. The !Kung data offer a special evolutionary perspective. When I did field-work with the !Kung, they were living primarily as hunter-gatherers, a mode of adaptation rare today, though *representative* of what was the universal pattern of human existence for 99 per cent of cultural history (Lee and DeVore, 1968). During that huge span of history, it is believed, basic patterns of human adaptation evolved (Lee and DeVore 1968). Lee (1979) goes as far as to say that 'basic human social forms, language and human nature itself were forged' during that span (p. 1). A study of !Kung healing may suggest principles fundamental to human healing and development, shedding light on their origins and evolution.[4]

Furthermore, !Kung and Fijian healers are teachers, generating and conveying the culture's central mysteries and wisdom. They are highly respected and viewed as approximating cultural ideals as they participate in the healing process and manifest the healing power. The healers are respected as guardians of the culture's ultimate powers, not for their personal achievements. Their transformation represents an ideal of development for the culture.

The concept of healing explored in this chapter suggests a transformational model which can be applied to understanding processes of education, development and community. The model is directly relevant to the healing enterprise, while offering an implicit generic perspective. For example, 'education as transformation' describes a model of healer education, while offering a generic perspective on education. The transformational model emphasizes psychological and social transitioning and the sharing of valued resources, in striking contrast to comparable models which predominate in contemporary Euro-American culture with their emphasis on linear stage-wise progressions and the individual competition for and accumulation of valued resources.

While the cross-cultural relevance of this transformational model must be established with extreme care, the model presents an alternative to euro-western approaches which seems worth consideration. The healing transition is an important key to a society's dominant issues in human potential; the transformational model suggests ways a society can encourage the communal generation and utilization of valued resources, which Rappaport (1978) posits as critical for the survival of the human species.

II ETHNOGRAPHIC DATA

The field-data presented are drawn from two studies of community healing systems: a three-month study in 1968 among the Kalahari !Kung (e.g. Katz, 1982b); and a twenty-two month study in 1977–8 on the outer Fiji Islands (Katz, 1981). Standard ethnographic methods, including participant observation, spot observation, and interviewing were used. In addition, psychological tests were given to matched samples of healers and non-healers to delineate specific healer characteristics, and survey questionnaires were given to community members to delineate characteristics of social organization.

A Accepting boiling energy: transformation and healing among the
!Kung

In Botswana, Namibia and southern Angola there are about 50,000 San people, of whom some 5,000 live primarily as hunter-gatherers. The fieldwork for this paper occurred among a group of nearly 500 !Kung-speaking San, living as hunter-gatherers in the northwestern Kalahari Desert, Botswana.[5]

The economic system of the !Kung is based on sharing collected food resources (Lee, 1979; Lee and DeVore, 1976; Marshall, 1976). Local groups do not maintain exclusive rights to resources or defend territories; a reciprocal access prevails. Frequent visiting among different groups mitigates the effect of localized shortages. Allied groups co-operate, coming together in a given area, living apart when sources of food and water are widely scattered.

Resources of all kinds circulate among members of a camp and between camps, so that any one person draws upon resources far beyond his or her capacity. Little investment in a capital sector of the economy is necessary; elements of the material culture are easily made, with ample leisure time to make them. Since individuals must move around to get food, personal property is minimal, usually less than 25 pounds per adult (Lee, 1979). The environment itself acts as a storehouse. There is a marked absence of disparities in wealth and possessions among the !Kung. Egalitarianism is the rule (Lee, 1979).

The primary ritual among the !Kung, the all-night healing dance, epitomizes these characteristics of sharing and egalitarianism (Katz, 1981, 1982a, 1982b; Lee, 1968; Marshall, 1969). In the crucible of intense emotions and the search for protection which is the healing dance, sharing and egalitarianism are put to the test, relied upon as vehicles for survival. The healing power, or *n/um*, is the most valued resource at the dance, and one of the most valued resources in all community life (Katz, 1982b). It is released by the community and, through its healing effects, helps to recreate and renew that community. Though 'strongest' at the dance, *n/um* has a primary significance throughout the !Kung universe of experience. Its existence and functioning harmonize with and help maintain !Kung life.

!Kung healing involves health and growth on physical, psychological, social and spiritual levels; it affects the individual, the group, the surrounding environment and the cosmos. Healing is an integrating and enhancing force, far more fundamental than simple curing or the application of medicine.

Sometimes as often as four times in a month, the women sit around the fire, singing and rhythmically clapping as night falls, signaling the start of a healing dance. The entire camp participates. The men, sometimes joined by the women, dance around the singers. As the dance intensifies, *n/um* ('energy') is activated in those who are healers, most of whom are among the dancing men. As *n/um* intensifies in the healers, they experience *!kia* ('a form of enhanced consciousness') during which they heal everyone at the dance. The dance usually extends far into the night, often ending as the sun rises the next morning. Those at the dance confront the uncertainties of their experience, and reaffirm the spiritual dimension of their daily lives. 'Being at a dance makes our hearts happy,' the !Kung say.

A healer talks about the !kia experience:

> 'You dance, dance, dance, dance. Then n/*um* lifts you in your belly and lifts you in your back. . . . N/*um makes you tremble, it's hot. . . . When you get into !kia, you're looking around because you see everything, because you see what's troubling everybody. . .* ' (Katz, 1982b, p.42).

Held in awe, *n/um* is considered very powerful and mysterious. As healers learn to control their boiling *n/um*, they can apply it to healing. They learn to heal, to 'see the sickness and pull it out.'

A powerful healer spoke of the feeling *!kia* gives, that of becoming more essential, more oneself: 'I want to have a dance soon so that I can really become myself again.' A transcendent state of consciousness, *!kia* alters a !Kung's sense of self, time and space. *!Kia* makes healers feel they are 'opening up' or 'bursting open, like a ripe pod.'

Through *!kia*, the !Kung transcend ordinary life and can contact the realm of the gods and the spirits of dead ancestors. Sickness is a process in which the spirits try to carry a person off into their realm. In *!kia*, the healer expresses the wishes of the living to keep the sick person with them and goes directly into the struggle with the spirits. The healer is the community's emissary in this confrontation. When a person is seriously ill, the struggle intensifies. If a healer's *n/um* is strong, the spirits will retreat and the sick one will live. This struggle is at the heart of the healer's art, skill and power. In their search for contact with transcendent realms and in their struggle with illness, misfortune and death, the healing dance and *n/um* are the !Kung's most important allies.

Fiercely egalitarian, the !Kung do not allow *n/um* to be controlled by a few religious specialists, but wish it to be spread widely among the group. All young boys and most young girls seek to become healers. By the time they reach adulthood, more than half the men and 10 per cent of the women have become healers. Still there is no stigma attached to those who do not become healers. An unlimited energy, *n/um* expands as it boils. It cannot be hoarded by any one person. The !Kung do not seek *!kia* for its own sake, but for its healing protection. At the healing dance, *n/um* is shared by everyone, all are given healing. As one person experiences *!kia* at the dance, others likely will follow. Though *!kia* may be experienced most intensely in the healers, they are channels to aid in the distribution of *n/um* to those at the dance.

The dance provides healing in the most generic sense: it may cure an ill body or mind, as the healer pulls out sickness with a laying on of hands; mend the social fabric, as the dance promotes social cohesion and a manageable release of hostility; protect the camp from misfortune, as the healer pleads with the gods for relief from the Kalahari's harshness; and provide opportunities for growth and fulfillment, as all can experience a sense of well-being and some, a spiritual development.

These integrated functions of the dance reinforce each other, providing a continuous source of curing, counsel, protection and enhancement. The healing dance is woven into !Kung hunting-gathering life without undermining the execution of everyday responsibilities. Healers are first and foremost hunters and gatherers, their primary obligation being to help in subsistence activities. A public, routine cultural event to which all have access, the dance establishes community, and it is the community, in its activation of *n/um*, which heals and is healed.

To heal depends upon developing a desire to 'drink *n/um*', not on learning a set of specific techniques. Teaching focuses upon helping students overcome their fear, helping them to regulate the boiling *n/um* and resultant *!kia* so that healing can occur. The *n/um* must be hot enough to evoke *!kia*, but not so hot that it provokes debilitating fear. Accepting boiling energy for oneself is a difficult process because *n/um*, painful and mysterious, is greatly feared. The healer's education stresses not the structure of the dancing, but the importance of dancing so one's 'heart is open to boiling *n/um*'; it emphasizes not the composition of the healing songs, but singing so that one's 'voice reaches up to the heavens.'

The experience of *!kia* brings profound pain and fear, along with feelings of release and liberation. *N/um* feels 'hot, like a fire that is inside.' A respected healer described another dimension of this fear: 'As we !Kung enter !kia, we fear death. We fear we may die and not come back!' When potential healers can face the fact of death and willingly die, they can overcome fear of *n/um*, and there can be a breakthrough to *!kia*. An older healer talks about this death and rebirth:

> '(In *!kia*) your heart stops. You're dead. Your thoughts are nothing. You breathe with difficulty. You see things, *n/um* things; you see spirits killing people. You smell burning, rotten flesh. Then you heal, you pull sickness out. You heal, heal, heal. Then you live. Your eyeballs clear and you see people clearly' (Katz, 1982b, p. 45).

The process which teaches the !Kung to become healers, also supports their continual efforts at healing. It is a process of education which engages the community.

Healers are similar to non-healers in a broad range of social, economic and political variables. While healers are not a privileged group, they do differ psychologically from non-healers in ways that both prepare them for the healing work and result from that work (Katz, 1982b).[6] It is a distinction they are meant to carry within. 'We (!Kung) are not meant to boast of our healing. It is . . . something we do to help others.'

B Traveling the straight path: healing and transformation among the Fijians

The island nation of Fiji, consisting of 100 inhabited islands and 500,000 people, is situated in the South Pacific, north of New Zealand. Approximately 50 per cent of the population is indigenous; the rest descended from emigrants from southern India, who came as indentured servants more than 100 years ago. The field-data on healing deals only with indigenous Fijian culture in the rural outer islands, where people live in villages of about 100 located several hours from each other by foot.

Fijians live primarily by subsistence farming and fishing (Sahlins, 1962; Nyacakalou, 1975, 1978; M. Katz, 1981). A village consists of several groups of closely related kin who jointly own land and choice fishing areas, often working them communally. Sharing of resources is highly valued. When Fijians sit down to eat, their doors must remain open. When anyone passes by, they call out, 'Please come in and eat.' Fijian social structure is hierarchical, but humility, regardless of status, is valued.

Ceremonial life is essential in Fiji, promoting economic and social exchange and celebrating the religious dimension (Thompson, 1940; Spencer, 1941; Ravuvu, 1976). Three main elements characterize Fijian ceremonies generally and the healing ceremony in particular (Katz, 1981): the *Vu* ('ancestors'); the *mana* ('spiritual power'); and the *yagona* ('a plant with sacred use') that brings this power to humans.[7] *Mana*, the ultimate power, is an invisible, irreducible force that 'makes things happen.' As Fijians say, '*Mana* is *mana*,' and its effects are often described as miraculous.

Fijians conceive of sicknesses in two major categories, with different etiologies. The 'true' or 'real' sicknesses are caused by natural events. For example, one may have painful joints from being in the cold ocean too long while net-fishing. The second type, 'spiritual' sicknesses, are caused either by witchcraft or by some violation of cultural norms, punished directly by the ancestors.

While Fijians may seek western medicine for treating 'true sicknesses,' both true and spiritual sicknesses are brought to the traditional Fijian healers. The same symptom pattern often can express either etiology.

In times of doubt, crisis, or illness, the spiritual healer is the primary community resource.[8] No problem is excluded from his or her domain, but the majority of cases are illnesses with accompanying physical symptoms. Requests for help range from a boy with a swollen neck, to a childless woman who wishes to become pregnant, to a family seeking protection against other's evil intentions, to an entire village wanting to make amends for violating a sacred custom. As one villager remarked about the spiritual healer in her village: 'He can't get sick, because without him, we would all be lost.' Compared to non-healers, healers are rated as significantly more 'respected' and 'hard working' and closer than most to the 'ideal Fijian'; they remain fully contributing community members.

The healing ceremony, centering around the ritual exchange of yaqona, typically begins when the client comes to the healer with a request for help whether it be for protection or cure. The client incorporates the request within a ritual presentation of yaqona to the healer. The healer accepts the yaqona on behalf of the ancestors from whom he or she draws healing power. Yaqona may be prepared with water and drunk by the healer, but that is not necessary. In that very act of acceptance, the critical initial exchange between healer and client is completed, and the healing is accomplished. In that moment, the *mana* is said to become available, making possible accurate diagnosis and selection of an effective treatment. The client returns after four days for the conclusion of the treatment, or, if needed, further treatment in the same or some new direction. Herbs and massage are used in about 20 per cent of the instances to carry out the healing.

Mana, like *n/um*, is the most valued resource in the healing ceremony and one of the most valued in community life generally. It is omnipresent. Though meant for the protection and healing of humans, *mana* can be turned to opposite purposes. Only by following the *gaunisala dodonu*, the 'straight path', can persons direct *mana* toward healing. The path itself is not straight, but the way one travels it should be. The path is discovered by traveling it.

Traveling the straight path means living out attributes that characterize the ideal Fijian. The straight path provides a concept of

49

ideal development for all Fijians, an aim pursued with special intensity by healers. The education of healers is an education for living in an ideal manner, and thus becomes a paradigm for education in and of the community.

The following attributes are often mentioned when prescribing the way a healer must live in order to follow the straight path: telling and living the truth (*dauvakadina*); love for all (*dauloloma*), so that all who come receive help; proper or traidtional behavior-(*i tovo vinaka*); humility Å*sega ni vukivuki*); respect for others and tradition (*vakarokoroko*); single-mindedness (*sega ni lomaloma rua*); and service (*veigarvai*), so that the power is used only to heal and not for personal gain. Though these attributes are often phrased in terms of the healing work per se, they generally prescribe the way a healer, and by extension all Fijians, must live. Together, they constitute character.

While being the source of character, traveling the straight path simultaneously challenges character. The education of the healer deals with subtle movements back and forth along dimensions of character, at increasingly demanding levels. The movement itself releases increasingly potent healing power. The healer's character creates the possibility of healing work, and the development of character marks the continuation and deepening of that work. Information about healing techniques is available only to those with character. There is respect for the technical aspects of healing, but character precedes and provides the context for healing technology.

The healer is constantly tested to betray the attributes that define the path. Increased healing power is determined by how one meets increasingly severe tests. For example, a healer's gain in power must be set within a reciprocating process whereby the community likewise gains in power.

A first vision lays the foundation of the healing work – the connection with the ancestor who will be the source of power, and the commitment to use that power for healing. It inspires the appearance of the path and sets in motion a life-long process which is more than carrying out the intent of the first healing vision. A continuous recreating and reshaping of that initial vision into an unfolding life pattern is required. That process involves advice and instruction from a teacher, if there is one; subsequent visions; lessons learned from one's patients; and most of all the actual practice of healing and learning to live with that practice in one's community.

A common metaphor of the straight path is that of a path cut by hand with a bush-knife through the heavy underbrush of the Fijian forests. In creating the path one must follow, dead-ends and shortcuts, tortuously difficult passages and relatively easy ones cause the person's movement to fluctuate in rhythm and speed, sometimes circling back on itself.

III TOWARD A TRANSFORMATIONAL MODEL

From the data on healing among the !Kung and the Fijians we can extrapolate models of psychological development, education, and community, at whose crux are transformational experiences. For the !Kung, these experiences are epitomized in the process of 'accepting boiling energy;' for the Fijians, in the process of 'traveling the striaight path.'[9] One expression of this transformation is a dramatically enhanced state-of-consciousness, such as *!kia*; but the transformational experience can also unfold during more subtle shifts in consciousness within the context of ordinary life events. Whether in its dramatic or ordinary context, transformation brings on an experience of reality in which the boundaries of self and social organization become more permeable to contact with a transpersonal realm. Accessing the enhanced state of consciousness and applying its effects within the community combine to constitute the transformational experience.

These transformational experiences can be said to unfold within and into a transformational model of psychological development (Katz, 1982a; Katz and Kilner, in press); to be guided by a transformational model of education – 'education as transformation' (Katz, 1981, 1982c); and to be structured by a transformational model of community – 'synergistic community' (Katz, 1983/4). In fact, there is one transformational model, which, as it is applied to the areas of development, education and community, interrelates those areas: education and development merge, and community is a stimulant for, as well as expression of, both. The model is offered as generic; originally derived from but not necessarily limited to *healer* or *spiritual* development and education, or *healing* communities. Though in contemporary euro-American culture the spiritual is

51

considered a separate or separable dimension, and healing a separate or separable role, the !Kung and Fijian data describe a situation where the spiritual is inseparable from other aspects of life, as is healing. The model reflects this integrated conception and offers an integrated perspective for understanding development, education, and community in the west.

The transformational model as applied to psychological development is clarified when compared with the Piagetian model, probably the most commonly accepted theory of development psychology in the west.[10] For example, the spiritual dimension plays a central role in the transformational model in contrast to the focus on psychological, and especially cognitive, dimensions in the Piagetian approach.[11] That spiritual dimension is extraordinary only in its depth and intensity, not in its separation from ordinary life. It includes, in an integrative manner, the psychological and cognitive dimensions, as well as other dimensions such as the emotional and physical. The validity of the transition into an enhanced state, and the state itself, is dependent on its application within daily life.

The transformational model emphasizes transitioning rather than stages achieved, process and experience rather than structures. *A continual* process of transitioning over the life-course is viewed as the crux of development, rather than the Piagetian focus upon a linear (or spiral) progression through fixed stages which culminates in an equilibrated end-state or stage in adulthood. Unfolding like a path cut through the bush, the straight path is not a linear progression through defined levels of attainment. Life history in the transformation model becomes the continuous dialectic of meeting and being overwhelmed by one recurring developmental challenge: transcending the self to channel transpersonal resources to the community. This contrasts with the idea of different developmental challenges at different stages in the Piegetian model. Though healers have careers, and can be said to move through stages in their work, these are surface categories, which do not organize the transitioning experiences.

The process of transitioning is neither unidirectional nor the basis of permanent structural gains, unlike the developmental process in the Piagetian model. Transitioning occurs toward and away from meaning, balance, connectedness and wholeness; and each movement is considered important in and of itself – regardless of direction – because it deals with the basic developmental challenge of transitioning. Once a particular meaning, for example, has been achieved in a certain setting, it is not thereby permanent. Meaning is undone as meaninglessness inevitably appears and old and new meanings are established. In their continual struggle to regulate their access to and control of the healing power, healers exemplify this fluidity in the developmental process. With each opportunity for transition, knowledge of how to transit must in the existential sense be relearned with each opportunity for transition; at times it is unavailable, even to the experienced healers. The process of transitioning is also accompanied by a fundamental experience of vulnerability, both more frightening and liberating than the feelings of perplexity, confusion, surprise and insight which are spoken of as accompanying the developmental transitions in the Piagetian framework.

Finally, the merging of individual and social development in the transformational model contrasts with the more individualistic, even personal emphasis in Piagetian models. In the transformational model, development is a shared enterprise, a joining of self and community with unexpected benefits to both. It is a way of giving support for the difficulties of transition as well as a way of distributing the benefits released by that transitioning.

By understanding the healer as a 'moral explorer,' we can see evidence for this merging of individual and socio-cultural development. Fijian healers must find and stay on the 'straight path.' It is this continual struggle which allows the healer to contact the most profound power in Fijian life and, more important, apply that power to healing. Healers are faced with the task of defining reality in their interactions with cultural mysteries. Defining reality, they impart meaning. Imparting meaning, they make judgments about mortality. None of these activities is predetermined. Though the straight path existed for many before them, all healers must find and travel the path for themselves. The community sends healers on a journey to new territories of experience, to formulate new questions of reality, meaning, and morality; and then it looks to them for guidance in these areas. In dynamic interaction with changing times, they can provide guidance for the direction of change.

The transformational model as applied to education – 'education as transformation' – stresses character development rather than cognitive development as the critical context for knowledge (Hahn and Katz, 1985, Katz 1981, 1982c, in press). It is qualities of heart –

courage, commitment, belief and intuitive understanding – that open the healers to the healing potential, facilitate the learning of healing knowledge, and keep them in the healing work. Healing technologies become available to those with the necessary character. Technologies serve the healing aim, but they do not justify or measure the healing work. Character is the necessary foundation and result of developmental processes. To travel the straight path, one needs character, which can only develop fully as one travels that path. The straight path unfolds in this reflexive and reciprocating manner.

Education as transformation stresses process more than outcome, focusing on healing as a dynamic balancing rather than the achievement of specific cures. Such education respects both aspects of a dialectic that seem necessary to individual and community health (Turner, 1969; J. Rappaport, 1981). It connects experiences ordered by the structures of daily life as well as those that occur in transition between and beyond those structures. Education as transformation gives added weight to the experience to transition itself, emphasizing the intrinsic value of the psychological movement that animates that transition. The experience of the transpersonal is intensified during these transitions but not restricted to them. In a process we can call 'envisioning', the experience of enhanced consciousness is continually reenacted and reaffirmed in the healers'daily lives. Transformation initiates the intensive phase of becoming a healer and also characterizes the healer's subsequent development.

Education as transformation is based upon a service orientation. The healer's commitment is to serve as a vehicle that channels healing to the community rather than to accumulate power for personal use. Education aims to connect the teaching-learned process to its community contexts. The cure of a particular patient assumes importance in the larger context of the general sense of dynamic balance in the community. Healers become a community's focal point of intensity, embodying a dedication to the healing work and reaffirming the community's self-healing capacities.

The transformation model as applied to community – 'synergistic community' – is epitomized, for example, in the !Kung healing community. In a synergistic community valued resources are renewable, expanding, and accessible (Katz, 1983/84; Katz, 1985; Katz and Seth 1985). As these resources are shared equitably with all members of the community, the whole becomes greater than the sum of the parts and what is good for one member becomes good for all. As a result, benefits to the community grow exponentially.

Synergy and scarcity represent paradigmatic alternatives, two ends of a continuum which in actual situations exist in some combination (Katz, 1983/84). What might be called a 'scarcity paradigm' dominates western thinking about the existence and distribution of a wide variety of resources. The paradigm assumes that valued resources are scarce; their presumed scarcity in fact largely determines their value. It further assumes that individuals or communities must compete with each other to gain access to these resources, struggling to accumulate their own supply, resisting pressures to share.[12]

An alternative paradigm is based on synergy. The term synergy describes a pattern of relationships among phenomena, including how people relate to each other and other phenomena (Fuller, 1963; Benedict, 1970; Maslow, 1971; Katz, 1982b). A synergistic pattern exists when phenomena are interrelating so that an often unexpected, new and greater whole is created from disparate, seemingly conflicting parts. In that pattern, phenomena exist in harmony with each other, maximizing each others' potential. Within the synergy paradigm, a resource such as healing becomes renewable and expansively accessible, yet it can remain valuable (Katz, 1981).[13] Individuals and communities activate resources. They function as guardians, not possessors of resources, and while guided by the motivation of service to others, they allow resources to be shared by all members of the community. Greater amounts of the resource become increasingly available to all, so that collaboration rather than competition is encouraged. Paradoxically, the more the resource is utilized, the more there is to be utilized.

Synergistic community is a perspective for understanding the functioning of synergy within a community as well as a guideline for increasing that synergy (Katz, 1983/4).[14] If, for example, healing is a valued resource for a community, the existence of a synergistic community would mean that that resource would expand and become renewable. The community would heal and become healed.

Synergistic community is initiated when members experience an enhancement of consciousness. As the boundaries of self become more permeable to the spiritual dimension, a transpersonal bonding between people can occur so that individuals realize and activate communal commitments. As persons 'die to' or go beyond their individual needs, sharing of resources becomes possible, even predictable. Realizing their deep connectedness, persons realize they do not have to compete for resources, which have become shared and thereby expanding.[15] Synergistic community is established by the full transformational experience.

The transformational experience is based on access to and working with a resource which is highly valued in the culture and is also renewable and expanding when activated – for example, *n/um* for the !Kung, *mana* for the Fijians. Transformation itself activates that resource. Given its socio-culture context, transformation releases that resource – now in the form of healing – to the community, making it accessible to all. A reciprocating web of valued resources becomes renewable and shared – for example, the *n/um* or *mana* is released in the process of healing which stimulates and expresses developmental processes so that access to *n/*um or *mana* is facilitated.

The recurring developmental challenge is on behalf of one's community and the benefits channeled to that community, whether or not the challenge is met. In either case the community shares in the process of transitioning, supporting the healer's movement back and forth as it itself so moves. As one healer makes the transition, it becomes more likely that another will; it is not a zero-sum game, but a situation of renewable and expanding resources. The !Kung healing dance exemplifies this – healers, by their own !*kia*, stimulate !*kia* in others. In synergistic fashion, effects are produced which are far beyond what is possible from separate actions.[16]

The transformational model we have just presented has been deduced from the field data on !Kung and Fijian community healing systems. But to what extent is this model culture-dependent, embedded in specific demographic, economic, technological and other socio-cultural conditions? The general validity of the model awaits further empirical work in other cultures. How valid is transformation as a paradigm for the process of psychological healing, and in particular to healer development and education and healing communities? How valid is healing as a paradigm for generic processes of development, education and community? A first step in this empirical effort demonstrates that 'education as transformation' characterizes healer education among hunter–gatherers (Hahn and Katz, 1985).

Despite the provisional nature of the proposed transformational model, its striking contrast with Euro-American models deserves comment. Transformational experiences are relatively absent in Euro-American models. These transformational experiences, epitomized in the healing transitioning, take individuals beyond the self and take communities beyond the usual boundaries of social organization. The result is a network of interconnections between individuals and within communities that makes sharing of resources a simple fact of living. The absence of such transformational experiences makes such sharing difficult, in spite of human motivation and intention.

Compelling arguments document the necessity of sharing, as well as other characteristics of the transformational model for the survival of the human community (see e.g. Caplan and Killilea, 1976; Eliade, 1965; Jung, 1952; Lee, 1979; Light, 1980; Maslow, 1971; Rappaport, 1978; J. Rappaport, 1981; Sarason, 1977). There is for example the need to appreciate the non-linear oscillation about a recurring central developmental issue rather than the relative Euro-American preoccupation with linear, 'progressive' models of development; the need to focus on character and community service in education rather than the relative Euro-American emphasis on technical training in isolation from character and on the personal accumulation of skill and power; and the need to view resources as renewable and expanding rather than the relative Euro-American orientation that valued resources are scarce, requiring competition to access them.

From the perspective of most contemporary Euro-American communities, establishing a synergistic community would require a radical paradigm shift – a major shift in the way persons experience meaning and interpret data (Kuhn, 1970). Accepting, even cultivating a sense of vulnerability, would create the possibility for such a shift (Katz, 1985). Experiencing the self-embedded-in community as a desirable state, along with the sense of the separate and separating self, would be one result. In a synergistic community, self and community work toward the common good while seeking to fulfill their own perceived needs. As healing is given, more rather than less becomes available. These apparently 'illogical' events can be accepted or even encouraged when the synergy paradigm prevails. If change is to occur and persist, socio-political structures which initiate and express these new ways of making sense of experience must be established.

R. Rappaport (1978) suggests that rituals in which we experience a transpersonal bonding are essential for the survival for the species. He claims that only through participating in such rituals can we overcome our separateness as individuals and, by knowing the reality of the transpersonal, become able to accomplish the communal tasks so essential to the survival of the human community. The present individualism and consequent fragmentation of these communal efforts in industrialized society is well documented (Berger, Berger and Kellner 1973). The transformational model offers an alternative to this fragmentation, stressing a transpersonal bonding within a supportive socio-cultural context.

NOTES

1 I wish to acknowledge the kind permission of the Governments of Botswana and Fiji, to do the research reported in this paper. The research was possible only because of the caring and wise support of the !Kung and Fijians I lived and worked with who gave me so much. I hope this paper begins to reflect that understanding. I also want to thank Michael Murphy, Linda Levine, Susan Pollak, Becka Reichmann and Merry White for their helpful comments. generously offered.

2 The terms 'transformation' and 'transformational' have wide usage in the social sciences (see e.g. Gould, 19; *Harvard Educational Review*, 1981; Jung, 1952). But rather than working within a strictly comparative framework, I wish to devote this paper to generating a particular meaning constellation for the terms, and for the purposes of the paper, restrict the terms to those developed meanings.

Among the !Kung and Fijians, and in most traditional non-western cultures, there are no significant differentations between 'physical' and 'psychological' healing. But I have chosen the term 'psychological healing' when dealing with the transformational model extracted from that data because the main application of that model in this paper will be to contemporary Euro-American thinking and practice, where such differentations remain crucial. Assuming the validity of those distinctions, the model proposed would be more relevant to the psychological and socio-cultural context of health and illness than e.g. the specific issues of tissue damage and repair. Yet this conservative stance may soon be unnecessary, as evidence is increasing within western social science and medicine for the confluence of the psychology and physical elements of healing (see e.g. Sobel, 1979).

3 Healing systems are among those parts of a culture most sensitive to

change. Dealing as they do with points of crisis, confusion, and opportunity – transitions which are the essence of cultural change – healing systems often function as the barometers of, as well as the responses to, such change. Therefore the study of healing could be focusing upon patterns of adaptation to change, perhaps even upon aspects of the culture which are most changed.

4　Contemporary hunter-gatherers or foragers are different from ancient foragers, changed as they are by their own history, which includes contact with other types of societies. Also, there are differences among contemporary foragers, such as the !Kung, the Inuit, and the Australian aboriginal (Lee, 1979). Yet the !Kung remain one of the few living groups whose life style may be similar to that ancient foraging way:

> The modern foragers do offer clues to the nature of the [foraging] way of life, and by understanding the adaptations of the past we can better understand the present and the basic material that produced them both (Lee, 1979, p. 433).

5　The research on healing was part of the larger Harvard Kalahari Research Project (Lee and DeVore, 1976).

6　Significant psychological differences were based on T.A.T. and Draw-a-Person test findings. Due to the small sample size and lack of longitudinal data, it was not possible to pinpoint the exact degree to which these differences were preexisting conditions, influencing the selection of healers, and/or were effects of the healing practice itself.

7　Yaqona's botanical identification is *Piper methysticum*. It is widely used in the South Pacific, and is also called 'kava kava'.

8　There are a variety of traditional healers. The type we are considering is called a *dauvagunu*; they can be considered as spiritual healers in distinction to the herbalists and massage specialists. Spiritual healers treat the broadest range of problems as well as the most severe; sicknesses with a spiritual etiology are their special province.

9　!Kung egalitarian social structure, with its emphasis on sharing, ensures that *n/um* is applied as healing which is distributed throughout the community. Therefore there is a relative emphasis in the !Kung data on accessing the enhanced state of consciousness. Fijian social structure cannot so clearly ensure that *mana* is applied to healing and distributed throughout the community. Therefore there is a relative emphasis in the Fijian data on applying the enhanced state toward healing in the community.

10　Piaget's focus is on intellectual development and the development of moral reasoning, and thus has limitations as a general theory of development for the whole person. But other theorists have extended the Piagetian framework to such areas as social development (Selman, 1980) faith development (Fowler, 1982) and community development (Higgins *et al.*, 1984). Our discussion of the Piagetian model is based upon this broader conception of the Piagetian model.

　　The transformational model can be particularly confusing at this point because some of those working within the Piagetian framework use the term 'transformation' to refer to processes which are different from those described in this paper.

11 Fowler's (1982) work considers the influence of spiritual factors throughout development. But it is not until the final stage in his theory, 'Universalizing Faith,' that he deals with a spiritual influence as direct and pervasive as that which occurs in the transformational model of development. Even then Fowler's Universalizers are rare and often exist at odds with their culture, in contrast to the spiritual dimension of the transformation model which is consonant with cultural context.

12 The relation of actual scarcity of particular resources to co-operation or competition remains an empirical question. The relationship may differ according to the resource in question as well as the social structure governing access to and control of that resource. Water is a scarce and valued resource for the !Kung people of the Kalahari Desert, while building materials for their shelters are a plentiful and valued resource. Both resources are shared among the !Kung (Lee, 1979).

13 It can be argued that resources created at least in part by human activity and intention, such as healing, are intrinsically expanding and renewable. Yet the scarcity paradigm can dominate the generation and distribution of these human resources. In most western psychotherapy techniques, healing is seen as existing in scarce supply. Value, expressed in varying fee schedules, becomes entrained to scarcity. People are forced to compete with each other for their share of healing. Here the scarcity paradigm seems to function more as an ideology than an empirically-derived framework.

14 Synergy, it seems, is an inevitable aspect or phase of community. It exists in a dialectical relationship with its opposite. Most Euro-American communities function primarily within the scarcity paradigm, but they require moments of synergy in order to remain intact. Synergistic community refers both to the phase of synergy that is intrinsic to community, and those particular communities in which there is relatively more synergy. But community cannot always function synergistically. In Turner's (1969) framework, anti-structure cannot exist without structure.

15 Synergistic community can exist even though its members are not altruistic, i.e. intentionally wishing to share or to help others. Sometimes the structure of synergistic communities is the dominant feature, overriding individual motivations. Members can act out of what they perceive as their own best, even individual interests, but the structure makes what is good for one, good for all.

16 An important source for concepts of community in contemporary western culture, as well as for strategies of introducing community change, is the discipline of 'community psychology.' (Caplan, 1964; Caplan and Killilea, 1976; Rappaport, 1981; Sarason, 1977). Community psychology operates primarily within scarcity paradigm thinking; its view of community is in sharp contrast to that of synergistic community. For example, community psychology assumes there is an

inherent conflict between the individual and the community because resources are insufficient to satisfy both; often one is satisfied at the expense of the other. The inability of community psychology to fulfill its mandate to encourage individual and community change may be due in part to its commitment to the scarcity paradigm.

REFERENCES

Benedict, R. (1970). 'Synergy: Patterns of the good culture.' *American Anthropologist*, 72, 320–33.

Berger, P. L., & Neuhaus, R. J. (1977). *To empower the people: The role of mediating structures in public policy*. Washington, DC: American Enterprise Institute for Public Policy Research.

Bourguignon, E. (1979). *Psychological anthropology*. New York, NY: Holt, Rinehart & Winston.

Caplan, G. (1964). *Principles of preventive psychiatry*. New York, NY: Basic Books.

Caplan, G., & Killilea, M. (eds). (1976). *Support systems and mutual help*. New York, NY: Grune & Stratton.

Carp, J. (1981). 'Youth's need for social competence and power: The community building model.' *Adolescence*, 64, 935–51.

Durkheim, E. (1968). *The elementary forms of religious life*. New York, NY: Free Press.

Eliade, M. (1965) *Rites and symbols of initiation*. New York, NY: Harper & Row.

Erikson, E. (1964). *Childhood and society*. New York, NY: Norton.

Firth, R. (1940). 'The analysis of "mana": An empirical approach.' *Journal of the Polynesian Society*, 40, 483–510.

Fogelson, R., & Adams, R. (eds). (1977). *The anthropology of power: Ethnographic studies from Asia, Oceania and the New World*. New York, NY: Academic Press.

Fowler, J. (1981). *Stages of faith: Psychology of human development and the quest for meaning*. New York: Harper and Row.

Frank, J.D. (1973). *Persuasion and healing*. Baltimore, Md.: Johns Hopkins University Press.

Freire, P. (1970). 'Cultural action for freedom'. *Harvard Educational Review*, Monograph Series No. 1.

Fuller, B. (1963). *Ideas and integrities*. New York, NY: Macmillan, Collier Books.

Gould, R. (1978). *Transformations*. New York, NY: Simon and Schuster.

Hahn, H., & Katz, R. (1984). 'Education as transformation; A test of the model.' Unpublished MS.

Harvard Educational Review (1981). 'Education as transformation' (Special Issue), 51(1).

Higgins, A.; Power, C.; and Kohlberg, L. (1984). 'The relationship of moral atmosphere to judgements of responsibility'. In W. Kurtines and

J. Gewirtz (eds) *Morality, moral behavior, and moral development.* New York: John Wiley and Sons.

James, W. (1958). *The varieties of religious experience.* New York, NY: Mentor Books.

Jung, C. (1972). *Transformation.* Princeton: Princeton University Press.

Jung, C. (1972). *Two essays on analytical psychology.* Princeton: Princeton University Press.

Katz, M.M.W. (1981). 'Gaining sense at age two in the outer Fiji Islands: A cross-cultural study of cognitive development'. Doctoral Dissertation, Harvard University.

Katz, R. (1981). 'Education as transformation: Becoming a healer among the !Kung and Fijians'. *Harvard Educational Review,* 51(1), 57–78.

Katz, R. (1982a). 'Accepting "Boiling Energy": Transformation and healing'. *Ethos,* 10(4), 344–68.

Katz, R. (1982b). *Boiling energy: Community healing among the Kalahari !Kung.* Cambridge, MA: Harvard University Press.

Katz, R. (1982c). 'Commentary on "Education as Transformation." ' *Harvard Educational Review,* 52(1), 63–6.

Katz, R. (1982d). 'The utilization of traditional healing systems.' *American Psychologist,* 37(6), 715–16.

Katz, R. (1983/4). 'Empowerment and synergy; Expanding the community's healing resources'. *Prevention in Human Services* (Special Issue on Empowerment), 3.

Katz, R. (1985). 'Synergistic community: Towards expanding educational resources'. Unpublished MS.

Katz, R., & Kilner, L. (in press). 'The "straight path": A Fijian perspective on development'. In C. Super & S. Harkness (eds), *Studies in Comparative Human Development.* New York: Academic Press.

Katz, R., and Seth, N. (in press). 'Synergy and healing: A perspective on western health care'. *Prevention in Human Services.*

Kuhn, T.S. (1970). *The structure of scientific revolutions.* (2nd edn. enlarged). Chicago, Ill: The University of Chicago Press.

Lee, R.B. (1968). 'The sociology of !Kung Bushman trance performances'. In R. Prince (ed.), *Trance and possession states.* Montreal, Canada: Bucke Memorial Society.

Lee, R.B. (1972), 'The Bushmen of Botswana'. In M.G. Bicchieri (ed.), *Hunters and gatherers today.* New York, NY: Holt, Rinehart & Winston.

Lee, R.B. (1979). *The !Kung San: Men, women and work in a foraging society.* Cambridge: Cambridge University Press.

Lee, R.B., & DeVore, I. (eds). (1968), *Man the hunter.* Chicago, Ill: Aldine.

Lee, R.B., & DeVore, I. (1976). *Kalahari hunter-gatherers: Studies of the !Kung San and their neighbors.* Cambridge, MA: Harvard University Press.

LeVine, R. (1979). *Culture, behavior and personality* (2nd edn.). Chicago, Ill: Aldine.

Lévi-Strauss, C. (1963). *Structural anthropology*. New York: Basic Books, 1963.

Light, D. (1980). *Becoming psychiatrists: The professional transformation of the self*. New York, NY: W. W. Norton and Co.

Marshall, L. (1969). 'The medicine dance of the !Kung Bushmen', *Africa*, *39*, 347–81.

Marshall, L. (1976). *The !Kung of Nyae Nyae*. Cambridge, MA Harvard University Press.

Maslow, A. (1971). *The farther reaches of human nature*. New York, NY: Viking Press.

McClelland, D. (1975). *Power: The inner experience*. New York, NY: Irvington.

Nayacakalou, R. (1975). *Leadership in Fiji*. Oxford, England: Oxford University Press.

Nayacakalou, R. (1978). *Tradition and change in the Fijian village*. Suva, Fiji: University of the South Pacific.

Press, I. 'The urban curandero'. In D. Landy (ed.), *Culture, disease and healing: Studies in medical anthropology*. New York: Macmillan, 1977.

Rappaport, J. (1981). 'In praise of paradox: A social policy of empowerment over prevention'. *American Journal of Community Psychology*, *9*(1), 1–25.

Rappaport, R. (1978). 'Adaptation and the structure of ritual'. In N. Blurton-Jones & V. Reynolds (eds), *Human behavior and adaption*, 18. New York, NY: Halsted Press.

Rappaport, H., & Rappaport, M. (1981). 'The integration of scientific and traditional healing: A proposed model'. *American Psychologist*, *36*, 774–78.

Ravuvu, A. (1976). 'Fijian religion'. Unpubd. MS, University of the South Pacific.

Sahlins, M. (1962). *Moala: Culture and nature on a Fijian Island*. Ann Arbor, MI: University of Michigan Press.

Sarason, S. (1977). *The psychological sense of community: Prospects for a community psychology*. San Francisco, CA: Jossey-Bass.

Scheff, T.J. (1971). *Being mentally ill: A sociological theory*. Chicago, Ill: Aldine.

Selman, R. (1980). *The growth of interpersonal understanding: Developmental and clinical understanding*. New York; Academic Press.

Shweder, R. (1977). 'Likeness and likelihood in everyday thought: Magical thinking in judgments about personality'. *Current Anthropology*, 18, 637–58.

Sobel, D. (ed) (1979). *Ways of health*. New York: Harcourt Brace Jovanovich.

Spencer, D. (1941). *Disease, religion and society in the Fiji Islands*. New York, NY: Augustin.

Tambiah, S. (1973). 'Form and meaning of magical acts: A point of view'. In R. Horton & R. Finnegan (eds), *Separate from modes of thought*. London: Faber.

Tart, C. (ed.) (1969). *Altered states of consciousness: A book of readings*, New York, NY: Wiley.

Thompson, L. (1940). *Southern Lau, Fiji: An ethnograph*. Honolulu, HI: Bishop Museum.

Turner, V. (1969). *The ritual process*. Chicago, Ill: Aldine.

Van Gennep, A. (1960) *The rites of passage*. Chicago: University of Chicago Press.

IV

SOCIAL CHANGE AND PERSONAL CRISIS: A VIEW FROM AN INDIAN PRACTICE

B. K. Ramanujam

ABSTRACT

In 'Social change and personal crisis: a view from an Indian practice,' B.K. Ramanujam looks at illness and healing through the lens of traditional Hindu philosophy. In this Indian system, emphasis is not placed on individual selfhood and goals, but on the individual's capacity to integrate into 'corporate selfhood'. Dr. Ramanujam uses two case studies, of Mr. T. and Ms. R., to illustrate the role of 'field' relationships in Hindu society. Most theories of personality development are based on western ideals of autonomy and individuation, yet in Hindu society, the individual is seen as developing in a large network which determines his goals and shares his destiny.

'Give me the benefit of your convictions, if you have any; but keep your doubts to yourself, for I have enough of my own.'

Goethe

The Hindu belief system has persisted over millennia, and this continuity is due to the enduring existence of three basic concepts. They are *dharma*, *karma*, and *samskaras*. The concept of dharma holds a central place in the Hindu ethos. There are two notions of dharma: Sanatana Dharma (universal and eternal dharma) which is applicable to all, and *Swadharma* (one's particular dharma). According to O'Flaherty, 'Absolute dharma demands that all of us behave properly in several certain general ways, in addition to the

65

particular requirements of social class and stage of life.'[1] Theoretically, there should be no contradiction between the two. O'Flaherty, however, points out the inherent contradiction between the two. She comments, 'The problem raised by the conflict between swadharma and eternal dharma was inherent in the very condition of existence, for it is a conflict between the real and ideal.'[2] An average Hindu does not experience this conflict. He strives to adhere to his swadharma as much as possible and keeps sabatana dharma as an ideal. This is accomplished by emphasizing proper behavior in any given context. This flexibility allows one to bow down before a family deity in home worship, make obeisance to the village god on one's way to work, visit the temple every day, or perform elaborate rituals. The understanding of religion and dharma may vary widely among all these individuals, but the conviction that one is adhering to the code unifies all who follow the faith. As Marriott has pointed out: *'Each person is a unique composite of having a personal code for conduct whose observance in appropriate conjunctions will bring him to the particular kind of perfection.'*[3]

Mimansa is defined as, ' . . . designation of a philosophical system which is divided into two distinct branches; the former, called Purva or Karma mimamsa, and founded by Gemini, is chiefly concerned with the correct interpretation of Vedic ritual; the latter, called Uttara-Bramha-, or Saririka Mimamsa, but best known under the name of Vedanta, and founded by Badarayana, is a pantheistic system discussing chiefly the nature of Brahman or the universal soul.'[4] However, the reference to Karma as mentioned here is to be found in Uttara Mimamsa. According to Mimamsasas, (600–200 BC), an individual's ultimate destiny and fulfillment in action (kharma) and right action (dharma) is essential for the spiritual wellbeing.[5] Even Buddha, who steered away from traditional Hindu dogmas, continued to emphasize dharma, albeit the focus was different. According to him life was bondage and the release could be obtained through right faith, right knowledge and right conduct. He described right conduct as *ahimsa* (nonviolence), satya (truth), aparigraha (not stealing), bramhacarya (celibacy) and anasakti (non attachment to worldly objects). These notions are part of Hindu cognition even today.[6]

The individual's duties vary according to the various stages of life cycle (varnasramadharma). Different models are prescribed for each stage. According to Marriott, 'The embodied code (dharma) of a person is understood as comprised of actions, powers and qualities.'[7] Robert A. LeVine has suggested that in such a system there are different models or codes available for individuals to choose from.[8] According to this concept, a code is a system of symbols acceptable to the community which contains assumptions about the nature of reality and the normative rules of behavior in that reality. The reality varies with each stage of life cycle, thus the code also has to modify. For example, a householder has several dharmic obligations. In order to fulfill these obligations he may have to use different codes. As the head of the household he is responsible for nourishing and sustaining the family, and this obligation is part of the 'household code.' Also signified in this code are the social obligations toward the jati and the community. Besides completing these tasks the householder also aspires to his personal evolution which may be represented by samskaras. There may be many other codes and one can switch from one code to another as necessitated by temporal demands. For example, when performing care-taking functions of a householder, the nature of the relationship between various family members and their recip- rocal obligations are clearly defined. In the social role, convention clearly determines the exclusiveness and inclusiveness of various kin groups in certain social functions. They include meditation, reciting prayers or joining a *bhajana* group.

It is very common in the present Indian scene for people to gather for community prayers at regular intervals. This provides a forum for people without distinction of state or creed to come together for devotional activities. The bhajana group may gather in an indi- vidual's house, or in a community hall, or in a temple. Milton Singer has interpreted bhajana as '. . . the bhajana is a kind of acting out in dramatic form and bodily gestures an ideal, for the purpose of evoking in men's minds the sentiments and attitudes that may eventually bring their behaviour closer to the ideal'.[9]

It is important to note that such a system should not be too rigid. An individual has a relative choice in determining his priorities. This choice is available because the individual behaviour is affected by the three criteria of *desa* (the locus where action takes place), *kala* (temporal dimension) and *guna* (individual predisposition). People who are comfortable with circumscribed action within a well-known arena can follow injunctions and models to determine their behaviour. For example, the more orthodox can perform a ceremony in its full ritual purity. Others who are less tradition-bound observe the same events through the mediation of a priest with or without personal participation. Those who prefer to move outside the convention, and integrate other systems, can always justify their behaviour within the constraints of *desa*, *kala* or *guna*. In this way tradition becomes integrated with the existing reality through 'institutionalization' and 'compartmentalization.'[10] According to Singer, 'The outward traditionalism of Eastern religions masks a wide latitude for individual choice and inner development.'[11] This should not be construed to mean that any behaviour is acceptable. The tradition has various notions of perfectability. The notion of perfectability is built into the life cycle. The individual's behaviour should reasonably accord with the ideals set up by the family and *jati*. Since his actions not only affect him but also the family and *jati*, the choice has to be exercised within the constrains of accountability to the family, *jati*, and, finally, the community.

The second major tenet of the traditional Hinduism is the doctrine of *karma*. The concept first appears in the Upanisads about 800B.C.[12] According to the law a man's desire determines his actions since he will go in pursuit of his desires. These actions have consequences in the future. An individual can transfer the fruits of his actions to his son. If he dies his sins of commission and omission can be compensated by the good deeds of the son, one reason for desiring a son. The son also plays an important role in family rituals. Conversely, the son can also be the recipient of the results of his father's good deeds. This is the popular version of the doctrine of karma. A more abstract conceptualization is offered by Majumdar, who wrote:

> The significance of the term karma is equally deep, if not deeper still and this may be realized from the text of *Aitreya Aranyaka* in which the entire process of cosmos, starting from the creative will of the Prajapati, the lord of beings, is said to reach its consumation in Brahma and Karma, both together denoting the final stage of evolution of the universe of life as self-acting system, guided by supreme intelligence, and endowed with harmony throughout.[13]

Karma is envisaged as the ultimate dynamic for the creation of the universe.

Social change and personal crisis

As mentioned earlier, the Mimamsas put a premium on right action which the *Bhagavadgita* endorsed. There are three paths to self-evolution: *Gnana-yoga* (through knowledge), *Karma-yoga* (through action) and *Bhakti-yoga* (through devotion). *Gnana-yoga* requires both capacity for discipline and intellect. *Karma-yoga* on the other hand is within reach of everyone. Hans Jacobs offer another perspective: 'Work for the welfare of the many, for the happiness of the many (Bahujana-hitaya, Bahujana sukhaya) makes for the forgetfulness of the ego, and is itself a means of self-realization (karma yoga).'[14]

Samskaras

A Hindu is brought up to recognize his duties and obligations through a series of life cycle rituals (samskaras). Each ritual marks the beginning of a new phase with its attendant identity, duties and responsibilities. According to Majumdar, samskaras enable a Hindu to be sanctified and lead to self-evolution (atmasamskritih).[15] Each ritual is a symbol of the beginning of a new task of learning to function in a new role. In the new role he has to acquire a new value system as well as a guiding ideology which is interpreted by each individual to discover a personal meaning. The adults in his environment facilitate the passage through the life cycle.[16]

Hindu Self

In the light of the above discussion a legitimate question to ask is if there is a Hindu self different than others. A corollary to this question is, if so, in what way is it different?

It seems that the Hindu self is 'allocentric,' i.e., determined by a focus on how others look at you.[17] There is a great need to present a positive social image. This is primarily because the individual's sense of self is based not on 'self-regard' but 'we-self regard' (as Alan Roland terms it) the *we* being represented by the family and jati.[18] The social system in which the individual is brought up becomes a significant parameter. This is true of all societies. However, I wish to emphasize a characterization of Hindu society

69

as a 'field society' distinct from western cultures which might be called 'particle societies.'[19] These terms are borrowed from physics but provide a useful metaphorical model for a distinction in the definition of boundaries between self and community. I define 'field' to represent the psycho-social space and not in the Lewinian sense.

Kurt Lewin defined the field as, 'the totality of coexisting facts which are conceived of as mutually interdependent'. The three major components of Lewin's theory include the statements, '1. Behavior is a function of the field which exists at the time the behavior occurs; 2. Analysis begins with the situation as a whole from which are differentiated the component parts, and 3. The concrete person in a concrete situation can be represented mathematically'.[20] The field for a Hindu is predetermined in the sense that he comes into this world with the imprint of past karma. The home in which he is born, the nature of his parents, etc., is preordained. Since the field consists of many persons in the family, the individual's position is determined. Thus, the field creates a place for the individual. He is expected, through his actions, to maintain continuity from generation to generation. The field acts as a facilitator in presenting a model of behaviour. These paradigms are reinforced by exposing individuals to 'ideal' patterns of behaviour as expounded in mythology. It is obvious that in such a system the ultimate goal is to be accepted by the family and experience a sense of belongingness. According to Lasker, in a field system the individual sense of self is not personally generated but derives from the collective expectation of others.[21] There is a substantial elaboration of social capacities to 'read' the wishes of others and locate oneself in the field. This requires the suppression of selfhood and denial of one's own needs. Self-sacrifice for the good of all becomes an ideology. Given all these conditions, the field acts as a support system for the individual and the absence of such support can create basic anxiety. The virtue of a field system is that if the primary object such as the father or the mother is absent there are others who can take over that role. This, however, depends upon the ability of the individual to utilize the resources of the field. If he isolates himself, no matter what the reason, the support will not be available. At the same time the individual experiences guilt for isolating himself.

We have noted that in a field system the facilitating agents are provided by the field. During the course of the life cycle changes take place in the individual. This also changes the field which has to provide a new modality by means of transformation. Thus the field becomes the unit of transformation. Implicit in this whole discussion is the fact that relationships are highly important in the Hindu context. In the psychological literature, one finds frequent mention of the mother–child relationship. Scant reference is made concerning the significance of fathers. In the Indian context Roland has mentioned the term 'symbiotic reciprocity' to describe the intimate nature of the mother–child relationship.[22] For a Hindu these relationships are significant but do not cover the whole gamut of experiences. The degree of dependency and intimacy relates to certain placement in the social nexus. A Hindu measures the relationship parameters along a family paradigm, and the relationship with a person is assessed in terms of the degree of intimacy one can achieve with the person as well as how much one can ask of (depend upon) the other person. It is by these criteria that one finds one's place in the society. Many subtle nuances of intimacy and dependency are explained in the forms. The term 'dependency' carries a pejorative connotation in the western context, but for a Hindu it is only natural that the family should depend upon the head of the household. The guru expects the disciple to depend upon him. Both will feel offended if it were not so. Thus, intimacy implies merger as well as transformation.

In these relationships, one becomes aware that multi-level transactions are taking place all the time. Family, communication, both verbal and non-verbal, is based upon the hierarchical positions of various members. Different permissible and forbidden behaviours determine the individual's place in the family matrix. To function in such a field an individual has to develop a high degree of sensitivity to the various interacting forces within the field which Roland terms as 'radar sensitivity.'[23] This is not a cognitive exercise, nor an information processing device. It is hypothesized that in such a system the field has the knowledge which is made available to the individual. In order to benefit from it he has to develop certain competences which are intertwined with the social values. In such a system, an individual's identity is a continuous reconfiguration of oneself in an interpersonal matrix.

The hierarchical position in the family nexus has been referred to earlier. Roland has described the nature of this in elaborate detail.[24]

Individual behaviour is determined by one's position within the hierarchy. Desai comments:

> The boundaries around such a self are built by limitation of the personal world, of those in the immediate childhood experiences and by a complex consideration of rules of hierarchy which govern interpersonal transactions.[25]

In such a system emphasis is not on individual selfhood but on the capacity to integrate into the corporate selfhood. An individual, ideally, has to pay less attention to his own affective status. Even if one recognizes a personal affect, its value has to be minimized. One's goal is not personally generated but is derived from the goal of the field. Consequently, one has to put one's energy into thinking of strategies to arrive at the derived goals. For Hindus, basic anxieties include fear of loss of support from the field, concern over a sense of not belonging, and shame and guilt for having failed the field. Whether the sense of failure is due to not fulfilling one's obligation or having failed the field, the sense of isolation is similar. In such an event many restorative strategies are available such as participation in religious functions, withdrawal strategy in which purification rituals play a role, meditation leading to transcendental experience, cathartic strategy in which one can participate in group rituals, etc. Irrespective of the particular strategy, the field agents are co-participants with the individual, as Kakar has graphically described.[26] The significance of the field as a support system has been amply documented by Marriot,[27] Raheja,[28] Inden and Nicholas,[29] Suzanne and Lloyd Rudolph.[30] Two case reports are presented which illustrate some of the theoretical constructs described above.

The Case of Mr. T.

Mr. T. was referred at the age of twenty-four years by his family physician because of multiple somatic complaints. During the evaluation and subsequent therapy the following facts were revealed. Mr. T. was the younger of two children, a boy and a girl, born in a well-to-do merchant class family. When he was very young his older sister married and had moved to her husband's house. His early childhood was described as happy because he was constantly

cared for by his parents and the servants. When he was approximately twelve-years old, his father was diagnosed as suffering from
tuberculosis, and was advised to move to a country house so that he
could be isolated from the other members of the family. His mother
went with him, leaving Mr. T. under the care of the servants. He
saw his parents once a week for brief periods when he was taken to
visit them. He missed them but was not too unhappy because the
paternal aunt, uncle and the servants were very attentive. When he
was approximately eighteen years old his father passed away.
Following this, the family business was managed by his paternal
uncle who became the head of the family. Unfortunately, the uncle
also died six months later. Mr. T. then became the head of the household consisting of his widowed mother and his widowed aunt with
her two small children. By then he was married and his young bride
came to live with the family. In addition he had the responsibility of
the family business about which he knew very little. Suddenly Mr.
T. was catapulted into several roles for which he was little prepared.
Overwhelmed, he attempted to engage his father's cousin as a
mentor who could guide him not only in his household responsibilities but also in business affairs. The cousin, however, refused to
take on this role. Mr. T. felt as if he was forced to handle multiple
obligations without any guidance or adequate preparation.

When he came to see me he had established a very constricted
life-style for himself. He had an almanac which indicated the
auspicious and inauspicious hours for every day of the week for all
twelve months in the year. He had to fit all his business, social and
other transactions according to this daily calendar. In practice, this
meant that he had to leave home to go to the shop at a particular
hour and return home according to a rigid schedule. He had to buy
and sell according to planetary injunctions. Since he was not
familiar with the trade he depended upon his employees to look
after the business. At this appointed time he would go to the shop,
sit for the fixed number of hours and return home. While in the shop
he would invite neighbouring shopkeepers for tea and pass the time
in idle gossip. They would oblige by coming, sitting for a while and
then would go about their business. During the course of the day
there would be four or five visitors who took advantage of his
hospitality without compromising their own business. Very soon
the employees also fitted into this pattern by humouring their
employer and conducting minimal business.

Being of shy temperament, Mr. T. socialized minimally. His time constraints also impeded socialization, leaving him to his own resources most of the time. While at home he did not have the companionship of the women because they would be busy with household chores. He spent time listening to taped religious discourses and reading philosophical literature. By the time he came to see me he was the father of a son. There was an unspoken family myth that the fathers would die at an early age after having a male progeny. This was true of his father and his uncle both of whom had only sons.

He began to realize that the once prosperous business was not faring so well. He was making profits, but barely enough to take care of the needs of the family. He wanted to expand his business after seeing others do so, but did not know how to accomplish this goal. Meanwhile, the demands of the family were increasing as the children grew up. He was not only a father but the guardian of two other children. All these pressures made him increasingly anxious. This stress was manifested by sleeplessness and stomach ailments. Mr. T. suffered constipation which itself made him anxious. He had a veritable pharmacy at home consisting of both western medicines and Ayurvedic (indigenous) drugs. In addition, he was very selective about eating 'hot' and 'cold' foods according to the Ayurvedic theories of health. Finally he had involved himself in religious and philosophical pursuits to the exclusion of all other activities appropriate to his age.

This case highlights some of the cultural factors which may have an impact on Hindu individual development. The first and the most important issue is the lack of field support during his growing years to facilitate his development according to the stages of the life cycle. He was brought up in total dependency, his parents not anticipating the future events. Ordinarily, in such families children are indulged but are also exposed to the various family rituals. They learn the family trade by active participation from a very young age. Mr. T. was physically separated from his parents, denying him the opportunity of learning by emulation. Because of the father's illness, Mr. T. had only minimal participation in social and religious functions. If the uncle had lived longer he would have been a role model and teacher. His death left a vacuum which Mr. T. attempted to fill with his father's cousin. When the latter refused this responsibility, Mr. T. was left without any 'shaping' agents in the field. His mother and wife could only fulfill their obligation of carrying on the household responsibilities and, perhaps, some of the family traditions. The relationship was awkward because they made demands on him as the head of the household without taking into consideration his lack of competence to fill the role. In his work world his employees looked for leadership and when they perceived the lack of it, they also became passively incompetent. Increasingly, Mr. T. became aware of his incompetence which resulted in a negative self-perception. The only way he could avoid being confronted with situations he could not handle was by fulfilling minimal obligations and insulating himself from interactions. The almanac provided him with a legitimate rationale consistent with the cultural beliefs for limiting his life-style. The only way he could maintain a semblance of positive self-image was by priding himself on his erudition in philosophical and religious matters. This also acted as a restorative strategy to minimize his anxiety. Under the ordinary circumstances I predict that he would have gone on this way until he came upon a *guru* who would have fulfilled all his unmet psychological and emotional needs. As an epilogue to this narrative I may add that Mr. T. was in treatment for a period of six years. I was not only a therapist but also acted as a mentor and thus was seen as the fulfilling *guru*. By the time we had terminated our contract, Mr. T. was the proud father of two more children, a son and a daughter, putting the family myth to rest once and for all. He had put away his almanac and had expanded his business considerably.

The therapeutic process involved several phases. Initially, a dependent relationship was allowed to evolve over a period of time. During this phase Mr. T. would bring to the sessions issues of day-to-day concerns. This involved decisions regarding his business or minor family problems. Most of the time he would make decisions on his own after exploring all the aspects during the sessions. Occasionally, I would have to offer direct suggestions. In a sense he was using me as a father surrogate, not in the transferential sense. When he realized the positive outcome of his decisions he felt encouraged and his self esteem improved. At this stage he was ready to introspect regarding his interpersonal transactional patterns. He could accept interpretations without experiencing anxiety. He was able to acknowledge the inner rage which was at the root of his difficulties. He was ready to recognize the ambivalences in his relationship with his mother, his wife and even his children without feeling annihilated because of the negative feelings. The burden of guilt was gradually reduced. The fear of death of which he was not aware began to surface and he was able to talk about it. With the reduction of the castration anxiety he was able to be more assertive in his interpersonal relationships. He could take new initiative which not only resulted in increased financial returns, but also contributed to a new status among his business associates. An indirect impact of all this was greater productivity on the part of his employees. His social activities, inevitably, increased. In this process his dependency on the almanacs began to be reduced until he had no need for it. The final phase was used to consolidate the gains he had made. As an epilogue I may mention that I had an opportunity to confirm that Mr. T. was doing well five years after the termination of treatment.

This account would be incomplete without a psychodynamic explanation of Mr. T's psychopathology. In the early years the parents were very indulgent which had resulted in Mr. T's helplessness and, at the same time, increasing sense of impotence. The reason for this was because he was not permitted to do anything on his own. He was even spoonfed by the servants until the age of eleven. He was not permitted to go out and play with friends for fear that he might get hurt. This resulted in a conviction on his part that he could not cope with life's demands on his own, and this feeling was reinforced by the adults around him. There was no scope for his experiencing his specific place in the family matrix. It must be mentioned that in spite of the field expecting that an individual function within a network of relationships, there is still scope for an individual to have psychological space in which he can evaluate his own values and determine his goals consistent with the family goals. Mr. T. was left in a psychological vacuum by the loss of significant objects when his identity was being formulated and crystallized. The reality was so painful that he experienced a great deal of anxiety. This was compounded by the secret fear of his own death as indicated in the family myth. Even minor indispositions were perceived as precursors to serious illness. The feedback from the people around him was continuously negative. In order to experience some self-affirmation he was constantly condoning other people's disrespectful behaviour, which gave him a feeling of self-righteousness. Over a period of time, however, he began to realize that he was being exploited. This provoked a great deal of anger, but because of his sense of vulnerability he suppressed it to a great extent. He also avoided placing himself in conflictual situations for fear of being hurt. For example, he avoided travelling great distances from home. This fear had three distinct components. One was that of being involved in a scuffle with co-passengers while travelling by train in which he would be hurt. In order to understand this fear one has to be familiar with train travel in India. As trains are overcrowded there is a last minute scramble for seats in the unreserved compartments. Even if a seat is reserved an aggressive passenger can claim it as his own. Mr. T., as he saw himself, was unable to defend his seat. Second, he was afraid of being robbed in a strange city, without any resources to return home. Also, there would be no one to turn to in case of an emergency (the nature of which was never clearly defined).

It is obvious that Mr. T. perceived himself as vulnerable in a hostile environment. This reflects considerable disturbance in early object relations. Given his experience of being totally protected up to a certain point, and then suddenly being abandoned without any inner resources, it is no wonder that Mr. T. felt so helpless. As Erikson has pointed out, 'Now, to have somebody to "look up to" in general, and in a variety of settings, to recognize and be recognized in a ritualized manner remains a basic need of a human being throughout his life.'[31] This is more so in the case of a Hindu family when field agents are resources when one moves on in the life cycle. Mr. T. came for professional help with a feeling of despair. During therapy he could experience a sense of support which enabled him to mobilize his marginal ego capacities to achieve in all areas. He was able to evolve strategies to improve his business. He was able to assert his leadership in such a way that his employees became more productive. He was also able to weed out and fire inefficient staff. The monetary returns were the best testimony to his efficient functioning. All this enhanced his position in the social group. He had no further reason to isolate himself which resulted in increased socialization. He was no more a slave of the almanac but became aware that he himself was the arbiter of his future. All this resulted in developing a positive self image. Once he reached this stage he could be more realistic about his aspirations and more pragmatic in his dealings. He continued participation in rituals; they were not a defensive manoeuver but a meaningful performance of life-cycle tasks.

The Case of Ms. R.

The case of Ms. R. represents a different vignette of a Hindu woman who had to negotiate her way in a traditional household which, over a period of time, was passing through change of revolutionary proportions. When she was first referred to me she was twenty-one and single. After completing undergraduate studies she was contemplating going to graduate school when a series of physical ailments intervened which forced her to stay at home for a period of time. The family was expecting that, according to custom, she would marry and become a housewife. Ms. R., however, had other ideas. None of these could be accomplished because she developed various fears – the most prominent of which was fear of travel. This kept her housebound and gradually, she became totally housebound and socially isolated. Increasing depression and self-destructive thoughts precipitated her referral.

Ms. R. was one of two children born into a prosperous and socially prominent family. All the members of the extended family were successful professional people except her father. In spite of it he had a respected place in the household, and his bride came from an equally well-to-do and respectable family. Ms. R., being the first grandchild, was the favourite of all and enjoyed a life of ease and luxury. Due to various circumstances her parents had to establish an independent household when Ms. R. was in her early teens. This changed the whole field structure because the father became the head of the household without the necessary competence. This necessitated the mother's going back to school to prepare herself for employment so that she could help support the family. This took her away from home most of the time when Ms. R. was going through much emotional turmoil as a process of growing up. Ms. R., realizing that she had led a sheltered life all those years, wanted a different experience. Also, the pressure for marriage was mounting. She did not want to be constrained to a restricted life so soon. Much against their will she prevailed upon them to send her to a college. Entry into college was a totally new experience. Up till then she had studied in a girl's school, and joining a co-educational institution was overwhelming. For the first time she was not under constant supervision. She saw other boys and girls interact with great freedom. This particular college was known for its educational excellence and also for its unconventional freedom. Many students found it to be a fashion to be non-comformist in their dress and behaviour. Ms. R. found that young people aspired to different intellectual pursuits and a non-traditional life-style. Nevertheless, due to her upbringing, she could only marginally participate in their activities. She concentrated on her studies and did very well. As was inevitable, she became emotionally involved with a young man. In her naivete, she expected this to be a serious relationship ending in marriage. The young man had other ideas and his ardour cooled towards her. She began to develop various psychosomatic symptoms and was barely able to complete the academic year. She left college and stayed home thinking that it would be for a temporary period of convalescence. Unfortunately, this was not a brief period and extended into almost a year. The family again started to seriously arrange a marriage. Without definitely informing them of her reluctance to marry, she went on rejecting one suitor after another. This is unheard of in an Indian, especially Hindu, family. It is the relative privilege of the young man to make the choice and not that of a young woman. After some time no more offers came and the prospects of marriage became remote. The parents also gave up making any attempts since they did not want any more humiliation. Ms. R. recovered her health and began to go to work. This brought her into contact with people who considered themselves avant-garde. She became exposed to unconventional life-styles and adopted them with a vengeance. This further alienated her from her family. After initial attempts to bring her in step, they gave her up as a lost cause. They did not approve of the people she met and the company she kept. It appeared as if she did not care, and this is important to keep in mind if we want to understand her dilemma. During this period she met a young man of a different caste. It started as a platonic relationship since both shared common interests. Over a period of time she began to love him and contemplated marriage. Without asking him she had assumed that he reciprocated her feelings. The parents were not too happy about the choice but gave their consent thinking that a conventional marriage was out of the question. When she proposed to the young man his response was equivocal. Gradually, he began to distance himself from her. Finally, when she confronted him for a definite commitment he made it clear that he had no intention of marrying her. This was a severe psychological trauma and resulted in a depressive illness which brought her to my attention.

B. K. Ramanujam

Ms. R.'s case represents a situation in which many cultural factors lend a unique quality to her personality development, her symptom formation and the resolution of her conflicts. The most important issues are those of role reversal, isolation and intimacy. Both her parents came from traditional but successful families. After separating from the extended family her father's limitations became apparent. This necessitated her mother taking up a career in which she became highly successful. In spite of this the father was given due deference as the head of the household, although there was an unspoken understanding of his limited role. Such a situation is not infrequent in Hindu families. I have encountered many instances in which mothers, because of their greater competence, would take over the decision-making role and the fathers would willingly give up their status. Such an arrangement worked out as long as the mother stayed at home and the father was the *de facto* breadwinner. In Ms. R.'s case the father had literally to take a subordinate role. His own sense of failure made him set up exacting standards for the children both in academic performance and general behaviour. Both the parents shared a common interest in the religious area. Both were strong believers and found companionship in shared rituals. They had strong views about male–female relationships and sexual mores which were transmitted to the children in no uncertain terms. When she left home to go to a residential undergraduate school she was exposed to a life-style totally alien to her. In this new environment she became aware of her suppressed sexual needs. These, however, overwhelmed her because she did not know how to cope with them. She made attempts to establish heterosexual relationships without sexual overtones. She soon realized that men viewed such relationships differently. This realization in itself was a shock since she had learned to accept that her values were universal. Torn between her sexual needs and superego prohibitions she developed physical ailments which, after a time, totally incapacitated her, forcing her to return home. This provided a safe haven in her turmoil. At the same time it also meant that she would have to observe the traditional code of behaviour. After being exposed to a relatively free milieu she could not reconcile herself to a restricted life-style. Being an attractive and intelligent girl, coming from a respected family background, she had no shortage of suitors. If she had agreed she could have ended up marrying a young man desirable by any standards. Since she had decided upon making all major decisions herself without interference from her family, she did not avail herself of the field resources. This alienated her from the field which, as I have described earlier, left her to her own resources. Her experimentation with a bohemian life style brought her face-to-face with different sexual and ideological mores. She could only superficially adopt the new life-style without being able to identify with it. In choosing a young man for marriage, she made the very first decision of her life. Unfortunately, he did not believe in any permanent commitment. When he refused her offer the narcissistic injury was too painful. It was as if the reality was too painful to cope with and she reacted by total withdrawal from all social contacts. She ended up at home, an environment which she had tried so hard to escape. She could have utilized many culturally available reparative measures. Since she had disallowed allegiance to traditional values she could not make use of them. The family was physically available to her, but since they could not understand her, their ability to help her was limited. Thus we see an individual, a product of one set of values, trying to adopt a different ideology and finding herself without any moorings. According to the theoretical frame of reference presented, she could not use the codes the culture provided because she rejected the symbol systems.

As the treatment proceeded she began to reidentify with the values she had given up. She even went to a guru to regain a sense of belongingness. The reconciliation with the family was facilitated by the fact that they fully co-operated by being constantly available. They were also willing to reexamine their actions and behaviour which had resulted in this unfortunate interlude in their daughter's life. Some time after the treatment ended Ms. R. went through a traditional marriage. Although the young man was of her own choice, parents on both sides approved of the choice.

From all accounts Ms. R. had a very protective childhood. In a large household there were many caretakers. Her mother, however, was not available as much as she demanded because of the mother being busy with the household chores as happens in a traditional Hindu family. Also, being the only daughter-in-law at the time, she had more than her share of responsibilities. Her mother-in-law was a demanding person and the mother was afraid of her. It is possible that the mother took upon herself more than she could manage to please the mother-in-law. Ms. R. had anticipated greater intimacy with the mother when the family separated from the joint household. Since the mother had to go back to school and later to work even this wish was not fulfilled. It is interesting that during the acute phase of her loneliness she would not leave the mother out of her sight, so much so that the other had to stay away from work almost for a year. She blamed the father for not fulfilling his legitimate role which required the mother to go to work and be away from home. She was very angry at both parents but could not express it. Going away to school represented two different emotions. She wanted to create a distance between herself and her parents who had failed her. Also this was her first attempt to establish her own individuality. As explained earlier this did not work out. After returning home she attempted to show anger by defying parental values. She was not ready and prepared for the new style of life she had selected for herself. After a short acting out phase her dependency needs came once more to the fore and her regression was total. Both literally and figuratively she had returned to the womb. When I went to see her in her house, since she could not travel, she had isolated herself in her room with the door and windows closed. Meals were brought to her room and she had minimal communication with her family members. This arrangement had gone on for months. The parents felt helpless since she was not willing to seek psychiatric help. Prayers were the last resort until a family friend brought me into the picture.

Summary and conclusions

Many theories of personality development are based upon observations of western nuclear households where ideals of individuation, setting goals for oneself and aggressively pursuing them, are highly valued. The Freudian model, Erikson's epigenetic theory, and later object relations theory all, in one way or another, have this as a basic frame of reference. The model presented here of the Hindu society is different. In such a society the individual is a part of the corporate system, the whole system determining his goals and sharing his destiny. He, on his part, strives to maintain his place within the family and the community by following the traditions allowing for continuity from generation to generation. The collective wisdom of the family is available to him to facilitate his growth and development. This should not be construed as a total merger of his individuality without any scope for individual self-expression.

Once he has fulfilled his obligations to the family and jati he can aspire to his own perfectibility. The system recognizes such aspirations and provides various codes for achieving the same. In order to achieve mutual aims, certain harmony in relationships is essential. This is accomplished by developing a high degree of sensitivity to others, and the individual has to subordinate his own needs for the good of the whole system. This does not mean that there cannot exist a dissonance between the individual needs and the expectations of the family and the community. Except under extreme situations where such dissonance leads to rupture in interpersonal relationships, various restorative strategies are available in times of crises. This presupposes two basic premises: ability of the field to be supportive and act as a competent facilitating agent, and the individual's competence to use the field agents. In the two case reports presented we see an illustration of the failure of both components. In the case of Mr. T. the field agents were absent, and in Ms. R.'s case they failed in their obligations, resulting in her withdrawal from them. Without such support both determined their own strategies to cope which were maladaptive.

A larger issue which emerges is how such field societies respond to change. No one denies that vast changes are taking place in Hindu society. Different theories have been presented about how the society is adapting to these changes. They include Srinivas's concept of 'sanskritization' and 'secularization,'[32] Singer's 'compartmentalization' and 'vicarious ritualization,'[33] Marriott's 'parochialization,'[34] Redfield and Singer's 'universalization, etc.,'[35] Hindu society has been flexible enough to adapt to historical imperatives over millennia. This, however, was possible because changes took place gradually over a period of time. Current changes are taking place too rapidly for such adaptivity. Social changes have not yet, however, caused massive cultural disruption.

Individuals, however, are experiencing varying degrees of discomfort. This varies from minor problems to extreme degrees of anxiety. As Erikson had commented,

> Some periods in history become identity vacua caused by three
> basic forms of human apprehension: *fears* aroused by new
> facts such as discoveries and inventions (including weapons),
> which radically change and expand the whole world image;
> *anxieties* aroused by symbolic dangers vaguely perceived as a

consequence of the decay of existing ideologies; and in the wake of disintegrating faith, the dread of an existential abyss devoid of spiritual meaning.[36]

The average Hindu is undisturbed by the change since his faith and ideology have not been shaken. He is quite content to benefit from modern technology without being encumbered by its oppressive domination. He is happy to enjoy it without self-consciousness. Nandi explains this phenomenon as, 'I suspect that a clue to this contradiction lies also in the Indian concept of temporally and spatially embedded norms. These norms allow one to live with positions which seem totally contradictory to each other or may both be derivable from an overreaching principle.'[37] Of course he is referring to the concept of desa, kala and guna which we have already discussed. It is those Hindus who are torn between traditionalism and modernism who are haunted by the spectre of 'identity vacua.' This is because modernity is equated with rationality and traditionalism is seen as blind superstition. It is those who cannot manage 'compartmentalization' satisfactorily who experience conflict. In the Hindu society today it is not totally an 'existential abyss,' but a continuing effort to find a meaning of human existence in a world of different values, a world in which the sense of 'we-self regard' has to give place to 'self-regard' alone.

NOTES

1 Wendy D. O'Flaherty, *The Origins of Evil in Hindu Mythology*, Berkeley, Los Angeles, London, University of California Press, 1976, p.95.
2 ibid., p.99.
3 McKim Marriott, 'The Open Hindu Person and the Humane Sciences', unpublished manuscript, 1979. p.2.
4 Arthur Anthony Macdonell, *A Practical Sanskrit Dictionary*, Oxford University Press, Oxford, 1979 edn.
5 P.G. Majumdar, *Some aspects of Indian Civilization*, Published by the author, Calcutta, 1938.
6 Premnath Bazaz, *The Role of Bhagavadgita in Indian History*, New Delhi, Jullunder, Sterling Publishers, 1975.
7 McKim Marriot, op. cit. p.3.
8 Robert A. LeVine, *Personal communication*.
9 Milton Singer, *When a Great Tradition Modernizes*, New York, Washington, London, Praeger Publishers, 1972.

10 ibid.
11 ibid., p.41.
12 P.G. Majumdar, op. cit.
13 ibid., p.297.
14 Hans Jacobs, *Western Psychotherapy and Hindu Siddanta*, London, Allen & Unwin 1967, p.70.
15 P.G. Majumdar, op. cit.
16 Sudhir Kakar, *The Inner Word; A psychosocial study of childhood and society in India*, Delhi, Oxford University Press, 1978.
17 A term used by Valentine Daniel.
18 Alan Roland, 'The Familial Self, Individualized Self and Transcendental Self, Psychoanalytical Reflections on India'. Unpublished manuscript.
19 Harry Lasker, Personal communication.
20 Calvin S. Hall, *Theories of Personality*, Gardner Lindzey, New York, London and Sydney, John Wiley & Sons Inc., 1957, p.240.
21 Harry Lasker, Personal communication.
22 Alan Roland, 'Intimacy as viewed from a cross-cultural perspective: Aspects of Self in India and America', *Modern Psychoanalysis*, 5:2, 1980.
23 Alan Roland, 'The Familial Self, Individualized Self and Transcendental Self, Psychoanalytical Reflections on India'. Unpublished manuscript.
24 Alan Roland, 'Towards a Psychoanalytical Psychology of Hierarchical Relationships in India'. Unpublished manuscript.
25 Prakash Desai, 'Affection and Cognition in Hindu Psychology.' Paper presented at the ACLS–SSRC Joint Committee on South Asia sponsored seminar, Chicago, 1980.
26 Sudhir Kakar, *Shamans, Mystics, and Doctors*, New York, Alfred P. Knopf, 1982.
27 McKim Marriott, 'Hindu Transactions: Diversity without Dualism,' in *Transactions and Meaning: Directions in the Anthropology of Exchange and Symbolic Behaviour*, Bruce Kepfere (ed.), Philadelphia, ISH Publications, 1976.
28 Glora Goodwyn Raheja, 'Transformational Process in Hindu Ritual: Concept of 'person' and 'action' in the performance of a vrat'. Paper presented at the CLS–SSRC Joint Committee on South Asia Sponsored seminar, Chicago, 1976.
29 Ronald B. Inden and Ralph W. Nicholas, *Kinship in Bengali Culture*, Chicago, London, University of Chicago Press, 1977.
30 Lloyd I. Rudolph and Suzanne H. Rudolph, *The Modernity of Tradition: Political Developments in India*, Chicago and London, University of Chicago Press, 1967.
31 Erik H. Erikson, *Life History and the Historical Moment*, New York, W.W. Norton and Co. Inc, 1975, p.71.
32 M.N. Srinivas, *Social Change in Modern India*, Berkeley, University of California Press, 1966.
33 Milton Singer, op. cit.

34 McKim Marriott (ed.), *Village India; Studies in the Little Community*, Chicago and London, University of Chicago Press, 1955.
35 ibid p.200.
36 Erik H. Erikson, *op. cit.*, p.21.
37 Ashis Nandy, 'The Traditions of Technology or an essay on Technological Consciousness'. Paper presented at a seminar on traditional technology and the development of the poorest section of the rural communities. Paper presented at a seminar organized by the Quaker International Affairs program at Khatmandu, Oct, 1977, p.16.

PART II

SOCIAL ORGANIZATION AND ENVIRONMENTS FOR LEARNING

This part maps the range and diversity of the learning environment, taking the reader from the urban ghettos of Colombia for a discussion of math education, to a storefront in Morocco to explore questions of traditional education in Islamic culture, and to a music lesson in Japan where four- and five-year-olds perform Mozart sonatas with astounding proficiency. The skills we value are often produced in different environments, just as the settings, as well as the goals of education, differ from culture to culture. In this chapter, different definitions of learning are examined, along with the variety and range of educational goals. Pedagogical techniques as well as diverse psychologies of education are also discussed. In this chapter, the question of 'cross-cultural fertilization' or 'transplantation' is explored – for example, what are the problems that arise when the techniques of 'new math' are introduced into a third-world country? Can educational methods be successfully transplanted? In this discussion, the figure of the teacher, and the qualities that make a good teacher, are also examined, as well as other dimensions of education not usually addressed in the United States, such as character development, sensitivity, and the spiritual goals of the educational process.

V

THE MAKING OF A *FQIH*: THE TRANSFORMATION OF TRADITIONAL ISLAMIC TEACHERS IN MODERN CULTURAL ADAPTATION

Jennifer E. Spratt and Daniel A. Wagner[1]

ABSTRACT

In 'The Making of a Fqih: *the transformation of traditional Islamic teachers in modern cultural adaptation,' Jennifer Spratt and Daniel Wagner examine the development of the Qu'ranic school through the person of the* fqih *or teacher. The Qu'ran, the primary text used in such schools is considered to be the word of God, and is recited aloud. Learning how to recite the holy book can only come about with the help of a teacher trained in proper phrasing and pronunciation. In this paper, Spratt and Wagner focus on the individual's experience of these schools, using interviews from students, teachers and community figures. They conclude that although the role of the* fqih *in Moroccan society has undergone significant transformations, these changes mirror larger changes in the society. Thus, the history of the* fqih *is the history of the evolution of Moroccan society in the twentieth century.*
society in the twentieth century.

I INTRODUCTION: INDIVIDUALS AS INSTITUTIONS

This paper considers the development of the Qu'ranic school through the figure of its teacher, the *fqih*. The Islamic educational system in Morocco can be said to be embodied in its teachers, and for this reason we focus primarily on such individuals' experiences, both as students themselves in the Qu'ranic school system, and as teachers and community figures. In the process, we trace the profound changes that the system has undergone in recent years – changes that these teachers have witnessed and experienced within the span of their lifetimes.

Tradition supports this 'teacher-centered' approach. The Qu'ran – the primary text to be mastered in Qu'ranic school – is believed to be the actual word of God and, as such, is meant to be recited aloud. Learning to recite can only be accomplished with the help of a master skilled in phrasing and pronunciation conventions. While much independent study of the text may also take place, it cannot replace the training and oral modeling provided by the *fqih* (Labib, 1975). Second, students in search of the higher levels of Islamic education such as exegesis, grammar, and law, traditionally travelled great distances to study with a scholar reputed to be particularly learned in one of these disciplines. The student's program of study at this level consisted not of attendance at one particular institution, but a series of apprenticeships with individual scholars who might be living all across the country. In the same vein, there was no single 'diploma' describing and capping one's course of study. Instead, a documentation of the scholars with whom one had worked (*ijaza*), sometimes including their recommendation and notice of satisfactory mastery of material, was the standard proof of education, and carried weight depending on the reputations of the scholars worked with. In many cases, an individual's reputation, along with a known history of study with renowned scholars, was more important in attracting students to establish one's own school than any document one might possess (Eickelman, 1978). And the Qu'ranic school, to this day, is often any available space – garage, single rented room – in which a master and his students can convene; the importance of the teacher is such that the schools themselves are often referred to simply by the name of the *fqih* who teaches there.

Islamic teaching as the enterprise of individual *fqihs* extended even to the university level, where one might expect a more complex administrative hierarchy. However, when the French decided to 'nationalize' the great Moroccan Islamic universities – the *Qarawiyyin* and the *Yusufiyya* – in the 1930s, their first attempts to negotiate with these institutions were frustrated by the lack of an administrative structure familiar to them. The French officials then set about imposing such a structure on a system that had previously operated as a confederation of recognized scholars and students, living and studying together in buildings erected and maintained by rich benefactors and the revenue of the religious community (Eickelman, 1978).

The centrality of the role of the teacher in traditional Morocco is a theme present at all levels of Islamic learning. In the words of one informant, himself a tailor, a former Qu'ranic school teacher, and known as a *fqih* by his community,

> I think that in everything, you need a teacher. It is possible to study by yourself, but it would be much easier with a *fqih*. For example, if you are traveling on a road you don't know, if you go by yourself without asking you might know some of it. But if you ask someone, 'the teacher of the road,' he will show you the easiest way to go.[2]

The range of meanings ascribed to the term *fqih* is of particular importance and requires some further clarification at this point. How may we differentiate between the Qu'ranic school teacher, the traditional healer, and the proverbial 'wise man,' all popularly hailed in Morocco as '*fqih*?' In its literal sense, the term designates a scholar of Islamic jurisprudence (*fqih*). But, in common Moroccan usage, it signifies more generally, an individual with a certain level and type of religious knowledge, usually attained through formal religious schooling. Just what knowledge is required, however, depends on both the scholarly level and social conditions of the community in which he operates. For example, in a rural or low-income urban area with a low adult literacy rate or little religious scholarship, an individual may be recognized as a *fqih* on the basis of his own greater, but still very limited, religious and literacy training. This same level of training, however, would not be sufficient to earn him the same title in a more literate or scholarly circle. In our interviews, the qualifications for becoming a *fqih* were frequently defined in broad, imprecise terms, open to interpretation:

> (The *fqih*) . . . knew religion in general. . . . His head was like a sea, he could talk about every field. That is why he was a *fqih*. . . . The Quran states that if someone is good with Allah, Allah makes him a *fqih* of religion, a *fqih* of both religion and life. A *fqih* is someone who is very knowledgeable about both religion and life. He knows what to do in life and after death.

The function and responsibilities of a *fqih* in his community are somewhat clearer. His role as 'teacher' in the broad sense, is central to his identity as a *fqih*:

> His duties are to teach people the message of what he has learned. He should tell people (what) Allah has told us to do. . . . If someone asks him about something in religion, he should answer him.

In the words of another informant, 'The *fqih* is someone who instructs people in their religion and guides them in their religion.' Therefore, while individuals recognized as *fqihs* may be found in many areas of employment – prayer leaders at the mosque, charm-writers, merchants, tailors, bath-house owners, even soldiers – the title of *fqih* still retains the sense of 'teacher'. The term is used here to refer specifically to the *fqih* employed as a Qu'ranic school teacher, unless otherwise noted.[3]

In the discussion below, we describe the traditional form of Islamic education as experienced by *fqih*s as students. We then juxtapose this picture with contemporary change in this traditional system of education. In doing so, related changes in status of *fqih*s are brought into relief, as well as the problem of adaptations of these scholars and their communities in times of rapid change.

II THE FQIH AND TRADITIONAL ISLAMIC LEARNING

In order to understand the present situation of the *fqih* in Morocco, it is important first to characterize his traditional place in the community and the process by which he acquired his title. A *fqih*'s training typically comprised three stages. First there was a period of study in his home-town Qu'ranic school, during which he completed a major portion of the task of committing the Qu'ran to memory. The second stage entailed travelling to other towns for study-apprenticeships with individual scholars. The final stage was marked by attendance at a formal center of islamic learning such as the *Qarawiyyin* in Fes or the *Yusufiyya* in Marrakech, where scholars and students of all subjects of the Islamic sciences were gathered. Depending on the quality of his teachers and the range of studies he had mastered during his period of travels, a student might earn a reputation as a *fqih* even if he chose not to continue to this third stage; the important thing was to have acquired that elusive quality called '*ilm*' or 'knowledge,' to the satisfaction of his community. The present section, based on the accounts of former students in Qu'ranic educational institutions, will describe this educational process in greater detail. These accounts are highly consistent with existing historical descriptions (Meakin, 1902; Michaux-Bellaire, 1911).

The long process of Qu'ranic education traditionally began when a young child was escorted by his father to join his peers at the neighborhood *jami'* ('mosque' in colloquial Arabic; but also used to denote the Qu'ranic school), and presented to the stern figure who would be his first Qu'ranic teacher.[4] Even for a youngster of seven, study would start early in the morning and continue to sunset, with a short midday break. A pupil's first task each morning upon arrival at the *jami'*, if he had mastered his previous day's lesson to the satisfaction of the *fqih*, was to perform the process of washing the *luha* (wooden tablet). He scrubbed off the Qu'ranic verses which had been written on it the day before; the washing solution was a water-and-clay mixture which, when dried before the fire, produced a whitened writing surface ready to receive the new day's text. Next, as pupils approached him one by one, the *fqih* would write a small section of the Qu'ran on each child's individual *luha* with a black ink. The *fqih* or an older student (*talib*) in the school, first read the segment aloud to the child, modeling pronunciation and phrasing; the pupil then spent the rest of the day memorizing the text on his board, word for word. The youngest children in the school received the most direct supervision and monitoring of their recitation practice, by the *fqih* or a *talib*, while others practiced on their own or in groups, reading the text aloud softly, over and over. At the end of each day, the *fqih* checked his students' progress, expecting each to recite from memory all that was written on his board (cf., Wagner & Lotfi, 1980).

Substantial memorization progress, such as a child's mastery of a fourth (*rubu'*) of the Qu'ran, was publicly recognized by a small procession and feast (*zarda*) given by the child's parents. The largest and most extravagant of these celebrations would take place when the child had successfully memorized the entire book. This level was generally achieved in six to eight years of study, although socioeconomic considerations and personal inclinations prevented the majority of young men from reaching even this point. But those few still able and willing, and now old enough to travel on their own, could opt to continue their studies by seeking out *fqih*s with special expertise in other towns.

The student, now called *musafir* or 'traveller,' having found a teacher in a new town willing to instruct him, would study and lodge in the mosque with the *fqih* and other students for a few years, until he had mastered the special training of that *fqih*. During this time, his sustenance was provided by a family in the village who had agreed to support him in this way, or by gifts of food given by villagers to the school community as a whole. According to one informant,

> The *musafirs* . . . were a contented lot, struggling for the sake of
> Islam and the Quran, and so without money because they
> received no pay. They were, in fact, unable to afford even to
> ride cars or buses from one town to another. They travelled
> bearing their wooden boards and their clothes on their backs,
> untroubled by the weight of their burden or the long distances,
> until they reached their destination on foot.

At certain times, the *fqih* and his students might make a tour (*adwal*) of homes in neighboring villages, chanting Qu'ranic verses and soliciting stores of butter, wheat, money, chickens, or oil from the villagers. The success of this lifestyle can be attributed to the belief that generosity to students of the Qu'ran would ensure the giver of *baraka* ('blessing from God').[5]

At this *musafir* stage, students would be expected to be able to write from memory the Qu'ranic verses on their boards, in order to review them. Such reviewing was an important procedure, intended to solidify one's acquisition of the holy text. At least one *fqih* has likened it to a voyage: 'If you are going to Marrakech for the first time, you learn some of (the route). Then a second time, you know some more; then a third time and so on (you will learn more) until you know all of it.' After the first complete memorization (*salka*) of the Qu'ran, achieved at the home-town *jami'*, the whole process was now repeated from the *opposite* direction: the last section that had been memorized was now first, the second-to-last now second, and so on. Before going on to memorize a passage again, however, the student would present his board to the *fqih*, who corrected any errors – and administered physical punishment (such as beating with a stick, or sharply twisting the skin of the neck) for every mistake. Oral reading (*tadwiza*) with the *fqih* would follow until the student had mastered the corrected words, whereupon he would return to reading and memorizing on his own. Ignorance of the meaning of the words being read and recited was common even at this stage:

Interviewer: Did you understand the Qu'ran when you memorized it?

Fqih: No. You can't understand the Qu'ran without studying *'ilm* (knowledge; science; the Islamic sciences).

Interviewer: Did you ever care about understanding the Qu'ran when you were memorizing it?

Fqih: When I was memorizing, I used to hear, 'This man went to study *'ilm*,' and so on. So I decided to go study *'ilm* as soon as I finished studying the Qu'ran. I was thinking of going either to a (rural) *madrasa 'ilmiyya* (institute of religious sciences; lit. 'school of knowledge') or going to Marrakech (to the *Yusufiyya*) because it was famous like the *Qarawiyyin* in Fes.

For this informant, the act of memorizing a text and that of understanding or acquiring knowledge, were two distinct stages in one's pursuit of an education. At their peak, the *Qarawiyyin* and *Yusufiyya* institutions enjoyed an international reputation at schools of Islamic learning, to the extent that one informant concluded, 'Knowledge (*'ilm*) was in Fes and Marrakech.' But upon reflection, most informants agreed that the higher levels of *'ilm* could also be acquired during one's studies as a *musafir* under the tutelage of individual scholars, or by attendance at certain smaller institutions (*mahads*).[6]

A *fqih* who attended the *Yusufiyya* explained that he studied Arabic grammar and verb conjugations,[7] and the primary texts of rules and legal principles of Islam. When he arrived there in the 1940s, the French reorganization of the institution had already taken place. the system was divided into three primary years of study, six intermediate years, and three terminal years, each year with a prescribed curriculum, as in the French secular school system. For a time, however, the traditional ambience of the school remained intact:

Fqih: There were no blackboards, no desks. The *fqih* brings his rug (*labda*) and the students bring their rugs and sit around the *fqih* and listen to him . . .

Interviewer: Were there separate classrooms for the different levels of students?

Fqih: It's a big mosque! (i.e., 'No, it was a single room!'). Concerning the *fqihs*, one doesn't hear the other. One is here, the other is there, and so on. The first year (was) in one place, the second year in another place. . . . Every class was in a (certain) place and no one could go to any class if he was not supposed to be there.

Lessons in the study circles would generally proceed with one student reading aloud from the text under discussion, of which there was frequently only one copy available to the group. At intervals, the master interjected his commentaries and elaborations, usually fixed and rather formulaic. The students (*talibs*) might take notes during the session or not, but in the evenings would prepare transcriptions of the teacher's commentary from their notes or completely from memory.

This depiction typifies such schools as they existed in the mid-1940s. However, the French administrative intervention was soon followed by curricular and legal modifications, which led eventually to important changes in the roles and status of *fqihs* in their communities.

III THE PERIOD OF TRANSITION: CHANGES IN THE TRADITIONAL SYSTEM

The bureaucratization of public services and the introduction of French as a second official language during the French Protectorate of Morocco (1912–56), brought on a host of new and secular literacy requirements which the *fqih* was unable to fill, either for himself or his community (Wagner, Messick & Spratt, in press). For access to jobs in the public sector, a new importance was placed on officially recognized written school diplomas, which *fqihs* and their students did not possess. Such changes are linked to another institution introduced in this period, the government public school system, which was based on the French educational model. The new schools rivalled the traditional system directly, for both students and prestige.

The government schools were at first regarded with skepticism by many Moroccans. Stories of resistance to attending the French schools abound, especially in rural areas. One woman remembers locking her children up in a room and feigning ignorance of their whereabouts whenever the local French-appointed truant officer came asking about them. She held a belief common at the time, that the foreigners planned to spirit her children off to France. Another story recalls an event in which a group of stubborn parents poured wine all over one hapless official, who tried (unsuccessfully) to convince them to send their children to the French school. Still another tactic employed by some, was to present the truant officer with sugar and other gifts, to persuade him *not* to send their children to school. A popular saying of the day ran thus: 'He who takes his son to (the government) school, will perish in Hell on the Day of Judgment.'[8]

Attendance at the modern primary school has grown substantially over subsequent decades, and is now said to comprise 60 to 70 per cent of Moroccan school-age children. Reasons for this increase lay in a combination of governmental legal pressures such as: mandatory public school attendance;[9] growing appreciation for the practical learning, including secular literacy, provided by such institutions; and hope of access to skilled jobs in the modern economic sector.

The *fqihs* we have described in this paper attended the intermediate and higher-level Qu'ranic institutions during this transitional period. One younger informant recalled being sent by his father, in the early 1960s, to continue his education in the Qu'ranic school despite pressures from the authorities to attend the new government school in his village:

A new school was constructed on the land next to us. . . . With the help of some notables, a count was made of all families with children (so that they should be sent) to the school. My father categorically refused to send me to that new school, so the local authorities summoned him and threatened him with imprisonment and other punishments. (His father responded:) 'If this is my child, then I am free to direct him whither I please, and if this matter concerns you more than it does me, then I do not want him to (learn to) read at all.'

I returned to the *masjid* (mosque; here, Quranic classes) to continue my studies, and my father was subjected to continued harassment from the authorities, who wanted the number of students at the school to reach the requisite level. My father's response was: 'I want my son to read the Quran only. As for your notion of instruction, it is incompatible with Islam.'

Before this (new) school was opened, the number of children studying at our *masjid* was thirty-five. After they entered school, only I remained.

A detail of particular interest in this informant's account, is that the authorities did not actually take any legal action against his father; it appears that they were not yet ready to deal with the difficult problem of suppressing a traditional religious stance.

In 1968 the Moroccan government announced 'Operation Qu'ranic School' in an attempt to reconcile the two educational systems, modern-western and traditional, once and for all. With government sanction, the Qu'ranic school would regain some of its flagging prestige and attendance, and be brought under a certain amount of national control and supervision. It was officially recognized as the preferred prerequisite for a child's entry into the modern system at age seven. In King Hassan II's speech which launched the project, he proclaimed:

For two years, (Operation Qu'ranic School) will allow parents not to have to concern themselves too much with the basic upbringing of their children. . . . It diminished the danger of juvenile delinquents. In Morocco, a child is started in school at the age of seven. It is vital that someone look after his upbringing between the age of five and that of starting school, especially when his father and mother both have to work away from home (King Hassan II, 1968).

Of special interest here is that his words are clearly addressed to a particular audience: the modern nuclear family with both parents working outside the home, interested primarily in child care facilities.

As discussed earlier, transformation of traditional Islamic schooling in Morocco had begun over two decades prior to Operation Qu'ranic School. And yet, the announcement of the new program marked a crucial turning-point for the traditional Qu'ranic school teacher. From an institution devoted to the complete mastery of the Qu'ran and the study of the Islamic sciences, Qu'ranic schooling now became officially legislated as a preschool charged with teaching the rudiments of reading, writing, and math in preparation for primary school. Certain traditional pedagogical features have remained in the *jami'*, such as memorization of a small number of the shortest Qu'ranic chapters, and some instruction on proper Islamic conduct. But the time allotted to these subjects each day has decreased, due primarily to the addition of government school-preparatory subjects. The *fqih* is no longer the head of a private enterprise, but subject to periodic inspections by a government official, required to follow curriculum set down by the Ministry of Education, and encouraged to attend pedagogical training sessions designed for Qu'ranic preschool teachers (Jordan, 1975).

As a result of this renovation of the educational system, teaching of the Qu'ran and religious sciences at the higher levels has undergone extensive renovations. Traditional *madrasas* and the travelling apprenticeship system still operate in remote rural regions, but they are without government sanction and have lost most of their clientele to the legal requirement of government school attendance. Officially recognized higher-level religious instruction is now available only in specialized branches of the modern national secondary school and university systems; and the old-style methods of teaching have been largely replaced by the trappings of a modern age, with lectures addressed to large groups of students in lecture halls and classrooms. The famed *Quarawiyyin* of Fes has donated its name to the Islamic Studies department of the national university, with a branch in Marrakech for the study of Arabic language, and another in Tetouan for Islamic law. In Rabat, King Hassan II has recently established the *Dar al-Hadith al-Hassaniyya*, a university institute devoted to the study of the traditions of the Prophet. The famous *Yusufiyya* of Marrakech, however, now functions primarily as a national historical monument, open to tourists.

Among our informants, we have encountered mixed reactions to these changes and to the increasing government involvement in religious education. For some, the decreased emphasis on complete memorization of the Qu'ran is a serious problem for the modernized *jami'*, as well as in the religious subjects included in the government school curriculum. As one *fqih* explained:

In the old method, there were the *jami'* (mosque), *talib*
(advanced student) and *msafria* (travelling students). Like this

we used to memorize the Qu'ran. Now there are modern schools
and universities where the Qu'ran has become just (a set of)
suras (chapters). In the first year (students study the chapter)
'Sabih,' second year, 'Ama,' and so on, fifth year 'Rahman.'. . .
Now in the new system, they don't memorize *hizb* (division;
one-sixtieth of the Qu'ran) after *hizb*, they just study some *suras*
from the Qu'ran. The old way, *salka* (complete memorization of
the Qu'ran), does not exist anymore. The teacher explains some
suras to the students. That's all.

Memorization of a few *suras* is still expected of students in the
government schools. However, the Qu'ran is not memorized in its
entirety, but at the rate of only a few *suras* per year – and there are
114 *suras* in the Qu'ran. Some *fqihs* also claim that the reduction of
time allotted to religious instruction in schools is one of the causes of
the decrease in religious observance among the younger, modern
school-educated generations of Moroccan society.

Despite their regret for losses in the scope and nature of Qu'ranic
education in modern times, *fqihs* also acknowledge practical advan-
tages of a more modern system. At the pre-school level, the
replacement of the wooden boards, pens, ink and clay, by slates and
chalk, has been a welcome convenience. One *fqih* described the
difference:

I used to teach students on these wooden boards before, but I
found that (the boards) are tiring. The students have to wash the
board, and the water is cold in winter. Then they have to put the
board in the sun until it becomes dry, and then write with a
stick. This takes too much time. But now we find that it is easy
to use 'modern *luhas*' (slates). If the student makes a mistake,
he doesn't have to wash the board and wait for it to dry, but can
just erase it and write the correct thing.

Also found to be beneficial, is the possibility for group teaching
around a large blackboard, rather than the 'old way' described
above, which was more individualized, but also more time-
consuming. We have observed the blackboard being used in several
creative pedagogical ways. The teacher may highlight target letters
in words with colored chalk; he may erase letters from a word and
then request that students fill them in again, writing from memory
on their individual slates. One *fqih* who employed these methods,

claimed he discovered them on his own, and has never attended a government training session.

Other innovative pedagogical methods have also been embraced by many *fqihs*, whether they have attended modern training sessions or not. Alphabet and single-word learning are frequently introduced, long before the child is expected to decode an entire Qu'ranic passage, traditionally one of the first tasks set before the child. Today, Qu'ranic passages are still practiced, but for the most part only orally, at this pre-school stage. A real concern for the children's understanding of the words they read and write also belies a new attitude to teaching. We have observed one *fqih* quizzing his class orally on Moroccan Arabic equivalents or explanations for written words presented in his lessons, and utilizing concrete items, pictures, and gestures to illustrate concepts. Several *fqihs* have verbally espoused the government view of the Qu'ranic school as a preparation ground for modern primary school. In addition, the age range of students is more restricted now than it had been in the past; this allows for adjustment of the lesson to the abilities of the whole group:

> We figured out that the method of teaching today is easier than the method by which we were taught. Before, children used to (start) coming to the Qu'ranic school when they were four years old. They used to sit and not do anything. At that time there were students of different ages in the same school, varying from four (years) to fourteen, and every one had his own way of thinking. Now students are of the same age, so they can talk to each other, discuss with each other, and learn from each other.

Perhaps because of the Qu'ranic schools' expanded curriculum established by the state, one *fqih* has noted a new inquisitiveness in the children: 'In the past, the child learned only what was in front of him. Now he asks for information from all fields and directions.' Another rural *fqih* advocated a diversification of subjects in the Qu'ranic school:

> In (traditional) religious education, it was said that the students had to memorize the *suras*, while it was not considered important that they understand them. . . . Here we prepare students to go into elementary modern schools. So we should teach them not only the Qu'ran, but also how to read, write, and

count, and also discuss with them the *suras* in the Qu'ran. Otherwise, if the students memorized only the Qu'ran, they would be like blind people.

Similarly a third informant, commenting on present-day higher-level study of the religious sciences, finds it 'protected by the university system and . . . presented in a modern way, in a clearer, more efficient way.' Such remarks are particularly striking in light of the traditional pedagogical approach encountered by these speakers themselves in their own schooling. That approach required the memorization of religious texts and commentaries while suppressing critical discussion of them, for criticism implied a challenge to the divine authority of such texts – in other words, heresy.

The impact of the field of child development on teaching is being felt among both modern and traditional teachers in Morocco. One Qu'ranic school teacher suggested, 'In the past, teachers didn't think about abilities of small children; they used methods that were too difficult.' Similarly, another *fqih* criticized teachers who ' . . . put letters, numbers, texts all on the board at once. It's like 100 kilograms; a child can't lift it all at once. Those (who do this) haven't had experience with children. (At my school) we only study one word per *week*.' The same *fqih* expressed interest in improving the children's home environment, as a way of improving attitudes and class performance.

For the most part, *fqihs* still see Qu'ranic pre-school as an important institution for the raising of Muslim children, despite change in school pedagogy. As one *fqih* put it, 'A house that we're going to build needs a foundation. That foundation must be Islamic.' When asked whether he expected that the Qu'ranic pre-school may one day be entirely replaced by the modern kindergartens already appearing, another *fqih* contended that such an event was highly unlikely. He argued that the Qu'ranic school is best, because it is where children learn the Qu'ran. In his view, 'the Qu'ran contains all the ideas that (any) other school could teach. The Qu'ran's importance does not disappear.'

The continuing importance of the *fqih* in his role as Qu'ranic teacher is not so clear, however, due to recent changes taking place in contemporary Morocco. The following section will explore the impact of these changes on the *fqih*'s position in his community, and its transformation over time.

IV CHANGING ROLES AND STATUS OF THE FQIH

The present section attempts to relate the past and present roles of the *fqih* in his community to changes in his social and economic status. In traditional Morocco, the *fqih* was a teacher, scholar, and religious guide, and, as an upholder of Sunni Islam, was scornful of the popular maraboutic worship widespread in rural Morocco. He was not an ordinary member of the community, being a literate figure, a memorizer of the Qu'ran, and one who had gone through the 'intense socializing experience' of full-time attendance in Qu'ranic institutions, living in a communal arrangement with teacher(s) and fellow students (cf. Eickelman, 1978; 1983a; see also 1983b).

Another facet of the *fqih*'s status, supported by our own observations, was his authority to punish a child for transgressions committed outside the Qu'ranic school. One informant recalled this kind of extension of the *fqih*'s authority to his own childhood activities:

> The *fqih* used to force his opinions and ideas on us forcibly and by means of his stick. For instance, the first time the *fqih* saw me learning to ride a bike, he said to my father, may God rest his soul: 'Do not let him ride on a bike, for this will cause him to forget the Qu'ran he has learned.' He was claiming that simply putting my hand on the handle would cause me to lose what I had stored in my mind from the Qu'ran.

Another former Qu'ranic student recalled the proscriptions of his *fqih*: 'He said to me, "My student, avoid modern urban centers and shun buses, for if you assume such a nature you will find it difficult to memorize the Qu'ran." '

The celebration (*zarda*) given by parents when a child had successfully memorized a sizeable portion of the Qu'ran, provides another example of the respect traditionally enjoyed by the *fqih*. Remembering his own *zarda* upon memorization of the entire Qu'ran, an informant recounted:

> It is a joyful occasion for the family and the *fqih*. . . . The (visiting) *fqihs* prayed for me and congratulated me on the event of my graduation. (The celebration) is at the same time an expression of gratitude for the great work the *fqih* has performed for the student and his family. The proof of his truthfulness, his faith and his industry is that he has borne his great message (i.e., 'that he has carried out his task').

This informant also recalled the practice among older students of organizing a *zarda* expressly for the *fqih*, as a show of their thanks and respect.

Such traditional respect for the *fqih* has not, in many instances, survived the effects of modernization of the school system. In the 1930s, with the nationalization of the *Qarawiyyin* and *Yusufiyya* universities by the French, one outcome was that the teacher became a paid government employee; he was no longer an independent figure who required and received support from the host Muslim community motivated by religious canons. Eickelman (1978) suggests that an erosion of status resulting from the French policy, led many of these university teachers to seek less remunerative, but more traditionally respected positions as *fqihs* in rural areas.[10] A Moroccan journalist reporting on the results of 'Operation Qu'ranic School,' observed that 'the community is (now) more attentive to the modern school teacher than to the *fqih*, to the extent that the latter has become one person too many, indeed even a subject of jokes' (El Koundi, 1983).

A loss of respect is further reflected in the following responses to one of our ethnographic questions:

Interviewer: It is said that long ago when a father brought his son to the Qu'ranic school, he would tell the *fqih*, 'If you kill my son, I will bury him.' What do you think of this saying?

Fqih A: This (saying) is very famous and very old. Anyway it is a good saying. In the old days people used to respect and give value to the *fqih*. That is why they used to say this. It is just a sign of respect to the *fqih*. That is why *fqihs* used to be serious and children used to memorize the Qu'ran in four, five, or six years. But now there is no respect. We are not respected by people. We teach students who become doctors, engineers, and so on, but they forget that it was we who taught them, and that it is because of us that they are what they are.

Fqih B: Long ago, when you wanted to read or write a letter, you looked in the whole quarter to find someone who was literate. That is why people used to respect the *fqih*, because he was the only one to teach children how to write and read. It was because of this that this saying (appeared). In fact it is not true that the *fqih* (actually) kills the student and the father buries

104

him, but it is just an expression that shows the respect and value
given to *fqih*s long ago.

Both informants clearly set their descriptions in the past tense.
Implied in the second response, is the fact that the spread of general
literacy through mandatory public schooling, has tended to strip the
fqih of his once-special status as one of few *literati* in the community.
A third informant, commenting on the question of whether special
privileges are still accorded the *fqih* in his community, responded,
'not today, not today. (These days), the people respect him for his
knowledge, they respect him for his correct behavior – if he behaves
correctly – and that's all.'

Status as measured by the economic recompense received for his
teaching services is a particularly sensitive issue for the contemporary Moroccan *fqih*. The promise of 'Operation Qu'ranic School' has
not included substantial financial support from the government for
individual *fqih*s. The community still provides the *fqih* with a
location in which to teach while the parents of students give him
occasional gifts and a nominal monthly fee. However, few *fqih*s find
this payment sufficient, and many employ themselves in other ways
as well. Among our sample of former or practicing Qu'ranic school
teachers are: several prayer-leaders (*imam*; or *murshid diniyy*) in
neighbourhood mosques, two tailors; at least two amulet-writing
traditional curers; and a shopkeeper. It has been argued that the
experience of higher-level Qu'ranic schooling, producing a network
of friendships, alliances and contacts useful in many areas of later
endeavors, is partially responsible for the substantial number of
Qu'ranic teachers (all former *musafirs* and madrasa students) involved in specialized economic networks that can utilize these
contacts to advantage. Eickelman (1983a) found that a considerable
number of Qu'ranic teachers were involved in the cloth trade in
rural central Morocco:

> . . . There was very little material profit (*rabh*) in being a
> Qu'ranic teacher and more to be made in making the rounds of
> rural markets and communities. Being a Qu'ranic teacher carried
> with it little sense of vocation or career. Memorization of the
> Qu'ran was an end in itself and gave a person status; being a
> teacher did not.

While Qu'ranic school teachers commonly sought other sources of income even before the Protectorate (Michaux-Bellaire, 1911), they have lately become much more aware of the relatively low remuneration levels for their own teaching when compared with those of salaried modern public school teachers. According to several *fqih*s, a major reason for the decline of Qu'ranic higher education is that graduates of that system can expect only low-paying jobs, for which the earnings are often described as *kif walu* ('next to nothing'). Most of our *fqih* informants who are now employed primarily in other professions worked for a period as Qu'ranic school teachers from a sense of duty to teach what they had learned, but left because of monetary problems. Several remember having learned tailoring or talisman-writing at the Qu'ranic school while still Qu'ranic students. Such skills were taught 'so that the learners could find a way to earn some money.' At least one *fqih* even considered working abroad as a migrant laborer, 'because it is a good way to make money, and everybody wants more. The sea, too, wants more water.' Explaining his decision to discontinue higher-level traditional Islamic studies, one informant stated, 'It became evident to me that this reading led me nowhere. It merely instructed the student to memorize and explain the foundations (of the Islamic sciences) and then leave with no guarantee of a job or a future.'[11]

The *fqih* as Qu'ranic school teacher has experienced the appearance of a new rival educational system, a society increasingly oriented toward western organizational ideals, and a host of shifting economic values and necessities – each with definite consequences for his own position in the community. While the new techniques which have been introduced in the Qu'ranic school may be effective for teaching general literacy skills, they have also compromised the traditional standards of rigor and concentration on the Qu'ran and related religious material. Attendance of pre-school-age children in Qu'ranic schools has no doubt increased, with the government's official requirement of a pre-school certificate for entry into modern primary school. However, mandatory public school attendance and the financial pressures of a modernizing society, have vastly reduced the number of older Qu'ranic students, who traditionally provided the *fqih* with help in teaching the young, and who would themselves eventually bear the title of *fqih*.

V CONCLUSIONS: HISTORY AS TRANSFORMATION AND TRANSFORMATION AS HISTORY

In this paper, we have considered several key issues in understanding the *fqih*'s function in Moroccan society, as possessor and teacher of religious literacy and religious knowledge. How has the significance of the term *fqih* changed with the changing roles of the Qu'ranic school teacher and his school in Morocco? More generally, how may we evalute change in a way that will illuminate the process of translating a 'traditional' institution into a 'modern' context? An answer may lie in approaching history as a process of continuous transformation. Such an approach would reject a static description of a 'traditional' institution as though it were etched in stone, and would soften the borders between those useful but problematic bipolar terms, 'traditional'/'modern', 'historical'/ 'contemporary', even 'then'/'now'.

The future of the Qu'ranic school appears to depend on the extent to which the *fqih* can perform functions of importance in a society undergoing rapid change. To assess his ability to do so requires a clear picture of where and how the *fqih* is embedded in the complex fabric of Moroccan society. He is possessor of the divinely unassailable content of Qu'ranic teachings, mastery of which is fundamental to the Muslim faith. By virtue of his central position in the Qu'ranic schools, the *fqih* has been intimately involved in the socialization of Moroccan children, sometimes over a period of many years. In addition, the *fqih* has been relatively free from Government control, when compared to teachers in the modern public school system.

All of these aspects of the *fqih*'s position have been seen to change over time. He now teaches more than religious material; his role is primarily as a pre-school instructor; and he has lost much of his age-old autonomy with the increase in supervision by government inspectors. Nonetheless, the number of children taught by the *fqih* is probably greater today than ever before. He is still sought out for a variety of religious, social, and medical problems, particularly in the lower socioeconomic strata of Morocco. Clearly, in one way or another, the *fqih* has demonstrated his ability to adapt to changing times.

One may ask, then, how Moroccans' conceptions of the *fqih* have been modified to accommodate these transformations in his role and position. One response is that the *fqih* is perceived in different ways across society, such that some bemoan his lost grandeur while others applaud his 'evolution.' The Qu'ranic school teacher is still a living concept among Moroccans, clearly differentiated, for better or worse, from the French-styled nursery school *monitrice* or the modern public school teacher.

The *fqih* has played a major role in the long history of Moroccan social life. This role, as we have seen, has undergone a number of significant transformations which mirror other changes in the broader society. As the *fqih* has given up a significant part of his independence to the state, so have the family and the tribal faction. As he has adopted a curriculum more in keeping with the literacy and numeracy needs of the child attending school, so too has western acculturation eroded the strict practice of Islam within numerous sectors of Moroccan society. As the *fqih* has relinquished some of his power (in the folk expression, that of 'life or death' over his charges) in the moral socialization of the child, so too have parents and extended families seen their control largely given up to the education provided by government schools, mass media, and life in the streets. Indeed, much of the strength and power left to the *fqih* seem to lie in the support of parents who view him as a potential counterbalance to these rapidly-changing times.

In conclusion, we see that the *fqih* is not merely a product of his times, but rather a part of the transforming process itself. This transformation is a history of the *fqih*, and at the same time, a history of the evolution of Moroccan society in the twentieth century. While a comparable statement might be made about many aspects of a society, the Moroccan *fqih* provides an especially interesting case, due to his centrality in traditional Moroccan society.

While some might claim that the contemporary adaptations of the *fqih* have given him a new and different identity, we would argue that the *fqih* still plays an important cultural role which is conceptually and ideologically very similar to his function in Moroccan society in previous centuries. Neither the *fqih* nor Moroccan society has remained static, but cultures have a way of reproducing themselves over generations, often through such key cultural agents as the Moroccan *fqih*.

NOTES

1 The research described in this chapter was undertaken in collaboration
with the Faculté des Sciences de l'Education of Université Mohammed
V (Rabat, Morocco). We gratefully acknowledge the help of several
Moroccan faculty colleagues as well as our Moroccan field research
assistants. The material presented here was undertaken as part of the
Morocco Literacy Project which has been supported by funds from the
National Institute of Education (G80–0182), the National Institutes of
Health (HD–14898), and the Spencer Foundation. Requests for furth-
er information should be addressed to: Daniel A. Wagner, Graduate
School of Education, University of Pennsylvania, 3700 Walnut Street,
Philadelphia, PA 19104.

2 Several methods have been employed in this research. These have
included many hours of structured interviews with nine traditionally-
educated *fqihs* employed primarily as Qu'ranic pre-school teachers;
and seven others, also traditionally educated and bearing the title *fqih*,
but who now teach in modern primary schools. Lengthy and more
informal taped discussions were also held with several of the above, as
well as with other *fqihs* not presently working as teachers; and a
number of written autobiographical sketches were also solicited.
Another method of ethnographic inquiry has been qualitative classroom observations of contemporary Qu'ranic schools, providing a
description of methods, materials, and activities. Finally, a review of
the existing historical, ethnographic, and government-policy literature
related to the topic has helped to corroborate our own findings and
situate them in historical and political context. Translations from the
Arabic and French were provided by Hussain Elalaou-Talibi, Hicham
an-Naggar, and Jennifer Spratt.

3 Other important figures in the hierarchy of Islamic scholarship are the
talib (advanced student, lit. 'seeker of knowledge'); *talb* (colloquial
deformation of *talib*, designating a mid-level scholar of Qu'ranic
recitation, and in common usage, virtually a synonym of *fqih* in the
sense of Qu'ranic school teacher and Qu'ranic recitation performer);
muqari' (the expert in several of the ten Qu'ranic recitation variants,
or *riwayat*); *imam* (prayer leader, himself a *fqih* usually elected by his
community for the task); and *'alim* (lit. 'scholar' in any domain,
although it generally refers to a scholar in the Islamic religious
sciences). Like the term *fqih*, the usage of *'alim* tends to be relative to
the educational background of the user, but it is generally agreed that
the *'alim* has attained a level of education and scholarship greater than
that of a *fqih*, and is usually engaged in pursuits of a more theoretical
and philosophical nature. As one amulet-writing *fqih* told us:

> The *'alim* knows the way to heaven and hell; he knows the stars, the
> seven heavens and what is in them, the seven earths and what is in
> them, the seas, engineering, medicine, geology. He knows the
> sciences. He knows what is between himself and his soul, that is,

whether his soul is on the path to heaven or to hell. He knows how to deal with things, how to judge, how to communicate with other countries, and so on. . . . He knows the Islamic *Shari'a* (law). . . . He knows how to be just in giving everyone his right.

4   While attendance at Qu'ranic school is a common memory for many Moroccan males, it was by no means universal. In poorer farming families that could not afford to give up the labor of their children, only one child might be sent to Qu'ranic school – the only son, perhaps, or the eldest, or the one deemed most serious or pious – long enough to learn the rudiments of reading and writing, and a few chapters of the Qu'ran. In certain sparsely settled mountain and desert regions of Morocco, neither Qu'ranic nor public schools existed until relatively recently.

5   This tradition of seeking sustenance from the larger Islamic community takes different forms in different societies. In Senegal, for example, groups of Qu'ranic students might travel together over long distances for a period of months. This activity is judged by some to be 'begging,' but in Senegal it is a typical way for those devoted to the study of the Qu'ran to survive while they are studying. It also appears to be a way for communication to be maintained by the relatively dispersed Islamic community of Senegal (Wagner & Lofti, 1982).

6   Special training schools also existed, such as *Sidi Zouine* south of Marrakech, for the perfection of Qu'ranic recitation variants, but these should not be confused with the *mahads*, which provided some comprehensive instruction in the Islamic sciences.

7   The centrality of Arabic language studies in the Islamic education system cannot be understated: As one religious scholar explained:

> (The *fqih*) . . . must have a thorough command of the Arabic language and of the sciences of the Arabic language. For that is the key that opens a true understanding of both the Qu'ran and the traditions of the Prophet. Without complete command of all the nuances of the Arabic language, of its rhetoric, its grammar, and all the sciences of the language, it is very difficult to thoroughly comprehend the sense of the verses of the Qu'ran . . . (and) the traditions of the Prophet.

8   In the Arabic, *Lli dda wilduh li-l-madrasa, rda youm al-qiyam fi-l-jehennem.*

9   Even today, despite a government requirement which states that modern elementary education through grade five is mandatory for all school-age children, this law is often not enforced or even practicable in the most remote rural and mountain areas, due to a lack of convenient schools and the need for child labor in shepherding and farming.

10   Another explanation for the retreat of many *fqihs* from larger educational centers during the French Protectorate, is that *fqihs*, as a literate

and influential group, were suspected (in many cases correctly) of activism in the Moroccan struggle for independence in the late 1940s and early 1950s. The *fqihs*' exodus to remote rural regions enabled them to avoid harassment, and in some cases imprisonment, by French officials. Our rural fieldsite, according to informants, appears to have been a popular spot for such 'fugitives,' as it is situated in the Middle Atlas Mountains and had relatively little official French intervention during the Protectorate.

11 This informant chose instead to attend a government institute in the province of Quarzazate, where a special program allowed former Qu'ranic students beyond the legal age (seven years) for modern school admission, to earn an elementary certificate recognized by the modern system. This certificate then enabled him to be 'integrated' in a modern secondary school program. Such routes, however, are no longer generally available for older Qu'ranic students. With respect to 'transfer of credits' and reciprocity between the Qu'ranic and modern school systems, it is important to note that in the early years after independence in 1956, a government mechanism was available to train *fqihs* to become primary school teachers. Interested parties were required to pass a qualifying examination, and to successfully complete a one-to three-year state-run program at a teacher-training center (*Markaz Takwin al-Mu'allimin*). After a number of years of teaching with probationary status, the successful candidate received the CAPS diploma, accrediting him officially to teach in the public primary school system. Of our informants, ten opted to enter the modern teaching system in this way, although two have since returned to Qu'ranic school teaching, and a third chose to return to school and is presently a full-time student in the public university system.

REFERENCES

Eickelman, D.F. 'The art of memory: Islamic education and its social reproduction.' *Comparative Studies in Society and History*, 1978, *20*, 485–516.

Eickelman, D.F. 'Religion and trade in western Morocco.' *Research in Economic Anthropology*, 1983, *5*, 335–48. (a)

Eickelman, D.F. 'Religious Knowledge in Inner Oman.' *The Journal of Oman Studies*, 1983, *6*, *Part 1*. (b)

Hassan II, King of Morocco. Speech inaugurating 'Operation Qu'ranic School,' October 9, 1968. Mimeo.

Jordan, P. 'Les écoles coraniques marocaines: attentes du milieu et perspectives d'évolution.' Report of the mission effected between 28 April and 21 May, 1975, for the Ministry of Primary and Secondary Education and for UNICEF, June 1975. Mimeo.

Kinany, A. Kh. 'Muslim educational ideals'. *Yearbook of Education: 1949*. London: Evans Brothers, 1949.

Jennifer E. Spratt and Daniel A. Wagner

El Koundi, H. 'Le m'sid et l'école en milieu rural: Apogée et décadence des deux institutions'. *Les Ruptures* (Morocco), January 1983, 15–17.

Labib, S. *The Recited Koran*. Princeton: Dorwin Press, 1975.

Meakin, B. *The Moors*. New York: Macmillan and Co., 1902.

Michaux-Bellaire, E. L'enseignement indigène au Maroc. In E. Leroux, ed. *Revue du Monde Musulman, Tome Quinzieme*. Paris: La Mission Scientifique du Maroc, 1911. Reprinted Nendeln, Lichtenstein: Kraus Reprint, 1974.

Michaux-Bellaire, E. 'La science des *Rouaya*.' *Archives Marocaines*, 1905, 5, 431–435,

Wagner, D.A. & Lotfi, A. 'Traditional Islamic education in Morocco: Socio-historical and psychological perspectives'. *Comparative Education Review*, 1980, 24, 238–51.

Wagner, D.A. & Lotfi, A. *Traditional Islamic education and literacy in five Islamic countries: A summary report*. Report to the Ford Foundation. New York, 1982.

Wagner, D.A., Messick, B.M., & Spratt, J.E. 'Studying literacy in Morocco.' In B.B. Schieffelin and P. Gilmore (eds), *The acquisition of literacy: Ethnographic perspectives*. Norwood, NJ: ABLEX (in press).

VI
CULTURAL CONTINUITY IN AN EDUCATIONAL INSTITUTION: A CASE STUDY OF THE SUZUKI METHOD OF MUSIC INSTRUCTION[1]

Lois Taniuchi

ABSTRACT

In 'Cultural continuity in an educational institution: a case study of the Suzuki Method of music instruction,' Lois Taniuchi discusses the philosophy and teaching techniques of the Suzuki Method from the viewpoint of their continuity with traditional and contemporary Japanese cultural beliefs about education. Although the method has been developed during the past fifty years, it represents a direct inheritance from the teaching of traditional Japanese arts, with the addition of contemporary overtones. During the past twenty-five years, the method has become very popular outside of Japan and is currently practiced in twenty-three countries. Using the case of the method's adoption in the United States, Taniuchi considers the ways in which the method as practiced in America has been readapted to provide better continuity with American educational values and practices.

Talent Education, or the Suzuki Method as it is better known internationally, is an interesting and highly successful method of teaching young children to play musical instruments. Although developed only forty years ago in Japan by Shinichi Suzuki, a Japanese violinist, it now has branches in twenty-three countries and approximately 300,000 students worldwide. The method's very young students have attracted considerable public notice through their mass performances of difficult works for violin and piano

113

which were previously the province of professional musicians and occasional child prodigies. Although the method itself remains a quintessentially Japanese approach to education which embodies deeply rooted Japanese cultural assumptions, its successful implementation in numerous foreign countries demonstrates its widespread appeal and ability to survive transplantation to other cultures. In the process of being adopted by other countries, certain aspects of the method have been modified to fit the indigenous educational attitudes and practices of the recipient cultures. This is particularly evident in the United States, where the method differs in a number of important respects from the way it is practiced in Japan.

This paper will briefly describe the Suzuki Method, and then consider various aspects in which the method demonstrates particularly striking continuity with traditional and contemporary Japanese educational attitudes and practices. Finally, some observations on how the American Suzuki Method has been adapted to better fit typical American cultural attitudes and practices will be presented.

A consideration of this particular method of musical training is pertinent to this volume's consideration of the role of education in developing human potential from several perspectives. Because the performance ability of students in the method challenges traditional assumptions about the limits of young children's potential to learn sophisticated skills, it is a striking example of the high level of ability which can be achieved in an optimally structured learning environment. Also, the considerable continuity between this newly developed method's beliefs and practices and traditional Japanese cultural attitudes may suggest new avenues of research concerning the manner in which each culture's own educational institutions reflect deeply rooted indigenous attitudes concerning the appropriate nature of teaching and learning. Finally, the manner in which the Suzuki Method as practiced in America has been modified in the direction of greater consonance with American beliefs and practices may serve as an interesting case study for policy makers who are considering transplanting their own culture's educational institutions to other countries. Previous discussions of the transfer of educational institutions have typically focused on the process of adapting western institutions to fit non-western cultures. The Suzuki method represents a case of educational institutional transfer in reverse – a non-western institution which has been widely adopted in the west and modified to better fit indigenous western educational beliefs and practices. Consideration of this example may illuminate aspects of the process by which imported institutions are modified to better fit different cultures, as well as reveal some of the implicit cultural attitudes about teaching and learning which shape educational institutions in the United States.

Data for this case study were collected during twelve months of participant observation at the Talent Education Institute headquarters in Matsumoto City, Nagano Prefecture, Japan. In addition to class and lesson observation and interviews with Suzuki and other teachers, interviews were conducted with mothers of local children taking lessons and visiting teachers and parents from the United States. The author also lived in Matsumoto from 1973 to 1975 studying as an apprentice violin teacher under Suzuki and subsequently taught Suzuki Method violin in the United States for a year.

DESCRIPTION OF THE SUZUKI METHOD

Shortly after the end of the Second World War, Shinichi Suzuki, a German-trained Japanese violinist, began to teach the violin to children in Matsumoto City according to a new educational concept which he had been gradually developing over the previous ten years. Noticing that all normal children learn to speak their native language easily and fluently by the age of five or six, he concluded that if this teaching method were adapted to other subjects, young children could learn equally effectively. This 'mother-tongue approach' became the inspiration for the founding of the Talent Education Method in 1946.

Suzuki's mother-tongue approach can be summarized in the following manner (Suzuki, 1974):

1 Structuring the home environment from birth in such a way that the child is in constant contact with the medium to be learned.
2 Beginning instruction with very simple tasks, using imitation and repetition as the basis of the teaching process.
3 Arranging for abundant daily practice.
4 Encouraging the child's interest in the medium to be learned by making it an integral part of positive interaction between the child and the family, especially the mother.

115

5 Making learning fun by showering praise and affection at each sign of increasing competence, and making lessons and practice sessions challenging and enjoyable.

The Suzuki method implements this mother-tongue approach in its teaching of violin, piano, cello, and flute to students beginning at the age of two years. Ideally, Suzuki recommends that children be exposed daily from birth to many repetitions of a selected number of recordings of great musical works, as well as the instrumental repertoire which they will later learn. More commonly in practice, when a mother decides that her child is ready to begin lessons, usually at around three years of age, the mother and child initially spend a month or two observing other children's lessons and listening at home to recordings of the repertoire.

When the child's interest in the instrument has been aroused, the *mother* begins lessons a few weeks before the child, and continues her lessons for several months to acquire a basic grounding in the instrument. Once the child's own lessons begin, the mother assumes the role of the child's home teacher, attending all lessons, directing all home practice sessions, and assuming primary responsibility for the child's progress on the instrument.

The first lessons involve only very basic and simple skills and explicit training in building the child's concentration ability. Each tiny step is repeated for several weeks at a time until the child can perform it easily and accurately many times in a row. Typically, it takes a three-year-old child about a year of hard work to accomplish all the steps necessary to play Twinkle Twinkle Little Star, the first song in the repertoire. After this point, however, the child's fundamental playing position, tone, and rhythmical sense have been solidly established, and progress through the repertoire rapidly snowballs in speed. Children continue to study and practice earlier pieces as they advance and on request can perform from memory any piece they have ever learned.

Weekly lessons occur in a small group, and group playing and instruction are interspersed with short individual lessons, with the other children and mothers looking on. Children progress through a set sequence of musical repertoire, learning the material completely by ear from the recordings until they reach an intermediate level.

Mothers are encouraged to maintain the amount of practice time at the upper level of their children's concentration and stamina, and to disguise the hard work in the form of games that they play together, with inculcation of the teaching points as the objective. Beginning with numerous one- or two-minute sessions per day, parents gradually build their child's ability to concentrate for longer periods. Over an hour of practice per day is not uncommon even for four-year olds, and enthusiastic mothers may practice even more. Not surprisingly, progress is rapid and children quickly progress to playing difficult professional concert repertoire. Average violin students master Vivaldi Concertos at age seven or eight, and Mozart Concertos at age ten or eleven; faster students perform these works at age five or eight, respectively.

Although the method is better known for its teaching of very young children, many students continue to study within the method through adolescence. As children mature, mothers gradually play a smaller role in home practice sessions and children frequently begin to practice largely on their own after the age of eight or ten. Although some students do go on to enter conservatories and make a career of music, Suzuki avows that the goal of the method is not to produce professional musicians. Rather than emphasizing career training, Suzuki desires to develop sensitivity, fine character, and well-developed general abilities in his students through the study of music.

American interest in the Suzuki Method began during the early 1960s, and by 1965 a few qualified teachers had begun to accept students. Membership in the method rapidly mushroomed, and currently there are approximately 150,000 students in the United States and Canada, outnumering those in Japan by a factor of four or five. Although most American teachers attempt to model themselves on the method as it is taught in Japan, in a number of respects modifications have been introduced which better fit American cultural beliefs and practices. The following discussion will describe these modifications as well as the ways in which the Suzuki Method as originally conceived in Japan is a product of Japanese educational beliefs and practices. These topics will be considered in regard to the following aspects of the method: early education and tailoring instruction to the very young child, the role of the mother, teaching techniques, theories of talent and ability development, and the ultimate goal of musical training.

Lois Taniuchi

EARLY EDUCATION

The Suzuki Method typifies indigenous Japanese folk psychological beliefs in its recommendation that children begin their formal training in the arts well before school age. Although Suzuki's recommendation that children begin formal lessons between the ages of two and three (Suzuki, 1982) anticipates common Japanese custom by a year or two, there is a widespread and very ancient belief that children learn many subjects, particularly music, second languages, and complex physical skills most easily and naturally during the pre-school years.

Fushikaden (ZeAmi, 1972) an ancient specialists' treatise on Noh Drama which has been preserved since the Kamakura Period (1185–1333) recommends that boys destined by birth to succeed their fathers as Noh actors begin their lifelong training in the art of Noh at the age of seven years, by traditional reckoning. By modern means of counting age, the child was actually only five and a half years old on the average, because traditionally, children were counted one year old at birth, and two years old when they celebrated their first New Year. Until the historically recent past, it was considered most auspicious for children to begin training in *okeikogoto*, or lessons of any type when the child was six years, six months, and six days old by traditional reckoning (approximately five years of age).

In contemporary Japan, the Suzuki Method is only one of several popular musical training methods for pre-school children. In addition to nearly universal enrollment in at least two years of parent-financed pre-school or day care centers (National Institute for Educational Research of Japan, 1983), during the past twenty years, extra enrichment lessons have also become very common for pre-school children. A recently completed pilot survey of the educational histories of all first-grade children in two Tokyo elementary schools (Taniuchi, unpublished 1983) suggests that a large majority of the 142 children surveyed began attending extra-curricular lessons during pre-school. In School A, a laboratory school attached to a well-known educational university which draws students from generally well-educated, upper-middle class backgrounds, 99 per cent of the children had taken extracurricular lessons during pre-school. In School B, a local elementary school in a middle and working-class neighborhood, 72 per cent of the

118

children had taken extracurricular lessons during pre-school. The most popular types of lessons, in order, were swimming, piano, calligraphy, and gymnastics.

When attempting to teach sophisticated skills in a formal lesson situation to pre-school children, considerable care is required in structuring and presenting the lesson material in such a way that the child's interest and motivation are maintained. The Suzuki Method has borrowed from a long Japanese tradition of folk teaching psychology in consciously stimulating the student's motivation to the greatest possible extent before allowing lessons to begin. New Suzuki students and their mothers observe the weekly lessons of the beginner's group that they will later join for a month or two, meanwhile listening daily at home to a recording of the first songs in the repertoire. During weekly lessons, the mother and child watch the other children from the back of the room and the teacher and other mothers combine in telling the new child how much fun it is to learn to play the violin. Mother explains that if the child is very good, he or she may someday be allowed to join in the fun.

Once the child's interest has been aroused, the *mother* receives from the teacher a tiny violin just the child's size, and the *mother* begins lessons and daily home practice sessions. The child is required to wait a few weeks longer, watching alone from the back of the room during weekly group lessons, and hearing and seeing the mother practice at home the same exercises that he or she will soon learn. At this point it is a rare child who does not daily beg to be allowed to practice the violin too. When the mother and teacher see that the child's motivation is at a fever pitch, the first lessons begin.

With the ingenious twist of adding the mother as primary role model for the pre-school child, the process just described is that of the time-honoured *minarai kikan*, or 'period of learning through watching.' Such varied contemporary institutions as Zen temples, junior-high-school tennis clubs, and salaried employment typically begin with a more or less rigorous and lengthy period during which the prospective applicant is expected to stand on the sidelines and watch the older members' activities. New applicants must demonstrate the seriousness of their intent to join the group by regular attendance, careful observation of group activity, and enthusiastic desire to be included. Once the group has judged a prospective applicant to have demonstrated sufficient staying power and

119

seriousness of intent, he or she is invited to join the group and provided with the necessary equipment.

Once lessons begin Japanese teachers recognize the importance of maintaining the student's initial enthusiasm for the subject by not dampening the beginner's clumsy but wholehearted attempts through excessively harsh correction. Most teachers believe that teaching is ineffective and the child's ability will not develop unless the child enjoys the learning process, and therefore tries hard to learn the material presented. Six hundred years before Rousseau ushered in an era of child-oriented, humanistic educational practices, the author of *Fushikaden* (ibid., 1972) recommended that teachers approach young students beginning the study of Noh drama in the following way:

> Allow children to develop their ability naturally by letting them follow their own inclinations freely. Don't excessively point out 'this is good' and 'that is bad.' If children are corrected too excessively, they lose their desire to learn and find Noh tedious and uninteresting. When this happens, their abilities cease to develop. (p.108)

Suzuki (1981) echoes his twelfth-century predecessor when he urges mothers and teachers of beginning violin students to remember that:

> Adults may want to teach numbers or mathematics, but a child wants to be petted and have fun playing. Tasks which are done happily are internalized and in this manner talent is grown carefully. The problem is how to combine interest and training. If a child is always scolded, his ability will not grow. (pp. 21, 23)

In contrast, Americans seem to have a different folk theory of the nature of motivation and interest. Interests are believed to arise primarily from an individual's personality and natural propensities, rather than being largely developed by the surrounding environment. American parents typically wait for their child to spontaneously evidence an interest in and readiness to undertake music lessons through such behavior as special interest in music-oriented play, or occasional requests for an instrumental toy to play with. Training in the arts, or the choice of a particular type of enrichment lesson is believed to be properly the product of the child's individual choice, rather than the result of a carefully orchestrated parental attempt to amuse the child's interest. Spending several months calculatedly stimulating a small child's desire to play the violin on the basis of a parental decision that the child should take lessons strikes many Americans as overly manipulative. Partly because American parents typically wait for the child to evidence spontaneous interest, children usually begin lessons slightly later, at age four or five.

The Suzuki Method as practiced in America rarely requires a substantial period of observation and daily home listening before the child is allowed to begin lessons. When a preliminary observation period is required, it is frequently considered more a test of the mother's demonstrated interest in the method than an orchestrated attempt to create strong motivation in the child. A child's simple indication of casual interest and willingness is usually sufficient for lessons to begin, without further delay for artificial inflation of the child's motivation.

Japanese Suzuki teachers believe that without an extremely high level of initial motivation, the child is unlikely to be willing to reliably produce the effort necessary to sustain the difficult process of daily coaxing the fingers and body to learn new and difficult combinations which constitutes violin or piano practice. Because a high level of student effort is seen as indispensable for the teaching process to translate into the development of abilities, the child's level of motivation is not left to the vagaries of individual differences and chance, but consciously maximized before beginning the teaching process. While the American reliance on the child's spontaneous interest may serve perfectly well in undertakings such as music lessons, where a child who does not evidence interest may not be forced to take lessons, such an approach may come aground in situations such as public school where children are required to learn subjects in which they may not be spontaneously interested. In such situations, Japanese folk psychological notions of gradually introducing the child to the subject in a manner carefully calculated to stimulate motivation may be of considerable use. It is worthy of note that a similar process of gradual introduction to the subject matter, designed to elicit the child's interest and motivation, is common in Japanese pre-schools and first grades (Taniuchi, forthcoming).

Lois Taniuchi

THE ROLE OF THE MOTHER

The mother's role in assisting her child's learning is central to the teaching process of the Suzuki Method. Indeed, the method could be summarized by saying that the Suzuki method teaches the mother how to teach her own child to play the violin at home. Mothers attend weekly lessons with a notebook and tape recorder and come forward with their child to sit under the teacher's scrutiny during lessons. During the lesson, the teacher explains directly to the mother what should be practiced at home during the week, and demonstrates the process with the student. The lesson ends with the child reciting a promise to practice hard according to the mother's instructions. Mothers are held solely responsible for their child's progress on the instrument, and although children themselves rarely receive less than generous praise and encouragement at weekly lessons, mothers may be quite strictly admonished by the teacher if the child has not been practicing hard enough.

Suzuki holds parents directly responsible not only for the development of their children's abilities, but for children's personality characteristics as well (1981). Stubborn, disobedient children are said to have acquired their parents' own habits of scolding and intransigence, just as cheerful, obedient children reflect their parents' happiness and agreeability. He therefore encourages parents to continually examine their personalities, honestly admit their own faults and openly strive for self-improvement as an example to their children. This idea that parents (particularly mothers) should constantly work to overcome their own personal weaknesses for the sake of their children has deep cultural roots in Confucian moral teachings for women such as Kaibara Ekken's *Onna Daigaku* (*Great Learning for Women*).

However, the idea of mobilizing the mother as a sort of full-time auxiliary private music teacher for the child is probably unique to the Suzuki Method. Traditionally, children who attended abacus, music, or any other type of lessons either did not practice outside of the lesson situation, or usually practiced at their teacher's house (Tsuge, 1983). Furthermore, the pattern of intense maternal involvement in children's educational achievement which is characteristic of contemporary Japanese families (E. Vogel, 1963; S. Vogel, 1978; DeVos, 1973) apparently has emerged only during the past few decades (Norbeck, 1978), as academic success has replaced family affiliation as the chief determiner of a child's occupational future.

Contemporary Japanese middle-class mothers are typically heavily involved in their child's educational activities. Although the Suzuki Method expects more maternal participation than do most extracurricular enrichment lessons, the previously described pilot survey of the educational histories of first-grade children (Taniuchi, 1983) showed that 65 per cent of first grade children's extracurricular lessons were either 'always' or 'frequently' observed by the mother. In addition to after-school lessons, most mothers maintain a busy schedule of school-oriented activities such as frequent PTA meetings, parent visitation days, and the like. At home, the pattern of the Suzuki violin practice session is recapitulated with school assignments through elementary school, as mothers assist with daily homework, monitor assignments, and ensure that the child is prepared for the next schoolday.

This habit of studying together with the child is established during the pre-school years. Japanese mothers informally teach their children many quiet games and activities which develop experience with educational materials such as writing and counting games, drawing, origami paper folding, and listening to story books. Most children also learn to read and write the basic phonetic alphabet (*hiragana*) and do simple arithmetic at home. A 1967 survey (Sakamoto, 1975) of five-year-old children who were to enter elementary school in five months showed that on the average, children could read 36.8 of the forty-eight hiragana letters. This average has risen over the past seventeen years, and currently most children can read almost all forty-eight letters by the time they enter first grade. This achievement is largely the result of mothers' assistance at home, as pre-schools rarely teach these skills.

Although in the United States mothers also assist their children's homework, they rarely do so to such an extent. Many parents may believe that it weakens a child's self-reliance and lessens the value of the child's achievement if parents are too heavily involved in the daily learning process. In contrast to Japanese theories of achievement, which tend to emphasize an interdependent network of co-operative effort and planning (Glazer, 1976), Americans prefer to emphasize individual effort and ability. Because American parents typically make a clearer distinction between the child's hobbies and learning tasks, and those of the parent, the demands of Suzuki music lessons frequently become a heavy burden for American parents. American Suzuki teachers find that only rarely are mothers willing to seriously practice the violin themselves for several months in preparation to teach it to their child. Observing all lessons and leading daily practice sessions often becomes much more than the mothers bargained for when signing their child up for lessons. One of the questions most frequently asked of teachers by American mothers is 'How soon will my child be old enough to practice by him (or her) self?'

TEACHING TECHNIQUES

From the point of view of classical western violin and piano pedagogy, perhaps the most unique aspects of the Suzuki Method's teaching techniques are the emphasis on group instruction, and the practice of having children initially learn to play by ear. In these respects, the Suzuki Method represents a grafting of traditional Japanese music teaching techniques to the study of a western instrument. When the Suzuki Method was transplanted to the United States, these Japanized aspects have usually been modified to resemble more closely typical western methods of music pedagogy.

For example, in Japan, Suzuki violin students usually receive their lessons as a member of an informal group of approximately ten or fifteen children whose lessons overlap each other on a given afternoon. Three or four less advanced students and their mothers arrive shortly before the teacher appears, and prepare their instruments and the lesson room for the teacher's arrival. Once the teacher arrives, relatively brief (five to twenty-five minute) individual lessons are interspersed with group instruction and remarks addressed informally to the entire group. Students carefully observe each other's lessons to pick up points which may be relevant to their own performance. Gradually, more advanced students arrive and begin observation and participation in the group activities. Earlier students linger once their lessons have finished to observe later students' lessons, usually spending most of the afternoon in the lesson studio. Scheduling is vague and flexible, and the length of an individual lesson may vary greatly depending on the child's attention span and the weekly assignment. The atmosphere is relaxed and friendly and lessons may be broken off while the teacher chats with the students over tea and cookies. Suzuki teachers believe that this type of group learning is more enjoyable and effective than exclusively private lessons because students have a chance to associate with and learn by modeling for other students, and to pick up hints for their own playing by watching the teacher work with other children.

This type of group lesson scheduling closely resembles that described by Malm (1959) as typical of traditional Japanese music lessons at the turn of the century. Even contemporary extracurricular lessons for children in traditional subjects such as abacus and calligraphy typically follow this scheduling pattern. In America, however, this type of group lesson is notoriously difficult to institute because many parents believe that private instruction in which the teacher's undivided attention is focused on only one child is more effective than either group activities or observation of other children's lessons. The tuition fee is seen as obligating the teacher to spend a fixed amount of time with a student each week, rather than being similar to a membership fee which allows the child to participate in group activities and to receive as much individual attention as the teacher deems his or her attention span and rate of progress requires. American teachers therefore experience pressure to schedule an individual half hour lesson for each child with the option of observing other children's lessons or participating in separately scheduled group rehearsal sessions. This relieves American parents of the frustration of 'waiting around' while other students have their lessons but also deprives the children of the chance for observational learning and fostering of relationships with other students.

To music educators trained in classical western music pedagogy, perhaps the most controversial aspect of the Suzuki Method is that the children initially learn to play by ear from listening to records which they hear daily at home. Typically, Suzuki-trained children do not learn to read music until they are at least seven or eight years old and studying on an intermediate level. Even after an advanced student becomes able to read music easily and well, musical scores are not used during the lesson, and the teacher hears only that part of a piece which the student has learned from memory. The decision to postpone teaching children how to read music until they are seven or eight is understandable in view of practical difficulties of trying to explain to a pre-school child why there are eight sixteenth notes in a half note. However, Suzuki holds that the main reason for this practice is to avoid focusing students' attention on the process of transcribing written symbols into sound and encourage their attention to musicality and tone production. He insists that because music is an aural medium, the performer should also experience it primarily aurally rather than visually (Suzuki, 1983).

It is significant, however, that traditional Japanese classical music was also primarily an oral tradition in which students learned to play by ear. Although an incomplete and rudimentary notation existed for traditional instruments, musical scores were typically preserved as privileged objects and only the most advanced students instructed in their use. Beginners learned pieces by imitating their teacher passage by passage, and through such additional teaching cues as singing and clapping (Malm, 1959). This is typical of the teaching and learning of traditional instruments in many other cultures, as well as western jazz and folk music (Trimillos, 1983).

For the past several centuries, however, western classical music has been passed on in written form, and taught and learned primarily through decoding musical scores. Such habits die hard, and currently in the United States, the Suzuki Method's postponement of teaching note reading and emphasis on learning by ear is one of the aspects which draws the most serious fire from the method's critics. It also causes considerable uneasiness among American Suzuki teachers themselves, and many teachers try to develop or borrow methods of teaching note reading to shore up what many consider a major weakness of the method. To address this problem, the American Suzuki Journal features a regular column on teaching note reading, which is not included in the Japanese monthly journal.

Suzuki has ingeniously adapted this traditional method of teaching by ear to the widespread modern availability of inexpensive record players and cassette tape recorders. Students can listen at home to the pieces they are studying until they learn them by heart. In addition, through constant exposure they also absorb the musicality and interpretation of the models. For this reason, even advanced students who read music easily are encouraged to listen daily to professional recordings of the works they are studying. Suzuki likens this process of absorption of musical sensitivity to the process of acquisition of the lilt and subtle intonation of one's native dialect (1982).

126

Many American observers however, feel uncomfortable about the degree to which Suzuki students are encouraged to listen to and imitate recorded models. In the western artistic tradition, 'creativity' or the ability to develop a uniquely individual rendition of even very well-known works is one of the most important goals of the artistic process. Conscious imitation of even artistically superior models is believed to be inimical to the development of such creativity. Perhaps for these reasons, American parents rarely play the recordings as frequently as recommended, and American teachers rarely encourage students past the beginning stages to use the recorded models as daily examples for direct imitation.

Japanese teachers, however, do not consider imitation in such a negative light. They believe that in the effort to approximate an ideal model, students will gain the superior qualities of a great performer, rather than lose that which is distinctive about themselves. Imitation of a superior model has traditionally been the core of the teaching–learning process in almost every Japanese art form or discipline (Malm, 1959; Gutzwiller, 1974). 'Creative' or merely different interpretations are not valued solely for their distinctive quality if they lack a concomitant excellence of artistic taste and high level of technical skill. Students are believed to gain such technical control through tireless attempts to approximate a worthy model, and to develop taste by becoming so imbued with the style of an excellent performer that it becomes their second nature. The Japanese approach does not altogether eschew creativity, but rather considers it more appropriate to the final stage of the learning process when the advanced student has acquired an exquisite control and understanding of the medium and therefore has the skills to produce a significantly important new interpretation rather than merely an idiosyncratic performance.

THEORIES OF TALENT AND ABILITY DEVELOPMENT

The Suzuki Method holds that all normal children can develop the ability to give a fine violin or piano performance of concert-level repertoire provided they have a conducive home environment, proper training, and practice well. Suzuki's belief that musical talent is the result of education rather than heredity is reflected in his choice of the name 'Saino Kyoiku,' or 'Talent Education'

Method. He is unshakably optimistic that just as all children learn to speak their native language fluently and confidently, any child can develop comparable musical abilities if proper effort is expended in moulding the environment and providing daily practice. For example (Suzuki, 1981):

> I am asked, 'Is there no superior or inferior ability?' I did not say, 'All children are the same.' There is no mistake in the genetical rule that there are no two people alike on earth. I am only saying that, 'Inborn greatness or mediocrity is not known.' When looking at a newborn baby, absolutely nobody can say, 'This child will be a talented musician,' or, 'This child will be a talented literary person.' Every healthy child in Japan has the ability to speak excellent Japanese by the age of six or seven. I ask all mothers, 'Does your child speak well?' If the answer is 'Yes,' then I say, 'If so, then that is the evidence that your child can develop excellent abilities with a good education. Have confidence.' (pp. 1–2)

As a Japanese, Suzuki is not unique in his belief that abilities are primarily determined by environment and training rather than heredity. A large-scale Japanese government-sponsored survey questioned 4,500 parents from a broad range of social classes in three different prefectures concerning various beliefs and attitudes related to intelligence (Miura, Nagano, Watanabe, 1976). Overall, 80 per cent of respondents indicated that they believed that intelligence is primarily determined by experience and education after birth, rather than heredity.

Cummings (1980) reports the prevalence of similar attitudes among teachers in his recent study of Japanese elementary schools. He notes the total absence of ability grouping of children within the classroom and remarks:

> Japanese teachers are, comparatively speaking, well qualified and experienced, and are confident in the learning potential of all students. They are not impressed by the scientific evidence that suggests school achievement is genetically determined. Instead, they believe anyone can learn if he tries and is appropriately guided. (p. 159)

Beginning in junior high school, many Japanese children experience increasing pressure to pass entrance examinations for prestigious high schools and universities (E. Vogel, 1962). In the popular imagination, gaining admission to a top university is the result of almost superhuman diligence and effort rather than inborn ability. Such popular sayings as 'pass with four (hours of sleep per night), fail with five' attest more to belief in the crucial role of hard work and perseverance than the actual sleeping schedule of successful applicants. Despite evidence of strong correlations between social class, financial background, early school achievement, and acceptance at elite universities (Cummings, 1980; Rohlen, 1983) the public continues to believe that any given child's chances of success are largely a matter of daily study until late in the evening with special tutors and attendance at after-school cram schools.

This Japanese belief in the necessity of great persistence and large quantities of hard work for the development of abilities has been noted by numerous writers, particularly Morsbach (1983) who describes the high esteem with which persistence is regarded by the Japanese. Continued effort in the face of a nearly impossible task is an indication of singleness of purpose and great strength of character and is glorified in many traditional and contemporary stories and sayings. In any type of study or learning situation, it is commonly accepted that the more valuable the skill to be learned, the harder it will be to acquire. Years of intensive self-discipline and training are expected to be necessary to acquire any really important ability.

Suzuki (1969) echoes this attitude when he writes:

Ability does not just come by nature without training. We have to educate it in ourselves. Stop lamenting lack of talent and develop talent instead. (p. 52) Practicing according to the correct method and practicing as much as possible is the way to acquire ability. If one is faithful to the principle, superior skill develops without fail. Those who fail to practice sufficiently fail to acquire ability. Only the effort that is actually expended will bear results. There is no short cut. (p. 109)

Repetition is central to this activity of diligent, persistent practice. Although the word in English connotes doing the same thing again and again in the same way, when a Suzuki teacher tells a student to repeat a particular passage 100 or 1,000 times, they expect that each time the student will strive to play it better than the last. Repetition is continued long past the point at which reasonable competence is reached, until correct performance becomes automatic. This is the process termed 'overlearning' in western educational psychology. Suzuki students for this reason continue to review and study every piece in the repertoire, on a comprehensive review schedule. Even advanced students are never considered to 'outgrow' the most elementary pieces, and Suzuki frequently re-teaches how to play open strings and Twinkle Twinkle to students playing on a professional level. He asserts that ability is more effectively developed through time spent in repetition and perfection of previously learned material than through learning new material.

The theory of learning embodied in this teaching tradition is beautifully summarized by Herrigel (1953) who describes the link that Japanese teachers perceive between repetition and ultimately creative performance:

> Far from wishing to waken the artist in the pupil prematurely, the teacher considers it his first task to make him a skilled artisan with sovereign control of his craft. The pupil follows out his intention with untiring industry. As though he had no higher aspirations he bows under his burden with a kind of obtuse devotion, only to discover in the course of years that forms which he perfectly masters no longer oppress but liberate. He grows daily more capable of following any inspiration without technical effort, and also of letting inspiration come to him through meticulous observation. The hand that guides the brush has already caught and executed what floated before the mind at the same moment as the mind began to form it, and in the end the pupil no longer knows which of the two – mind or hand – was responsible for the work. (p. 60)

In contrast, Americans prefer to de-emphasize the sheer volume of diligent daily practice which is necessary to develop competence in virtually any field. Textbooks for the popular market carry such titles as 'Learn German in Sixty Days', or 'Ballroom Dancing in Ten Easy Lessons.' Folk beliefs and popular stories usually describe superior abilties in already developed forms, or the progress of students who possess natural genius rather than focusing on accounts of average people who achieve prominence through years of determined hard work and perseverance. In learning situations, teachers and parents usually refrain from encouraging children to exert intense sustained effort in the absence of talent or affinity for a subject, preferring to scale the goal to their estimation of the child's abilities. Morsbach (1983) observes that American culture typically stereotypes those who spend years of intense self-discipline in pursuit of faraway goals as possessing rigid, compulsive personalities, rather than as examples to be admired and emulated.

The American Suzuki Method also tends to de-emphasize repetition and sheer volume of practice. Parents and teachers of preschool and lower-elementary-school-age students frequently believe that encouraging large amounts of practice (Suzuki recommends one to two hours per day for this age group) is not necessarily good for a child. Rather than building character through training in diligence and persistence, Americans feel that so much practice by such a young child may somehow be vaguely harmful. Perhaps for this reason, young American Suzuki students tend to practice less than they do in Japan.

Furthermore, the American cultural attitude that repetition is usually boring, whereas learning new material is fun, means that Suzuki students and parents become oriented toward rate of progress through the material rather than quality of performance. Students are less willing to continue to practice and study earlier material, and teachers meet resistance from both parents and students in spending lesson time in continued study of 'easy' songs. American Suzuki teachers are also less likely to prescribe their Japanese counterparts' favorite prescription for difficult passages 'Practice it 1,000 times this week and then see if it still seems hard.' Daily repetition of the records for home listening also suffers, with American parents being less willing to play the same record five or six times every day.

THE GOAL OF MUSICAL TRAINING

Although most Talent Education students develop surprising proficiency at very young ages, Suzuki asserts that the primary goal of the method is not to train children to become professional musicians, but rather to cultivate the qualities of sensitivity, service to others, and nobility of character in its students. The following quotation gives a sense of Suzuki's attitudes on the subject (Suzuki, 1969):

The mother of one of my students came one day to inquire

131

about her son. This student had good musical sense, practiced very well, and was a superior child. 'Sensei (Professor), will my boy amount to something?' When the mother asked me like that, I answered laughingly. 'No. He will not become "something." ' It seems to be the tendency in modern times for parents to entertain thoughts of this kind. It is an undisguisedly cold and calculating educational attitude. The mother was alarmed and surprised at my answer. So I continued, 'He will become a noble person through his playing. Isn't that good enough? You should stop wanting your child to become a professional, just a good earner. This thought is concealed in your question and is offensive. A person with a fine and pure heart will find happiness. The only worry for parents should be to bring up their children as noble human beings. That is sufficient. Your son plays the violin very well. We must try to make him splendid in mind and heart also.' (p. 25)

This emphasis on the spiritual rather than utilitarian goals of artistic training is common in traditional Japanese arts such as archery (Herrigel, 1953), *chadō* (tea ceremony), *kendō* (Japanese fencing), and *shodō* (calligraphy). The suffix *dō* is written with a Chinese character meaning way or path, and when used in this sense connotes a spiritual discipline. Suzuki shares his view of the goal of studying music and in his early writings (1946) coined the term *'ongakudō'* or 'Path of Music' to describe the properly spiritual nature of musical training.

These traditional arts were historically the province of the Japanese upper classes and have assimilated many characteristics of Zen Buddhism and *Bushidō*, the ethical code for samurai warriors. Because the arts were primarily pursued for the purpose of spiritual discipline, they were usually practiced in private settings, and making a living by their public performance for money was viewed as inimical to the spirit of the art. A distinction arose between *kurotō*, or 'professionals' such as impoverished teachers and geisha who made their living from performance or teaching, and *shirōto* or 'gentleman amateurs' who pursued it for other higher purposes (Tsuge, 1983). In modern Japanese, the meaning of these words has shifted to emphasize relative level of skill, and the original connotation of opprobrium in the term *kurōto* has been reversed. *Shirōto* now carries a slightly negative nuance and suggests a low level of mastery and understanding of an art, closely approaching the English 'amateur.'

Suzuki preserves something of the original attitudes toward the *shirōto* and *kurōto* distinction in his above advice to a mother and in his typical self introduction as 'an amateur violinist who is president of an international organization for training amateur musicians' (Suzuki, 1983). Not being professionally oriented, the method enjoys something of a renegade status in the Japanese musical scene because it is not linked to professional conservatories and music universities. Due to the Japanese tendency to maintain strict divisions between adherents of different artistic schools, Suzuki students who wish to pursue a musical career within the Japanese professional system must usually leave the method in their early teens to study with a teacher affiliated with a mainstream conservatory or music university.

Rather than mere professionalism or technical expertise, Suzuki's goal is to raise noble human beings who are splendid in mind and heart through the discipline of musical training. He frequently asserts 'to attain high art and musical sense, a pure mind is indispensable' (1969, p. 44). He directly links style and characteristics of violin playing to personality attributes, and attempts to change students' personal weak points through prescribing certain techniques of violin practice. In pursuing such training, he concentrates intensively on the more subtle aspects of violin technique, such as tone quality, musical sensitivity, and intonation. For example, a student who lacks the ability to carry out her intentions self confidently may find herself required to spend months practicing how to produce a clean attack on an open note, repeating a single note 10,000 times each week. A student with an egotistic and self-aggrandizing playing style may find himself the object of Suzuki's frequent teasing and be used as a model in public teaching demonstrations focusing on his weakest points until he learns to be more humble.

Although in his own teaching Suzuki actively attempts to develop student's chararcter through musical training, in practice few other Suzuki teachers even in Japan pursue this goal so purposefully. Most teachers continue to espouse Suzuki's attitude that the primary goal of the method is to develop fine character in their students, but pursue this through less radical methods, such as encouraging respect for the teacher and other students, using polite language and greetings, and maintaining a cheerful and positive lesson environment.

Suzuki frequently writes poems and inspirational sayings for distribution to students and presentation at graduation ceremonies which reflect the direct relationship he perceives between a musician's character and the quality of performance, and the almost mystical connection between the quality of a player's tone and the quality of their heart.

'A string has no heart, it sings only with the soul of the player.' (*Gen ni ha kokoro nashi, narasu mono no kokoro wo utau nomi.*)

'Tone has a living soul without form' (*Oto ni kokoro ari, sugata naku ikite*).

Contemporary students of traditional Japanese instruments such as the shakuhachi (Japanese bamboo flute) attest to a similar linking of the study of an instrument and spiritual discipline (Gutzwiller, 1974). Learning the instrument is a process of lifelong study of a few basic works of great antiquity which are studied and restudied at gradually deeper levels. The goal is personal and spiritual maturity, and mere musical pleasantry or technical brilliance in the absence of a concomitant spiritual understanding is devalued as empty mechanical wizardry. The quest to produce pure tone or 'the true sound of the bamboo,' assumes a function similar to that of a Zen *kóan* (a riddle-question whose solution accompanies enlightenment) in itself. The goal is *ichi on jō butsu*, the attainment of enlightenment through perfecting a single note.

The path to achieving this enlightenment through the study of a particular skill requires patient practice of the medium until its component techniques can be performed effortlessly and infallibly, without the benefit of conscious thought. This requires countless repetitions of fundamental techniques concentrating on achieving control of their minutist aspects (Morsbach, 1983). As described above, Suzuki frequently requests such practice from his students, prescribing, for example, 10,000 repetitions of an open tone, concentrating on improving the beauty of the after echo. The goal is for students to transcend the need for their conscious mind to monitor their efforts to achieve a high quality performance, at which time the medium can be practiced as a spiritual exercise in a selfless meditative state of transcendent calm and detachment. The discipline of practicing to attain such a level of performance as well as the insights gained in the transcendent state are believed to positively affect all other aspects of daily life.

Herrigel (1953) beautifully chronicles this learning process in his description of six years spent as a student of a master in the art of Japanese archery. Four years of intensive daily training were necessary before Herrigel could draw the bow and loose the shot with the required unconscious detachment, effortless strength, and infallible timing. The object of this arduous training was the psychological and spiritual attitude of Herrigel himself, and only after considerable spiritual maturity and flawless instinctive control in loosing the arrow had been attained was he allowed to turn his attention to where the shots landed. The goal of the years of patient practice is to become able to abandon the controlling self and to allow perfectly trained ability to function in a state of spiritual transcendence.

Such overtly spiritual goals are quite foreign to American training in the arts. Learning to play an instrument is undertaken either for enjoyment or the utilitarian purpose of pursuing a career. In its transplantation to the United States, the Suzuki Method has so completely lost its original spiritual aspects and character-moulding techniques that few American teachers or parents are even aware of their existence. The method focuses on the concrete task of teaching children to play an instrument and rarely espouses higher goals for moulding character than helping children learn to enjoy music and providing a warm, supportive lesson environment. This is in consonance with the typically pragmatic American approach to education, and disinterest in spiritual and quasi-mystical quests for self improvement through long practice and discipline.

The goals of the American Suzuki Method are also not inimical to the pursuit of a musical career. Indeed, in the eyes of many observers, the number of students who go on to pursue careers in music is in some way a measure of the method's success or failure. Many Americans perceive something wasteful in a child who plays concert repertoire at the age of ten yet does not go on to become a career musician but plays only for the enjoyment of family and friends or personal satisfaction. Also in contrast to Japan, US teachers and students in the Suzuki Method are not isolated from mainstream musical careers and several conservatories and university music departments sponsor programs in the method.

Lois Taniuchi

THE SUZUKI METHOD IN PERSPECTIVE

Besides those similarities enumerated in this paper, there are other aspects in which the Suzuki Method resembles traditional Japanese educational methods. For example, the relationship between Suzuki and his adult students resembles in some aspects the traditional master–disciple relationship, and the method's organizational structure shares many characteristics of the traditional *iemoto* system of fictive kinship. However, every educational institution shares aspects of continuity with its cultural roots, and the evidence of cultural continuities presented in this paper is not meant to suggest that there is nothing new about the Suzuki Method.

Particularly in the blending of traditional and contemporary practices, there is much that is innovative. The method's basic approach of teaching western instruments and classical concert repertoire through methods adapted from traditional Japanese instrumental and spiritual training is unique and diverges considerably from Suzuki's own western-style musical training in pre-war Germany. There are many ingenious examples of the blending of traditional and modern elements as in using the widespread availability of inexpensive cassette tape recorders in the home to supplement the time-honoured oral tradition of teaching by ear and greatly increase students' exposure to the music they must learn. Suzuki's idea of recruiting and training the contemporary educationally oriented mother as an auxiliary home music teacher also very effectively ensures that pre-school children will practice in a regular and efficient manner.

Furthermore, this paper's description of changes which the method has undergone in its transplantation to the United States is not meant to suggest that the American version of the method is incorrect or inappropriate within the American setting. This judgmental view is particularly common among both Japanese and American participants in the Suzuki Method, who tend to discount the legitimacy of culturally different educational attitudes and practices in favor of a unidimensional value system in which the original Japanese method is 'good' and the aspects in which the American version differs are 'bad' or 'wrong'. Perhaps, by understanding how these changes reflect deeply rooted American cultural beliefs and practices we may understand them not as mistakes or perversities, but as arising from different conceptions of the nature

136

of the process of teaching and learning which contributes to the strength and vitality of other American educational institutions and practices. In a different context, for example, the American penchant for utilitarian rather than character-building goals of training and emphasis on non-repetitive short-cut learning procedures may allow for a broader dissemination of practical skills and a greater willingness to attempt to learn things oneself without relying on a teacher's authority.

However, a teaching method as complex as the Suzuki Method functions as a carefully-balanced inter-related whole, and by changing some aspects of the method, one subtly changes the internal dynamics of the system and achieves a different end product. One example of how this has occurred in the adaptation of the Suzuki Method to American cultural values is the effect of different beliefs about the appropriate role of the mother in the child's learning. Because American mothers are in general less willing or able to be extensively involved for several hours a day in their children's music practice, they spend little time practicing the violin themselves, play the practice tapes less often, and find it difficult to supervise lengthy practice sessions. This means that American children either practice less or must accept more responsibility for their own music lessons at earlier ages, and this pays off in less efficient and careful practice which in turn affects the average level of American students' performance.

Rather than stubbornly attempting to urge the ultimately unsuccessful process of changing American mothers' conception of their own role so that it becomes more Japanese, successful practitioners must modify and readjust the method to compensate for highly resistant cultural beliefs and practices. By attempting to modify culturally discrepant demands and introducing new techniques which serve a similar teaching function, the method can adapt itself to the new culture without seriously decreasing its effectiveness. However, it is important in this process that the method does not only borrow those aspects which are congenial and ignore others as this can create serious imbalance and inefficiency in the overall system. For example, American reluctance to encourage students to learn primarily through imitation of models and impatience with large amounts of repetition means that many parents do not daily play and replay the practice recordings at home. This makes it difficult for children to learn new material and to memorize thoroughly that which they have learned. In compensation, many American Suzuki teachers have found it necessary to develop methods of teaching music reading to young students so that they can efficiently learn new pieces.

Perhaps this paper's description of the Suzuki Method can provide some ideas for those practitioners who contemplate transporting educational institutions across cultures. Ideally, in the process, both cultures can learn from each other and combine their own strengths with new ideas developed in different traditions. In the case of the Suzuki Method, a basically traditional Japanese method of music instruction has been adapted to local beliefs and customs in numerous countries throughout the world. In the process, it has demonstrated not only that very young children can learn a highly complex skill such as playing the violin, but also that they can learn to experience the joy of making music. This in itself is perhaps the most significant contribution of the method.

NOTE

1 Field research for this chapter was generously supported by a Japan Foundation Fellowship and a Sinclair Kennedy Travelling Fellowship from Harvard University. I am indebted to Merry White, John Singleton, Munir Fasheh, and Senichi Tsuge for their comments on earlier versions of the paper, and to Shinichi Suzuke and the members of the Talent Education Institute in Japan for their kindness and cooperation with the research.

REFERENCES

Cummings, William. *Education and Equality in Japan*. Princeton NJ: Princeton University Press, 1980.

DeVos, George. *Socialization for Achievement*. Berkeley: University of California Press, 1973.

Dore, Ronald. *Education in Tokugawa Japan*. Berkeley: University of California Press, 1965.

Glazer, Nathan. 'Social and Cultural Factors in Japanese Economic Growth.' In H. Patrick & H. Rosovsky (eds), *Asia's New Giant: How the Japanese Economy Works*. Washington D.C.: The Brookings Institution, 1976.

Gutzwiller, Andreas. *Shakuhachi: Aspects of History, Practice and Teaching*. Doctoral Dissertation, Wesleyan University, Middletown, Connecticut, 1974.

Herrigel, Eugen. *Zen in the Art of Archery*. London: Routledge & Kegan Paul, 1953.

Malm, William, *Japanese Music and Musical Instruments*. Rutland, Vermont: Charles E. Tuttle Company, 1959.

Miura, Kanae; Nagano, Shigefumi, and Watanabe, Keiko. 'Parents' Beliefs and Attitudes about Intelligence.' In *Bulletin of the National Institute for Educational Research of Japan* No. 38. Tokyo: NIER, February 1976.

Morsbach, Helmut. 'Socio-Psychological Aspects of Persistence in Japan.' In *Essays on Japanology, 1978-1982*. Kyoto: Bunrikakau, 1983.

National Institute for Educational Research of Japan, Section for Educational Cooperation in Asia. *Preschool Education in Japan*, NIER Occasional Paper 04/83. Tokyo: NIER, 1983.

Norbeck, Edward. *Country to City: The Urbanization of a Japanese Hamlet*. Salt Lake City: University Press, 1978.

Rohlen, Thomas. *Japan's High Schools*. Berkeley: University of California Press, 1983.

Sakamoto, T. 'Preschool Reading in Japan.' *The Reading Teacher*, December 1975, 29 (3), pp. 240–4.

Suzuki, Shinichi. *Nurtured by Love*. New York: Exposition Press, 1969.

Suzuki Shinichi. *The Law of Ability and the 'Mother Tongue Method' of Education*. Pamphlet privately published by Talent Education Institute, Matsumoto, Japan, 1974.

Suzuki, Shinichi. *Ability Development from Age Zero*. Athens, Ohio: Ability Development Associates, subsidiary of Accura Music, 1981.

Suzuki, Shinichi. *Where Love is Deep*. Saint Louis: Talent Education Journal, 1982.

Suzuki, Shinichi. *How to Teach Suzuki Piano*. Matsumoto, Japan: Talent Education Institute, 1983.

Suzuki, Shinichi. Opening Remarks at the Sixth International Suzuki Conference. Matsumoto, Japan: July 17, 1983.

Taniuchi, Lois. Unpublished results of a pilot survey of the educational histories of first grade children in two Tokyo first grades. June, 1983.

Trimillos, Ricardo. 'The Formalized Transmission of Culture: Selectivity in Traditional Teaching/Learning Systems in Four High Skill Music Traditions.' *East-West Culture* Learning Institute Report. Vol. 9. No. 1/2, May 1983. pp. 1–9.

Tsuge, Genichi. (Professor of Musicology, Kunitachi College of Music). Interview June 16, 1983.

Vogel, Ezra. Entrance Examinations and Emotional Disturbances in Japan's 'New Middle Class.' In R. Smith and R. Beardsley (eds), *Japanese Culture: Its Development and Characteristics*. Chicago: Aldine Publishing Company, 1962.

Vogel, Ezra. *Japan's New Middle Class*. Berkeley: University of California Press, 1963.

Vogel, Suzanne. Professional Housewife: The Career of Urban Middle-Class Japanese Women. *Japan Interpreter*, Winter 1978, *12*, pp. 16–43.

Lois Taniuchi

ZeAmi, *Kadensho (Fushikaden)*. (In Japanese) translated from classical to modern Japanese by Kawase, Kazuma. Tokyo: Kodansha, 1972. For an English translation see ZeAmi, *The Kadensho*, translated by Shimada, Shohei. Privately published 448 Okidome, Ikaruga-cho Ikoma-gun, Nara-ken JAPAN, 1975.

VII
LEARNING ELEMENTARY SCHOOL MATHEMATICS AS A CULTURALLY CONDITIONED PROCESS

Carlos E. Vasco

ABSTRACT

In 'Learning elementary school mathematics as a culturally conditioned process,' Carlos Vasco examines the 'myth' that mathematics is a 'universal language of science,' and thus a supra-cultural subject. Analyzing cases of Colombian children, he concludes that mathematics can be as culturally dependent as learning literature or history. Most teachers, Vasco states, believe that children know nothing about mathematics when they enter school; thus the teaching of the 'new math' is destined to reach only a small percentage of children. Vasco argues that only the students who can construct their own 'conceptual systems in spite of their teachers' and disentangle by themselves the maze of symbolic systems will be immune from 'mathofobia.'

I INTRODUCTION

Norma X lives in a slum up the steep hills to the East of Bogota, Colombia. When I met her six years ago, she was seven years old and was attending first grade at the local school. She used to help her mother sell food and soft drinks on Sundays at a nearby park. She could sell a dozen bottles of soft drink at 9 pesos a bottle and quickly and accurately return change from a 200-peso bill. But she flunked first-grade arithmetic.

141

Carlos E. Vasco

Luis Eduardo Y dropped out of the fourth grade in 1975. Some years later he wanted to pass the five-grade elementary school through a State examination, which is given twice a year to prospective high-school entrants. He did not dare take it, because he thought he knew nothing about fractions. But I knew that he was an able mechanic and had very good experience with nuts and bolts, wrenches and calipers. He could 'see' in a flash of his alert mind that a 3/8″ jaw would not bite a half-inch nut or even a 1-cm European bolt-head. I needed paper and pencil to verify that he was right. Once he realized that he knew a good deal about fractions, he had no trouble taking and passing the State examination with flying colors. Now he has just finished High School and wants to be a teacher (of mathematics, of course).

Mathematics is thought to be the most culturally independent of all academic subjects. 'New Math' textbooks printed in the US or Belgium were translated into Spanish and Portuguese with only minor variations in the story-problems and are now taught in most Latin-American countries. Looking backwards, it was not different in the years past: standard school textbooks used in Colombia copied each other in a chain going back to Spanish and Latin Renaissance arithmetics. The myth of mathematics as the universal language of science and the superficial image of mathematical truth as invariably and *a priori* structured in human reason, reinforced the stereotype of mathematics as a supra-cultural subject.

The distinction between Arabic and Roman numerals signaled a degree of cultural dependence. But it was thought to be due to the early stages of development of primitive peoples, to historical accident, and to the late development of writing. It was something archaic, located at the superficial level of symbolism, and wholly immaterial from the viewpoint of modern mathematics.

But the word 'archaic' points deeper than its superficial connotation of things obsolete. It points to the origins, to the sources, to the principles and the principals. Should we look deeper into the roots of mathematics?

Michel de Foucault's *Archeology of Knowledge* taught me to discover hidden strata through a close analysis of discourse. Jean Piaget's truly archeologic studies of the slow and tortuous development of logico-mathematical concepts in children taught me to listen to them very carefully and to interpret their apparent errors as symptoms of a different type of logical structure. The Russian

142

Psychologist Lev A. Vygotsky explicitly taught me where to start the search:

> That children's learning begins long before they attend school is the starting point of this discussion. Any learning a child encounters in school always has a previous history. For example, children begin to study arithmetic in school, but long beforehand they have had some experience with quantity – they have had to deal with operations of division, addition, subtraction, and determination of size. Consequently, children have their own preschool arithmetic, which only myopic psychologists could ignore.[1]

The purpose of this paper is to determine as accurately as possible the cultural dependence of the learning process in mathematics. What is essentially right in the claim to universality in mathematics? Where are the culturally specific aspects of mathematics to be located, both theoretically and empirically? How are they to be used to develop a culturally adapted curriculum for elementary school mathematics? These are the questions that guide the search.

2 THE CULTURAL SETTING

In Colombia, grade-school and high-school programs are centrally prescribed by the Ministry of Education and mandatory for all private and public, urban and rural schools. Sporadic curriculum reforms amounted to some additions, deletions and reshufflings of program contents. In 1975 a newly elected Liberal Government started a comprehensive school reform, called 'The Qualitative Betterment of Education.' An ambitious experimental curriculum for grades one to three was drafted and tested in a sample of schools scattered around the nation. In 1978 I was appointed by the National University of Colombia as Adviser to the Ministry of Education for the restructuring of school mathematics. Many evaluations and rewritings of the experimental programs have taken place since the first draft, and a newly revised set of programs for the five-grade elementary school has been submitted to teachers and universities for evaluation.

About half of the public schools are located in rural areas, and urban public schools are attended only by lower-middle and lower-class students. Cultural diversity among different regions of the country, among urban and rural school districts, and among slum dwellers and middle-class families cannot be properly accounted for by a centrally prescribed program, but curriculum differentiation (or even 'tracking') is politically unfeasible. A more flexible policy of adapting the programs of local conditions and of encouraging local rewriting of Integrated Units of Learning has been adopted; I find it basically sound, but it makes the evaluation of the experimental testing hard to obtain and harder to interpret.

As expected, more questions than answers have arisen from experimenting with the new grade-school programs. Teacher resistance to change is widespread, and the Teachers' Unions stall reforms as a strategy to add to their clout at the negotiation table. Far-right groups find most reforms 'dangerous' or 'inspired by world communism,' and far-left groups brand them as 'useless' or 'dictated by US imperialism.' Local research in education is minimal, and research made in other countries is often contradictory or easily disqualified. One could quote conflicting findings about most questions in mathematics education.[2]

The raging war between 'new Math' and 'Back to Basics' oversimplifies the issues. Arguments are heated and emotional, and the facts quoted by each side are easily reinterpreted by the other. But conspicuously absent from the evaluations, from the political bickering, from the research reports, and from the 'New Math' v. 'Back to Basics' polemics is the main issue of this paper: What conflicts arise between universal or standard mathematics and concrete mathematical systems found in the local cultures? How to detect, refine and utilize those culturally transmitted systems for a curriculum reform? What experience with those concrete mathematical systems do children already have before or outside school?

Children are routinely assumed, not only by myopic psychologists but by almost everybody else, to know nothing about real mathematics when they enter school, except perhaps counting up to a certain number. How true is this assumption?

And even far-sighted psychologists and practically everybody else think that school mathematics is a universal subject, whose cultural dependence is limited to the informal language, the mathematical symbols and the trivial examples and story-problems used in the classrooms and textbooks. Is that the important cultural dependence?

3 A TOOL FOR CULTURAL RESEARCH IN MATHEMATICS

It is well known that even illiterate cultures have often quite complex trading systems, astronomical and calendrical calculations, games and sports with complex scoring rules, intricate marriage systems with refined mathematical structures, etc. But it is not so well known that children handle complex mathematical – or at least proto-mathematical – systems in a very skilled way before going to school, or without having gone to school at all.

Many scattered but consistent findings suggested the development of a theoretical tool to handle the empirical data, to lay out the field in a wider perspective, to provide a framework for further research, to shape a disciplined language, and, above all, to enable the mind's eye to have a clear vision of holes. In my opinion, one of the main uses of theory is the possibility of making holes visible. By definition, holes are non-entities, and therefore not directly perceivable. The fact that one does perceive them, points to the existence of an underlying theory, be it only the anticipation of a smooth field of vision. If that much theory exists, and you see edges, you can construct holes. No theory, no holes. Everybody agrees that the teaching of school mathematics is full of holes. How to classify and analyze them? How to dismiss pseudo-holes and detect new ones? How to perceive cultural vacuums and pseudo-mathematical emptiness?

The abused fad of the 1960s, 'the systems approach,' by now hammered and chiseled through twenty years of hard criticism, yielded the clues to the understanding of mathematical systems taught in school and of those familiar to children at home and in their neighbourhoods. A refined version of a General Systems Theory applicable to mathematical education research is needed. It should cover the whole of existing mathematics without pedantic ambiguity; it should lay out the field and help to indicate holes; ideally, it should overcome the sets-and-logic approach of the New Math, and the numbers-and-routines approach of the Back to Basics people. But it should also meet a seemingly contradictory demand: in spite of the intended generality and universality, it should help detect very fine cultural differences in the proto-mathematical and mathematical systems actually used by children and unschooled adults.

145

In the late 1970s I attempted to develop an appropriate version of the General Systems Theory in a more general setting[3] and to refine it for the purposes of research and curriculum development in mathematics.[4] For the limited purposes of this paper, and for the sake of a minimal agreement in terminology, a short version follows.

4 THE INTERNAL SPLITTING OF MATHEMATICAL SYSTEMS

Let us think of systems in the present context as consisting of components, procedures and relations. More formally, we could think of a system as an ordered triple (C,P,R) consisting of a set of components, a set of procedures and a set of relations.

Components are discernible, multiple, passive with respect to procedures and subject to relations. They are things, objects, elements, points, individuals . . . to be recognized and handled. Either you see them, or you overlook them.

Procedures are active and point to the practical; they demand time, energy, adroitness. They are actions, transformations, processes, operations, algorithms, routines, functions . . . to be performed. Either you perform them, or you omit them.

Relations are more subtle and point to the theoretical; they bind things together or separate things from each other. They are bonds or repulsions, similarities or differences; they relate, structure, organize components. Either you get them, or you miss them.

It is instructive to try to define components, procedures or relations. All definitions turn out to be circular. There have been some attempts to reduce procedures to relations and relations to sets of ordered n-tuples. As useful reductions, they might be practical for particular purposes; as definitions, they completely miss the point. Components can be viewed as the building-blocks of systems. Procedures can be viewed as providing the dynamics of systems. Relations can be viewed as providing the statics, the structures of systems.

Systems have structure, not vice versa. Several systems may have the same structure. The same components may be rearranged in different structures. You may detect several different structures in the same system; but once you fix one definite structure and forget, neglect, abstract from the others, you start to speak of a definite system with that structure only. You speak about the ordered group structure of the system of integers under addition with the usual ordering, and abstract from the ring structure, or from the partially ordered structure determined by the multiplicative (divisor/ multiple) ordering. Here the integers are the components, addition is the procedure, and the usual additive ordering is the relation. But you may have a whole set of procedures, like addition, subtraction, multiplication, Euclidean division, among others; and a whole set of relations, like strictly less than, less than or equal, strictly greater than, greater than or equal, proper divisor, divisor or equal, proper multiple, multiple or equal, successor, predecessor, opposite (in sign), among others. All procedures mentioned were binary, in the sense that each handles two components at a time to produce others; but there are many procedures that take only one component at a time (unary), or three components at a time (ternary), or n components at a time (n-ary procedures). All relations mentioned were also binary, in the sense that each one holds or does not hold between two components at a time; but there are many relations that hold or do not hold of a single component at a time (unary predicates), or among three components at a time (ternary), or n components at a time (n-ary relations).

Each procedure defines a natural associated relation that holds between the components used as arguments and those produced as results: the raw-stuff-to-finished-product relation. These relations that result (but are different) from the procedures, along with the explicitly given relations, constitute the structure of the system. Relations structure, organize, systematize the system. A system without relations (and hence without procedures) is a 'dead' system: it has no structure. A set of components is therefore the corpse of a system. One can define, or mount, or build, many structures on that same set of components, which is called the universe, or the underlying set of the system.

Structures are abstract with respect to systems. In a sense, structures are that which several similar systems have in common: they may have the same structure in a sense easily made precise. Systems, in turn, however abstract they seem, are concrete with respect to structures. The additive group of integers is a concrete system; the abelian group structure is abstract: many other concrete systems do have the same abelian group structure.

This straightforward way of splitting systems into three very different sorts of entities was most fruitful in the conceptual analysis of every single mathematical system encountered in the mathematics curriculum from pre-school to college. Without the conceptual clarification brought about by this threefold internal splitting of mathematical systems, the cultural analysis would have been impossible.[5]

5 THE EXTERNAL SPLITTING OF MATHEMATICAL SYSTEMS

Once internally analyzed into components, procedures and relations, all systems of school mathematics and all systems culturally functioning as mathematical or proto-mathematical outside of schools were seen to exist at three very different levels:

5.1 Superficial level: symbolic systems

They are the only ones appearing in textbooks. No wonder: textbooks can print symbols only. They are the only ones taught to children. No wonder: teachers can only emit sounds, draw signs, form gestures, and all that is exclusively symbol transmission.

Formalist philosophers of mathematics think – or try to force themselves to think– that symbolic systems are the whole of mathematics. Fortunately they are not. Formal systems are not even the whole of symbolic systems in mathematics: most of written and spoken mathematics consists of informal symbolic systems.

Numbering systems (as different from number systems) are good examples of symbolic systems. Take for instance the Roman, or our own decimal Hindu-Arabic system.

5.2 Ground level: conceptual systems

Once formalism and behaviorism were assigned their proper niches, constructivist philosophies of mathematics and cognitive schools of psychology could talk again about constructing, handling and understanding conceptual systems, without guilt feelings. Conceptual systems are those that are assumed by good textbooks, even though they can only talk or write about them through symbolic systems (talking textbooks are now on the market). Conceptual systems are those that are constructed slowly – not always painfully – by children from the earliest months of their lives. Number systems (as different from numbering systems) are good examples of conceptual systems. Take for instance the so-called natural numbers or cardinal numbers with their usual procedures (operations) and relations. 'Natural' numbers are of course as 'artificial,' as much works-of-art, as much construed and constructed, as much man-made or woman-made as anything you name. But they are constructed so early that they seem natural. You may also realize that the conceptual system of natural numbers with their procedures and relations is independent of the numbering system you chose for it, either English-spoken, or Spanish-spoken, or Roman-written, or Hindu-Arabic-written, or binary-coded. It is essential to realize that a single conceptual system at the ground level can appear as a plurality of symbolic systems at the superficial level.

5.3 Archaic level: target systems

It took a lot of digging to discover the different strata running way underground. Piaget, Vygotsky and Bruner helped a lot. Language analysis and 'clinical interviews' of children helped more. But you can do a lot of analyzing and a lot of interviewing without knowing what you are looking for. The key ideas came from an unknown 1973 book by the French historian and philosopher of mathematics, Pierre Raymond. It is unknown to mathematicians and educators because nobody would guess from its title (*Le passage au matérialisme*) that it has anything to do with mathematics; and it is unknown to materialist philosophers because they stop reading it as soon as they find out that it is about mathematics. I happened to like mathematics, among other sciences, and to like materialist philosophy, among other philosophies, and found the book fascinating. It points the way for an archeology of mathematical constructions. It shows how newly constructed conceptual systems in mathematics come from abstraction of active transformations on deeper systems. These are then forgotten. The archaic systems are thus passive with respect to the active system that acts on them. They are concrete with respect to the newly constructed conceptual system, which is abstract by definition: it is abstracted, pulled-out of the concrete system or systems that gave rise to it. They are natural with respect to the artificial, artfully constructed conceptual system that supersedes or superates the archaic systems.[6]

To give an example of target systems giving rise to new systems at the ground level, let us go back to the threefold splitting of systems into symbolic, conceptual and target systems, but now going backwards, or better, forwards, but starting from the bottom up. Let us take up again the example of the natural number system at the ground level with its different numbering systems at the superficial level, and let us try to look for the target systems at the archaic level that give rise to the others.

6 ARCHAIC LEVEL: TARGET SYSTEMS

Let us think of children playing games with concrete collections of everyday objects. Thinking about collections of pictures, of toys, of silverware or dishware, or better still, about collections of rocks or bottle crown-caps, you may imagine a poor child from a slum in Colombia moving things around, observing, pondering, piling things up, inventing his own games. At first he has some objects to play with, performs some actions on them, and perceives some similarities and differences among them. That is precisely a system with its components, its procedures, its relations. Through grouping the objects by hand, by visual-neural 'Gestalten,' by common properties, by comparisons, his original system of rocks and bottle crown-caps becomes the target system for a new system of collections of such objects. The new objects are now collections, subcollections of the original one (usually not including the whole original collection or the empty collection). Then he begins to assemble and disassemble collections out of other collections; he groups them and splits them; he sets aside the crown-caps of a given brand of soft drink from the rest; he moves a whole pile or a train of crown-caps onto or next to another. He perceives some similarities and differences among the collections. That is precisely a new system: its components are the sub-collections; its procedures are reunion and complementation; its relations are inclusion, disjunction, not having anything in common with, having a larger number of objects than, having a smaller number of objects than, having the same number of objects as. . .

As the child plays with the original target system, he begins to construct a very interesting conceptual system, described by Piaget in detail, and classified by him as a 'Groupement': almost a group, but not quite; almost a lattice, but not quite. Mathematicians may not like this hybrid monster, but it is enough to play with crown-caps with your neighbourhood pre-schoolers for a half-hour to convince yourself that the conceptual system they are constructing is not the usual Boolean algebra of sets with union, intersection and comple-mentation, nor the usual Boolean lattice of sets with inclusion New Math fanatics think they are. But it is not the natural number system. Back to Basics fanatics think they are constructing either. My hypothesis is that the failure of the New Math is due to the dissimilarity of the conceptual system of teachers and textbook writers (the usual Boolean algebra of sets or its equivalent lattice), and the culturally constructed system of children: the system of collection games, which has, among others, a 'Groupement' – structure. But now, if you noticed the last three relations perceived by the child in his collection game, they seem to have more to do with number: less than, greater than, equal. But not yet. My hypothesis about the failure of 'Back to Basics' is that it tries to force numbers down the throats of children through symbolic routines (the words one, two, three . . . are also symbolic), before they finish enjoying the culturally (for their age and environment) more appropriate collection games.

Soon enough they realize that those relations they may express (at the symbolic level) as 'smaller than,' 'bigger than,' 'the same as,' naturally split the sub-collections into batches having the-same-number-of crown-caps. This equivalence relation is built out of the two other order relations 'smaller than' and 'bigger than' when the ordering fails. The dependence of many equivalence relations on order relations is not found in mathematical textbooks. But it is simply detected as a failure to order: ask a group of children to queue up in order of height; if you see two children pushing each other too long, they are the same height.

Notice that these relations we have expressed at the symbolic level as having-less-elements-than, having-more-elements-than, and having-the-same-number-of-elements-as, do not depend on the concept of number. On the contrary: the concept of number is built out of those three relations, when the game of sub-collections is taken as the target system for a new conceptual system: the natural numbers starting with 'one,' with 'going up one' as the natural procedure, and 'being next to' as the natural relation. The procedure is unary, not binary like addition. Peano was right in more ways than he thought, when he formalized the natural numbers in his first version, starting with one, and using the successor as the only operation. Children like his system.

But they do not like the natural number system of teachers and textbooks with its four operations (none of them the one they like) and their two relations of additive order: less than or equal, greater than or equal. Children accept rather the relations: strictly less than, strictly more than. But for mathematicians these relations are not reflexive, and hence, by definition of order relation, they should not be called 'orders'. Calling them 'strict orders' is a contradiction in terms, widespread usage notwithstanding, at first, children build a conceptual number system for each type of collection game: two-bottle-caps, two-rocks, two-candy. . . . The fleeting but real existence of these concrete number systems is widely attested to by linguistics and cognitive psychology. They are intermediate stages in the construction of the natural number system, abstract with respect to concrete games of 'smaller,' 'larger' or 'equal' sub-collections, games which in their turn were abstract with respect to games with the crown-caps, rocks, pictures or pieces of candy themselves.

Old-style arithmetics still talk about 'concrete numbers' like two caps, and 'abstract numbers' like two. This distinction is worth reviving. It marks the culturally relevant proto-mathematical systems out of which the mathematical system of the natural numbers with their operations and relations is constructed at the conceptual level. It is the one Norma X knew how to handle.

Once the natural number system is constructed as abstract, and the child has played with it for years, counting forward and backward, jumping two or three numbers at a time, he begins to notice that going-up-two, or going-down-two, are new and interesting procedures in themselves. Now he begins to take the once abstract natural number system as target system; the procedures that acted on the natural numbers moving them up or down begin to take up a personality of their own. He is beginning to construct the signed integers. Then he sees that the natural procedure between two

152

signed integers is to apply them successively to a natural number. New procedures and relations begin to be constructed conceptually, and a new system, abstract with respect to the target system of natural numbers, begins to take shape. What a mathematician would call the composition of two operators is for the child the natural addition of integers: if you go up four and then go back three, it is the same as going up one. Is that addition or composition? The child couldn't care less: he can perform the new procedure on the newly formed components of his conceptual system. Integers are natural when natural numbers become so familiar as to seem natural. But in the usual textbooks, all that is found about this culturally natural construction of the signed integers is a confused and complex double-talk about the integers being equivalence classes or ordered pairs of natural numbers. Only very fine archeological work could detect that those equivalence classes are precisely the dead bodies (graphs) of the live and active signed integers as up-and-down operators children love to construct. In fact, the active operator $+2$ applied to the natural numbers as target system has as its graph the set of ordered pairs $(0,1)$, $(1,3)$, $(2,4)$ . . ., $(n, n+2)$,. . . But using that as a definition for a child who can construct the active operator by him- or herself, is as awkward as defining one hour to be the set of ordered pairs (midnight, 1 a.m.), (1 a.m., 2 a.m.), . . ., (11 a.m., noon), (noon, 1 p.m.), . . . (11 p.m., midnight). Would you like that? And what about the hour from half-past one to thirty-to-three? Any honest youngster will tell you he doesn't like defining integers as equivalence classes. And you cannot list them all anyway, either. But you can certainly build the concept as soon as you can count up and down the natural numbers by ones or jumps And those are hard procedures to master. Back to Basics fanatics are right in insisting to New Math fanatics that they should not teach integers as equivalence classes; but they are wrong in trying to force children to master the integers through symbolic routines. They will be forgotten and confused right after the final exam if they are not articulated onto the up-and-down jumping procedures.

By the way, the infinity of natural numbers and positive integers (as operators they are not the same as their targets) is easily understood by young children as endlessness (infinity) once they master the going-up procedure. Let me finish this section with the following true story:

In 1978, Santiago Z, then a second grader, started a contest with me: he would name a big number and I would name a bigger one, and so forth. He started easy: 'Ninety!'. I said: 'Hundred ninety!'. 'Two hundred!' he said. 'Two thousand!' I said. 'Ninety thousand!' was his bid, and I retorted: 'Hundred thousand!'. He became exasperated and shouted: 'Infinity thousand!'. I lost the game.

7 GROUND LEVEL: CONCEPTUAL SYSTEMS

It should by now become clear that the ground level is shifting upwards as soon as a system is mastered and can become the target for the next construction. It is to Piaget's credit that he noticed that the new construction results as a 'reflexive abstraction' from procedures, not from objects or relations. Procedures acquire the status of objects when the archaic system is forgotten. This happens with the signed integers and with the rational numbers, which arise culturally as procedures on target systems, and then become passive objects, representable as points on a static line. Teachers and textbook writers think those are the integers or the fractions, and confuse the issues hopelessly for the youngsters that are trying to build the active procedures and master them. The first conceptual system which is mathematical with respect to the proto-mathematical target system of the crown-caps was the 'Groupement' of crown-cap sub-collections. Out of many such collection games arises a second conceptual system, that of the natural numbers starting with one and having as natural procedure going up to the next. Out of this initial conceptual system the full system of natural numbers with many operations and relations can be constructed at the conceptual level. The original conceptual systems of sub-collections are superated, forgotten. The procedures of going-up or-down by jumps give rise to a new conceptual system of signed integers with culturally natural procedures and relations. Once this basic system is built, it can be enlarged by introducing new procedures and noticing new relations. Then, this new conceptual system takes up a life of its own and nobody notices its archaic roots any more. The 'victims' of the going-up or -down procedures, that is, the target systems, are buried deep, and the conceptual system of signed integers with their usual operations and relations is ready to become the target system for a new conceptual system; the integer-

valued functions on the signed integers cherished by number theorists.

To divert attention from symbolic systems, I have tried to avoid
all mathematical symbols in the preceding text. To stress the point I
am trying to make, it must be said that the words I have used to
describe the target systems and the conceptual systems are not
really the objects, procedures or relations: they merely refer to
them; but the use of everyday language was meant to convey the
concept of archaic and ground-level systems as different from the
symbolic systems. I am sorry, but I cannot possibly print here a
target system or a conceptual system; I can only give you some hints
on how to construct a conceptual system once you have identified a
familiar target system. I wish I could spare you the construction
work (direct telepathy maybe?). But then you might also miss all
the fun.

8 SUPERFICIAL LEVEL: SYMBOLIC SYSTEMS

Now, when it comes to symbols, it is just child's play to devise a
symbolic system once they master the conceptual system. Try to
design a symbol system for the more primitive system of crown-
caps. Or for the system of collection games. Or a system for the
natural numbers, or for the integers, or for the rational numbers
which is different from the run-of-the-mill numbering systems.
Your design might not be very good for certain things, like adding
or multiplying large numbers; but it might be very good for other
things. A simple tally of equally spaced bars is very nice for the
newly formed conceptual system of natural numbers just pulled out
of the target systems of the collection games. You do not need a
symbol for the natural operation of 'going up to the next': you
simply write one more bar to the right. And if you are careful, the
order relations are easily checked by length comparison:

$$| | | | | |$$
$$| | | | | | | | | | | |$$

If you get tired of counting bars one by one, try the usual trick of
crossing out fives with the five-bar: 卌 is a very nice symbol for the
number five.

Different cultures have developed different symbolic systems for
the same conceptual system of natural numbers. How do we know it

is the same? The 'sameness' of the conceptual system can of course only be inferred out of coincidences, easiness of translation, success of trading practices, or other observable symptoms. It is clear that at this basic level we have called the ground level, a large degree of universality is attained. But is it only at the symbolic level where the cultural diversity is located? My answer is a definite 'No!' The cultural diversity is also located at the archaic level of target systems, and that location is more important and far deeper than the superficial diversity of symbolic systems.

9 PEDAGOGICAL CONSEQUENCES

The first general idea is that the teacher, the curriculum designer and the researcher should try to start from the bottom up: exploring the diversity of culturally concrete target systems that give rise to a conceptual system.

In the present theoretical framework, mathematics at the conceptual level cannot really be taught. One can conform the right environment and give the right cues to promote meaningful play with the culturally familiar target systems, to help children construct the conceptual system; once they have constructed it, they should be encouraged to invent their own symbolic systems. There will be a plurality of target systems that may give rise to the same conceptual system; the choice of those with which the children will be encouraged to play has to be made in terms of cultural familiarity and usefulness. There will be a plurality of symbolic systems that arise out of the same conceptual system; the choice of those the children will be encouraged to develop and master has to be made also in terms of cultural familiarity and usefulness; but if a child, or better still, a group of children, develop their own system, they should be encouraged to play with it and to compare it with the culturally more widespread systems. If they understand the conceptual system, they will easily make the translation; if they do not, they will not even know it is a translation.

A second general idea is a counterpoint to the first: it states that starting from the symbolic systems down is counter-productive. The mechanical mastery of symbolic routine blocks the concept-building process. Symbols can and should be used to help the conceptual construction along the way, and it can be argued that the concept cannot be fully developed without some form of accompanying symbolism. But the priorities should be clear.

If the children know some symbols, one can start down to the possible underlying concepts and the certainly underlying target systems. If they progress up from target systems to some concepts, one can start seeking symbols. One should foster these ups and downs, but remarks that the main trend has to be upwards, starting from different target systems that have the same structure. Once the conceptual system is partially built, and a particular symbol system is attached to it, try different symbolic systems that have the same meaning. Try to infer whether the meaning is really there: go all the way down to different target systems to see if the concepts are correctly applied to them. Then go up the ladder again.

In the book mentioned before [Section 5.3], Pierre Raymond shows how this simple pattern of using one or several target systems as concrete raw materials for the construction of abstract conceptual systems is repeated throughout the history of mathematics. My suggestion is to let 'ontogenesis,' the re-construction of those systems by children, follow at least some of the paths of 'phylogenesis,' the construction of those systems in the history of mathematics.

But I am not stressing the usual (and wrong) platitude of teaching mathematics only through so-called concrete methods or concrete materials. Raymond observed the above-mentioned relativity of the classification of a particular system as concrete or abstract also at the historical level. Piaget observed it at the genetic level. But the pattern is the same: once a good symbolic system is developed for the active system and enough familiarity is achieved, a new active system uses the former as target system, and the new conceptual system can be so successful that it now becomes concrete and the first concrete system disappears into the background and is easily forgotten.

I am advocating a rescue operation to recover those concrete systems, where the original cultural dependence will be found to lie. They might turn out to be very abstract themselves, but that does not matter. The word 'concrete' is very relative indeed.

Piaget has sharply criticized the confusion between these activities in school and the truly active methods. Any perception, any meaningful word of a three-year-old is already abstract: it lumps together many objects and forgets, or abstracts from, many otherwise important differences. It takes a lot of mental activity to construct that. It is the mental activity on the currently concrete systems that has to be stressed.

Vygotsky remarked also that teaching methods used for mentally retarded children, based on concrete, look-and-do techniques, had resulted in profound disillusionment:

> It turned out that a teaching system based solely on concreteness
> – one that eliminated from teaching everything associated with
> abstract thinking – not only failed to help retarded children
> overcome their innate handicaps but also reinforced their
> handicaps by accustoming children exclusively to concrete
> thinking. Concreteness is now seen as necessary and
> unavoidable only as a stepping stone for developing abstract
> thinking – as a means, not as an end in itself.[7]

The above ideas forced a thorough rethinking of all systems taught at the grade-school and high-school levels, from the natural numbers with their usual operations and relations, to the real functions of elementary calculus with their operations and relations. Many surprises were found at all levels, from the most concrete collections of familiar objects children use as target systems to build their counting numbers, all the way up to the bizarre behavior of functions and derivatives.

A full account of the research done on all those systems will be the subject of a forthcoming book. Many aspects of that research could be called cultural, anthropological, linguistic, psychological or mathematical. But the general pattern repeated itself over and over. Seemingly trivial details of language, learning troubles, apparent mistakes, negative reactions of children, led the way to unearthing the culturally relevant systems, pinpointing the conceptual system and relating the different symbolic systems attached to it. A few short examples follow in Sections 10 to 15.

No contention is made about the representativity or generalizability of these examples. It would be hard to separate what is specific to a particular child, a particular sub-culture or a particular country, from what is general or universal, or to pinpoint what is due to cultural factors, or to genetic factors, or to an interaction of both. It is clear, for instance, that the peculiar objects or local toys children play with are not the same in different cultures; they are not the same even in different strata of the population of the same city of Bogota. But why have children's games turned out to be more universal than was imagined? Why do developmental psychologists trace strikingly familiar patterns of growth for children from Geneva, Paris, New York or Jakarta? The hypothesis underlying the presentation of examples from my limited experience is that the action schemes of children will be found to be very similar in different cultures, no matter how different the targets of those actions or the linguistic labels attached to them may be.

If mathematics arises from the articulation of those action schemes, as Piaget contends, and not from the reactions of the target objects or the repetition of spoken or written symbols, the following pattern of a correct pedagogy of mathematics can be transferred to wholly different cultures and environments: explore first the mathematical and proto-mathematical activities of the local culture; pick up the language actually used by children and adults to represent the corresponding objects, procedures and relations; start from the concrete target systems found in that culture and use the local language to elicit those action schemes or activity patterns on the target systems. Watch for the symptoms of the actual construction of conceptual systems, and let several symbolic systems flow or attach themselves to those conceptual systems. My contention is that this pattern of educational activity is generalizable to the teaching and learning of mathematics in other cultures.

10 SET THEORY

Set theory as conveyed by New Math textbooks turned out to be very alien to our cultural environment. Of course, British and Dutch school teachers found that out very soon after the introduction of the New Math in their own cultural settings, and Japanese teachers rejected it out of hand after a few months.

Nevertheless, a little more digging showed deeper strata that were easily and playfully handled by Colombian children. Many culturally familiar situations that give rise to the counting numbers were found to be natural and interesting for children. I call them 'collection games.' Children readily identify, use, count, label, assemble and partition collections of everyday objects in and out of school: their marbles, their toys, their school utensils, furniture, silverware and dishware, postage stamps, picture cards, you name it.

Carlos E. Vasco

The theoretical key was Piaget's distinction between collections (both figurative and non-figurative) and operational classes. Concrete figurative collections have to be visible as one simultaneous 'Gestalt,' and they must have at least two elements. Concrete non-figurative collections must also count at least two elements, and all members of the collection must have a common property and fall under the same label. There are no empty collections, or unitary collections either. These collections are not mathematical sets: they are systems with many inner relations and active operations and procedures. Children never perceive members of their families or the buddies of their class by children as sets of loose, unordered, unstructured elements. The set with its dead elements, its frozen procedures and departed relations is just the corpse of a system. No wonder children do not like sets; but they love systems. Where in the world is the child that accepts that the set [a,b,c] is the same as the set [c,a,a]? Such equality is possible only at a high level of abstraction, when all the 'oblivious factors' have deleted all traces of structure in the original systems and have dumped them into the obscure depths of the category of sets.

I am not denying that it may be interesting, and even necessary, to study corpses of systems at later times. In biology it is also necessary to dissect dead frogs and to kill cells with dyes to see them through the microscope. I am only saying that children do prefer live frogs and wiggling cells. They also prefer live, bound and structured systems, to dead, loose, unstructured sets. If the words 'set' and 'element' are not forced on the child and one abstains from empty and unitary sets, the child is home free in that part of set theory that reflects concrete collection games. One is reminded that for the Greeks, and all the way down to Renaissance arithmetics, zero and one were not numbers: numbers started at two. We still agree with our ancestors that unity is neither prime nor composite; but we balk at the perfectly parallel statement that unity is neither even nor odd. But they accepted both, simply because unity was not a number.

The culturally natural procedures with collections were found to be union and complementation. Children refused to use the connective 'or' in connection with union of collections, as all set-theory textbooks prescribe: they prefer the connective 'and,' which textbooks say has to be used for set intersection. But children insist on saying 'The blue blocks *and* the disks' for the union, and use no connective for the intersection: 'The blue disks.' Children were right. So much the worse for textbooks.

Such simple explorations of the cultural world of children's collection games, carried out in the mood of a mathematically trained cultural anthropologist, allowed me to rewrite much New Math material that teachers used to repeat without much understanding, and children used to repeat without any understanding at all. Many virtues of the proper version of set theory were recovered, and at their root many well-known vices were detected.

11 LOGIC

Another surprise was the contrast between the 'New Math Logic' now taught in many grade schools, and the culturally specific logical language games played by children. It turned out that propositional logic is not understood by young children as textbooks assume children often have a pure reward–punishment idea of telling the truth. But an appropriate version of the so-called deontic logic of some wayward logicians was found out to be perfectly understood by youngsters in a very precise way: they are constantly given instructions, orders, prohibitions, promises of conditioned rewards and punishments. But in this culturally tuned setting the usual tautologies are no longer valid. The connective 'and' is not commutative; try to commute: 'Take off your shoes and pull out your socks.' Because of the time-dependence of conditions, the counter-reciprocal is not equivalent to the original sentence, and 'If p, then q' is interpreted by children as 'either p or not q'; textbooks assure you that such transformation is incorrect, and that the right one is 'either not p or q,' which children refuse to accept. In fact, 'If you behave, you may go to the movies' is always interpreted by the child as 'Either you behave, or you may not go to the movies,' and never as 'Either you do not behave, or you may go to the movies,' which is preposterous. Children are again right and textbooks wrong. Again I say: so much the worse for textbooks.[8]

12 NATURAL NUMBERS

Natural numbers are associated with concrete systems of collection games, with number-words attached as quasi-adjectives to plural nouns, or with rote-memory number lists attached to objects of a concrete collection through finger-pointing. Dice, dominoes or playing cards may be well known by very young children, who can tell the patterns as 'Gestalten,' without counting dots or spades. The words they use may collide with the decimal numbering system; for instance, 'ten' is a shorter word than 'nine', but '10' has more symbols than '9'. The numbers 11 and 12, when read aloud, have nothing to do with the symbols; 13 and 15 are not quite read 'threeteen' and 'fiveteen' as they should be. In Spanish, the numbers 11 through 15 present a similar problem. But we do not have the problem the Germans have: 21 is read in reverse as 'einundzwanzig'; compare with the Latin 'undevinginti,' which stands for our 19. And let us not even tackle the French problem of 'quatre-vingt-dix-neuf'. . .

To mention only one operation, a study of division guided by a few hints given by the Italian mathematician Emma Castelnuovo, led to the detection of two different types of culturally familiar division processes, none of which agreed with the one taught in school:

12.1 To give the same number of items from a given batch of candy to each one of the children in a given group. The result is a number of items.

12.2 To split a fixed amount of items into batches of a given size, each batch to a child. The result is a number of children.

Children in Colombia speak of the first process as 'dividing candy *among* children' ['Repartir *entre*']. The expression used for the second process is rather difficult to translate into English: they speak of dividing *at-a-time* ['Repartir *de a*']. But both processes can be carried out without using multiplication, and therefore do not coincide with the division process taught in school, or with the words used by textbooks: 'Divide *by* ['Dividir *por*']. The independence of the culturally familiar division processes from multiplication is easily observed outside the schools, in spite of the textbook identification of division as an inverse operation to multiplication. I was told by a French mathematician that there are native groups who practice addition, subtraction and division, but do not know how to multiply. If confirmed, their existence would support phylogenetically the ontogenetically observed independence of division from multiplication.

13 INTEGERS

Children were found to reject instinctively the negative integers. These constructs have best known for centuries, but they were not easily welcomed into mathematics. The master of Renaissance algebraists, Cardano, called negative solutions to quadratics and cubics 'fictitious,' 'useless,' and even 'false'.[9] We are never quite convinced that minus times minus gives plus; we decide to learn that by heart as a rote rule, without trying to understand.

But children can construct the positive and negative integers as active conceptual operators that move things around: natural counting numbers, streets along an avenue, steps in a staircase, and other things more familiar than debts or temperatures below zero. The integers are active operators that move things up n steps (+n) or down n steps (−n). The identity operator does not move things at all (0). But then, the natural procedure between two of these active operators is not addition: it is the successive application (or composition) of the two operators: we had already remarked in Section 6 that going up four (+4) and then going down three (−3), is the same as going up one (+1), that is: +4 o −3 = +1, where the small circle represents composition of operators, just a fancy and culturally foreign way of saying that you apply one after the other.

From this viewpoint it can be seen that debts or temperatures below zero are not the right models for the negative integers. They are rather two more target systems for the culturally familiar operators that act on the natural counting numbers, the steps in a staircase or the streets along an avenue. Indeed, walking n blocks north or south changes the numbering of the side streets that go east–west in a definite way: walking four blocks north and then three blocks south is the same as walking one block north. But I haven't told you what street we are at. The target system is one thing, and the active conceptual system is another thing.

The cultural dependence of the target system was evident in an experimental trial of this system in a slum school in Bogota. In this city, the north is a fashionable suburb, while the poor live in the south side. The obvious symbolic system for the integers in this system is 4N, 3S, 1N, etc. Identifying 4 and 4N by dropping the'N', and writing 4S for negative-four struck the slum kids as an insult: 'Why is it taken for granted that "4" means "4 North"? 'Why are northern numbers called positive?'. 'What is so negative about living in the south side?'. The kids were right, and we had to change the system to east and west, because there are very few more Avenues east of First Avenue, and nobody would feel insulted.

Finally, for those operators there is a natural change-of-orientation operator, called 'minus' and written '–'. It is obvious that if you change orientations twice, you leave them as they were before. There is no rote 'rule of signs': just the straightforward understanding of what happens if you reverse orientations twice. But notice that the 'minus' operator is now an active monster that eats integers. Functions are beginning to appear as active operators that act on the now familiar integers, which will in turn fade into a target system. The 'minus' is a unary monster that eats integers and spits them back reversed. If it bites you twice, you end up unharmed. Some boys in the State of Antioquia recalled hearing their grandfather tell this story about witches: if you cut a witch once with a knife, she will come back at you and cut herself once more, to cure the first wound with the second. Do you think those boys from Antioquia will ever forget what happens if you apply 'minus' twice?

14 FRACTIONS

This system is the headache of all math teachers. College freshmen seem to have forgotten all about fractions, as any teacher that has corrected tests about derivatives of fractional powers or integration of rational functions knows well. The proposed remedy of the Back to Basics movement is to drill much more on the fractions. It has been tried, but the number of rote exercises seems to affect little or not at all the difficulties with fractions in the years ahead; what those exercises are known to affect is the attitude towards mathematics: more kids hate math, and more adults fear fractions.

I began to think fractions were too hard for third graders. As I pondered moving them up to the fifth grade, I saw a group of first graders in a Gym class following without any trouble a series of instructions about half-turns and quarter-turns. There was a culturally friendly target system for fractions!

Very young children know a lot about half-gallons, quarters, pints and half-pints, as long as it is milk. Luis Eduardo Y and his fellow mechanics know a lot about fractions of an inch. Girls know a lot about fractional lengths, as long as it is string or ribbon. In metric

164

countries fractional lengths are even easier to handle: no jumps from twelve to a foot, three to a yard or God-knows-how-many to a rod or mile. But the same child that knows how much is it when you pour a half-gallon of milk into a container, and then a quarter-gallon more, will be totally baffled before the hieroglyph '1/2 + 1/4'. Should I add? multiply? cross-multiply? find the LCD? We must have jumped too fast to the symbolic system without any construction of the pertinent conceptual system.

'Fraction' is an ambiguous word: it refers to rational numbers and to fractional symbols. Is it 1/2 the same as 2/4? Obviously not! The first numerator is odd; the second is even. But somehow, they are supposed to be the same. The same what? Well, if the child has not built the right conceptual rational number, the question cannot be solved at the symbolic level. But at the conceptual level, rational numbers have no numerators or denominators. They are active monsters. Once you know the halving monster, you don't care if the teachers writes 1/2, 2/4, .5 or even 50 per cent. It is all the same. But now we know the same what: they are just funny disguises for the same halving monster.

For children from six to twelve (at least) it is very important to know what the monsters are supposed to eat. They eat turns, they eat lengths of rope, they eat certain natural numbers, like tens of dozens. They even eat quantities of milk or areas of concrete surfaces. I have studied all these target systems, and it is clear that the hardest is the one about areas. But it is the easiest to draw on the blackboard or on the textbook, and it is by far the commonest; but it is the culturally wrong target system to start from at least here in Colombia.

It is also clear that the usual words for transforming fractions, 'reducing,' 'simplifying' and 'amplifying' are culturally confusing; it is said that to simplify is the same as to reduce a fraction, and that the contrary is to amplify the fraction. But children associate a reduction with making smaller, and an amplifier with making sounds louder. So I propose to use 'simplifying' and 'complicating,' meaning just to make more simple or more complicated at the purely symbolic level. At the conceptual level, rational monsters really enlarge and shorten what they eat (except of course the tame monster, who does no harm to his victims, and he is 'Number One'). It is important to realize that these monsters do not eat pies or sheets of paper, as many teachers seem to think. They eat the mass

Carlos E. Vasco

or volume of pie dough or the area of the sheet. 'Half-pies' are quickly identified as phoney: if you will allow me to eat my half-pie, I'll choose the upper half, because it has all the frosting on it. Or if you allow me to choose my half-an-orange, I'll choose the inner half and leave you the rind. If you ask a child what do you get if you split a sheet of paper along the middle, he won't answer 'Two half-sheets' (unless he knows you want that answer). He will answer: 'Two little sheets of paper,' and he is right. The halving monster doesn't eat the objects themselves: just their areas, lengths, masses, weights or volumes.

Again, the natural procedure to apply to two monsters at the conceptual level is not addition: now it is again composition, or better still, applying them one after the other. Children learn fast that one-half of a half-gallon is a quarter; that one-half of a half-inch is a quarter of an inch, etc. But they do not know what it is if they see something like: '(1/2) × (1/2).' Why the multiplication symbol? Why read 'by,' or 'times,' when all there is to it is a simple 'of'? When the children get bored with the target systems because they have already constructed the rational monsters, they say simply 'a half of a half is a quarter.' If you ask them for the target systems, they shrug you off; 'It's the same.' When a child says 'It's the same,' he has constructed a conceptual system: he has learned mathematics.

15 GEOMETRY

Geometric systems were also packed with surprises. I must start by confessing that the New Math way of stating that line segments are sets of points used to leave me cold, or worse: frozen. There are too many sets of points that are not lines, and the dogmatic tone of infallibility assumed by the teacher who repeats the dictum is simply infuriating. When one day I saw a child looking at a line segment with a magnifying glass to try to see the points, I had enough of the New Math geometry.

Why not just play with line segments as primitive elements in a delightful system where points are unknown? Rethinking systems of segments, it was clear that there were many interesting operations or procedures to perform on them: sliding, turning, aligning them end to end, doubling them, bisecting them and what have you.

166

And a host of relations can be found: parallelism, incidence, congruence, perpendicularity.

I started playing segment games with children. Children in the slum areas found it hard to say in Spanish 'segmento'; they said 'semento,' which sounds exactly like 'cemento' ['cement']. Thus we decided to call them simply 'rayitas' ['little strokes']. The stroke games were simple but active; children were eager to move the sticks that stood for segments or strokes all over the place, turn them, join them, slide them. Questions about relations would stop them cold. One could almost see the neurons firing hypotheses; usually no words were uttered; maybe a quick sliding of a lollipop stem or a length check with thumb and index as calipers. One could see the eyes gleam at the flash of an insight. And a smile. All my philosophical training started to bubble in my mind: is this the long lost relation between theory and practice?

Indeed, procedures and operations reflect practice; relations reflect theory. Procedures are active; they have a priority in practice (you have to do something to perform them), and they have also a priority in theory (you have to do something to check a relation).

The priority of action is well documented by Piaget. He defines operations as internalized, reversible and co-ordinated actions. Vygotsky speaks of 'the internal reconstruction of an external operation'.[10]

Learning is, therefore, the performance of actions, operations, procedures and algorithms (at the symbolic level, procedures are called algorithms). Teaching is, therefore, the facilitation of such performance. These observations help one to appreciate functions as active transformations, not as relations, and much less, as sets of ordered couples. And they help one to rediscover active geometry.

Once, I drew a line segment downwards, and then labelled it A to B, starting at the point closest to the chalk:

Carlos E. Vasco

I said: 'Let this be the stroke AB'. One youngster objected: 'You drew it downwards! Shouldn't it be the stroke BA?' I was caught off-base. We forget the motion, the action; children do not. For us a segment is a segment, dead, cold, frozen. It is indifferent if it is called AB or BA. For children, it is still alive, warm, directed downwards. I tried to imagine how many teachers have answered the same question with a stern face and a dogmatic *ex cathedra*: 'It is the same. Period.' The same what? The same for whom?

The same group of children in the Gym class following instructions like 'A half-turn to the right!', who led me to the earliest target system for fractions, solved also the problem about angles. There it was, the long lost active angle-of-turn, right at the first grade. Children's geometry being dynamic, the right concept of angle is not the pair of half-lines (rays) joined by one end. It is the amplitude of a turn, and it has from the very beginning a definite orientation, an inside and an outside. But the angle drawn on the blackboard is already dead. It has lost the orientation, the inside and the outside.

In 1978 I started redesigning the geometry programs from first to ninth grade, reconstructing a whole array of geometric systems I called 'active geometry.' It starts acting on the child's own body and his toys as target systems. A conceptual system of transformations is constructed on those systems. And many possible symbolic systems can arise from the conceptual system.

Just an example: walking along line segments and turning with your own body at corner angles solved the eternal query of students about external angles of triangles.

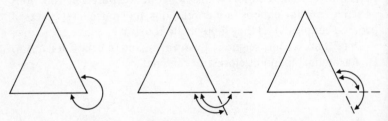

Question: Which one is the external angle?

If you look at the dead figure, you are lost. No definite answer is possible. But just chalk down a big triangle on the floor, and walk around it. There is no doubt about the meaning of the external angle you have to sweep with your front foot to regain the next side of the

168

triangle after you overstep the vertex. The obvious fact that, when you walk around the whole triangle, you end up facing in the same direction you started, gives dynamic, active, live meaning to the fact that the sum of the external angles is a full turn (360°).

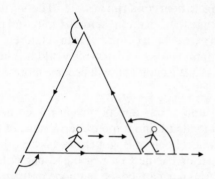

Answer: Just walk around the triangle!

But then, what is the meaning of the statement about the sum of the internal angles being 180° (that is, a half-turn)? Just try to walk around the triangle sweeping the internal angles with the foot that drags behind. Much to everybody's surprise, you end up facing backwards. Just try it. Don't miss the fun of active geometry!

Seymour Papert had also discovered this type of dynamic geometry around the same time. In his 1980 book *Mindstorms*, he talks about children mimicking the LOGO-Turtle with their own bodies, to be able to program a circular trajectory. He calls this 'body geometry' and 'syntonic learning':

> The Turtle circle is body syntonic in that the circle is firmly related to children's sense and knowledge about their own bodies.[11]

But to do active geometry one does not need a sophisticated computer or a well-implemented, interactive LOGO-language; my assumption is that you need only a sensitive ear to listen to unsophisticated children talking in their own underdeveloped language, and a sensitive eye to discover the culturally relevant target system. Then you can start developing active geometry, not only at MIT's Mathland environment, but in every grade school in the country.

Again, in Papert's language, I am advocating 'cultural

syntonicity.' He illustrates this concept by relating angles to navigation by means of the LOGO-Turtle:

> One of the most widespread representations of the idea of angle in the lives of contemporary Americans is in navigation. Many millions navigate boats or airplanes. . . . The Turtle connects the idea of angle to navigation, activity firmly and positively rooted in the extraschool culture of many children. And as computers continue to spread into the world, the cultural syntonicity of Turtle geometry will become more and more powerful. [12]

I cannot judge how firmly and positively rooted navigation is in America; in Colombia I find it too esoteric: none of the children I know in the public schools of Bogota have this experience. Perhaps in the Caribbean or Pacific Coast of our country there might be some children who navigate boats; but none of them will have any chance of interacting with the computer Turtles of the LOGO-environment, at least not before the twenty-first century. I do not think we should wait that long: I am advocating cultural syntonicity, not only of geometry, but of every mathematical system; and not only in a LOGO-environment, but at any school, however remote from yachts or computers. Let us start connecting any and every mathematical idea or system to an activity firmly and positively rooted in the extraschool culture.

16 CONCLUSIONS

This anthropological voyage into the uncharted regions of the Colombian grade schools changed my mind about learning mathematics: it revealed that making mathematics one's own can be as culturally dependent as learning literature or history, and not only at the linguistic or symbolic level. The apparent ahistoricity and aculturality of mathematics is a fiction of an adult mind that has reached the plateau of formal thought and has repressed the historically conditioned, culturally dependent reasoning of all children and most adults, at least when those adults are not trying to 'think mathematically;' that is, practically all the time.

The problem is that the math teacher is one of the few adults who is trying to 'think mathematically;' and the writer of math textbooks is even worse. The main obstacle the Colombian experimental reform has found is certainly not at the level of children: they love it. It is at the level of teachers, especially at the level of teacher instructors and supervisors. They know all the answers. They are sure mathematics is the universal language. They think they can evaluate objectively what children know about mathematics. I think they just evaluate what children remember about those disembodied symbolic systems most teachers think are mathematics.

A revered teacher and researcher of mathematics, Edward G. Begle, thought to the last minute of his life that mathematical systems were formal, symbolic systems. His survey of math education research hit on the notion of mathematical systems, but the prevailing formalist philosophy of mathematics misled him to identify mathematical systems at the conceptual level with formal symbolic systems and, of course, to forget target systems completely.[13] Most math education research starts from the same confusion and ignores target systems altogether. My prediction is that such research will progress little or nothing from now on.

Perhaps alternative teaching methods might accelerate learning of symbolic procedures; but the researcher will not know why. New methods based on Artificial Intelligence models will come to the fore; but up to now machines can perform only symbolic algorithms. Conceptual understanding, transference to new situations and production of new mathematical concepts from target systems will remain in the shadow.

As long as mathematical and pre-mathematical target systems are ignored, researchers, textbook writers and teachers will hold on to the wrong assumption that children know nothing about mathematics when they enter school. What language teacher would assume that six-year-olds know nothing about the English or Spanish language when they enter schools? Perhaps teachers at special education institutes for the deaf-mute. As long as teachers keep thinking that children are mathematically deaf-mute, the teaching of mathematics, 'Basic' or 'New,' is doomed to reach only the privileged upper 10 per cent that manage to construct their own conceptual systems in spite of their teachers, disentangling by themselves the maze of symbolic systems disembodied of all their cultural and imaginative content. Once they construct their conceptual systems, they can easily tune their receptors to the teacher's wavelength, keep learning mathematics, and start leaving their peers way behind. The teacher will teach the privileged students only, creating in the rest of them the 'mathofobia' so well described by Paper.[14]

A serious analysis of every mathematical system encountered in the school curriculum should be carried out in detail before designing a new research program, a new textbook, and even a new lesson or school activity in mathematics. Here are some of the questions that are being researched here in Colombia, and that should be researched elsewhere, in order to make real this utopian goal:

1 What experience with concrete systems, either mathematical or proto-mathematical, do children already have in their extraschool cuture?

2 How can we delimit those culturally familiar target systems to establish their components, their procedures, their relations?

3 What words, images, symbols, signals, gestures, tokens . . . are used by children and adults to talk about the components, their procedures and the relations of such concrete target systems?

4 What transformations, actions, procedures or operators on those target systems constitute the raw materials for the construction of a new conceptual system?

5 What does it mean to compose, or successively apply those operators to target components? What other conceptual combinations or operations can be performed on the operators that now form the components of the new conceptual system?

6 What relations hold among those operators?

7 What symbolic systems have been developed in the local culture, in the dominant middle-class culture, or in the mathematical literature to represent those operators, the procedures on them and their relations in the new conceptual system?

8 What procedures are used to manipulate and combine those symbols in the corresponding symbolic systems (algorithms)?

9 What relations hold among the symbols of each symbolic system, and among the symbols of different symbolic systems developed for the same conceptual system?

10 Do standard textbook notations and algorithms collide with the concrete, conceptual or symbolic handling of the culturally familiar target, conceptual or symbolic systems?

Thus, only two simple conceptual tools are used to analyze the mathematical totalities. We could think of them as two triadic prisms that decompose the white light of the mathematical totality that is being analyzed; the first prism shows three levels of systems: concrete target systems, conceptual systems and symbolic systems; the second prism shows three different types of entities inside each system: components, procedures and relations. Once the whole picture is spread out in detail and understood in its complexity, educational research and curriculum design in that particular aspect of mathematics will have a definite framework, where the direct cultural dependence of symbolic systems, the indirect cultural dependence of conceptual systems, and, above all, the determining cultural dependence of concrete target systems will stand out.

NOTES

1 Quoted with permission from Vygotsky, L.S., *Mind in Society. The Development of Higher Psychological Processes*. Harvard University Press, Cambridge – London, 1978, p.84.
2 See, for example:
   Begle, E.G., *Critical Variables in Mathematics Education: Findings from a Survey of the Empirical Literature*. MAA – NCIM, Washington, D.C., 1979.
   Fennema, E. (ed.), *Mathematics Education Research: Implications for the '80s*. NCTM – Reston, 1981.
   Suppes, P. (ed.), *The Impact of Research on Education*. NAE, Washington, D.C., 1978.
3 A first draft of the more general version was published by the Colombian equivalent of the NSF, 'COLCIENCIAS', in its journal *Ciencia, Tecnologia v Desarrollo*, vol. 4, no. 4 (October–December, 1980), 463–82, under the title: 'Teoria de Sistemas y Metodologias Cientificas'. A fuller account was published by the OAS Headquarters in Washington, D.C. or from the Colombian Ministry of Education: Ministerio de Educacion Nacional, Oficioa de Documentacion, CAN, Bogota, D.E. Colombia.
4 The special version for the mathematics curriculum was published by the Ministry of Education as a booklet for teacher instructors in several editions since 1978. It was read as a paper at the Fifth International Conference in Mathematics Education held in Campinas, Brazil, in February 1979. This paper was later published in the mathematics teachers' magazine edited by the National University of Colombia, *Notas de Matematica*, no. 10 (1980), 1–14. The title translation is: 'The

Carlos E. Vasco

Concept of System as a Key to the Mathematics Curriculum'. [El Concepto de Sistema como Clave del Curriculo de Matematica'].

5   The power to make holes visible is, as stated above, the main use of theory. The simple theoretical tool of splitting systems as directed enabled me to see the incompleteness of the usual Bourbaki-type of splitting structures into three 'mother structures': algebraic, ordinal and topological. First of all, Bourbaki confuses systems and structures; second, algebraic structures are those in which the only relations are those implicitly defined by the procedures; but ordinal and topological structures are just two examples – and not the only ones – of structures in which no explicit procedures are given. They should be called (purely) relational structures. Ordinal structures have only order relations (binary); topological structures have only vicinity relations (neighborhoods can be thought of as unary relations: V(x) holds if V is an open neighborhood of x; or as binary relations: (x,y) holds if V is an open neighborhood of both x and y). But there are many other relational structures not classifiable as algebraic, ordinal or topological. For example, a system of points with betweenness and colinearity as (ternary) relations; or a system of straight lines with parallelism and perpendicularity as (binary) relations. They are purely relational, but they are neither ordinal nor topological. Such a gaping hole in the Bourbaki system was invisible without the theory.

6   This is a typical case of the dialectical concept of 'Aufhebung': to superate in the sense both of making something obsolete and of recuperating the best, the gist, the essence of it. Good examples of target systems are hard to pinpoint, because they are easily forgotten once you have constructed the conceptual system. And you can swear there was nothing deeper than the systems now appearing concrete, passive and natural. It is essential to realize that a single conceptual system can appear as a single construction over a plurality of target systems at the archaic level.

7   Quoted with permission from Vygotsky, *op. cit.*, p.89.

8   A preliminary study of time-dependent connectives and their use in ordinary language was recently published in Spanish in: Vasco, Carlos E., 'Conectivas Secuenciales y la Formalizacion del Lenguaje Ordinario'. *Matematica-Ensensanza Universitaria* (Bogota), no. 27 (June 1983), 12–23.

9   Cardano, Girolamo. *The Great Art or the Rules of Algebra* Translated and edited by T.R. Witmer. The MIT Press, Cambridge, MA, 1968. See pp. 9,11 and 29.

10 Vygotsky, *op.cit.*, p. 56.

11 Quoted with permission from Papert, Seymour. *Mindstorms. Computers and Powerful Ideas*. Basic Books, Inc. New York, NY, 1980, pp. 58 and 63.

12 ibid., p. 63.

13 See Begle, E.G. *Critical Variables in Mathematics Education: Findings from a Survey of the Empirical Literature*. Mathematical Association of America – National Council of Teachers of Mathematics. Washing-

ton, D.C., 1979. Begle died in 1978 at the age of sixty-three. In the introduction to his book (pp. 1–3) he studies the basic notion of mathematical system. But he reduces mathematical systems to our superficial level: symbolic systems.

14 Papert, *op. cit.*, Chapter 2: 'Mathofobia: The Fear of Learning', pp. 38–54.

PART III

CULTURAL PERSPECTIVES ON THE LIFE COURSE

The ancient Greeks pronounced that man is the measure of all things. While our unit of measure has changed over the centuries, the question of what the human person is, how one can develop to one's fullest potential and live the most meaningful life has been asked continually. It is significant that even definitions of the very nature of the person are widely divergent. Cultures differ greatly in their conceptions of life stages and their markers, the goals and motivating ideals of life, and the ways in which these are implemented. This part explores conceptions of the person in a number of other societies. Essays on the traditional Indian conception of the self, the ways in which Japanese women have used culturally approved modes to develop their potential, the meaning and realization of relationships between the generations in China, however diverse in their treatment, all contribute to an understanding of cultural meanings in the life course. Finally, an essay on death in India elucidates questions related to the transitions in relationships and the trauma surrounding the loss of a member of one's kin and community which further continues the discussion of meaning in life.

VIII

THE WORK OF MOURNING: DEATH IN A PUNJABI FAMILY

Veena Das

ABSTRACT

In all societies, death has been a subject of mythology and folklore. Anthropologist Veena Das turns her attention to the ceremonies surrounding death and mourning in Punjabi culture. In this chapter, Das adopts a new perspective on this topic, and examines 'mourners to see whether we can discern a structure within which grief and loss are articulated, such that the connections between individual grief and societal patterns of mourning may be laid bare.' Unlike other researchers on this subject, Das does not focus on the separation of the mourners from their community, but on the mourning as bringing about a 'proper separation' between the living and the dead. This paper is based on fieldwork conducted among an urban Punjabi community in 1974–5, and centers around two case studies.

The subject of death has a perennial attraction for the human mind.[1] There is no known society, historical or contemporary, that has not ritualized death, made it a subject of mythology and folklore, speculated on its origins and its finality and tried to contain its disruptive effect on meaning in human life. No wonder philosophers have characterized human societies as communities in the face of death and described social reality as constantly threatened by lurking irrealities.[2] In the anthropological and sociological traditions, Durkheim (1947) gave special importance to piacular rituals as providing the means for healing the wound inflicted upon a

179

community by the death of one of its members. Malinowski (1948) characterized death as the final and supreme crisis of life and found in it an important source of religion. Nozick summarized the problem posed by death in the following words: 'Granting that life ending in death is in tension, at least with our existence having meaning, we have not yet isolated why this is so.' (Nozick 1981: 581).

Isolating why this is so may proceed on a route of philosophical enquiry, systematically examining and separating the various ways in which meaning may be threatened by the acknowledgment of man's finitude. Or else one could follow a different mode of enquiry, primarily historical or sociological in orientation. For example, Philippe Aries' (1981) masterly survey of changing attitudes towards death in western societies since the Middle Ages helps us to understand the social rather than universal location of these attitudes. Understanding the modes of being human in different societies and different periods of time shows us the limits of our own experience and this is the most valuable lesson of history and anthropology. They demonstrate the power of human imagination in resolving the tension between our finitude and our attempts to lead a meaningful life.

THE PRESENT STUDY

Both Durkheim (1947) and Malinowski (1948) emphasized the function of death ceremonies in creating a secure world of meaning for the individual. In the ceremonies of death, said Malinowski, the culturally valuable belief in immortality is given body and form. Nowhere is this statement more beautifully illustrated than in Hertz's classic essay on death (Hertz, 1960). Hertz showed that if we concentrate on collective beliefs relating to death, these may be best discussed as three separate complexes – beliefs relating to the body, beliefs relating to the soul and beliefs relating to the mourners. He argued that visible changes upon the body consequent upon death are related to beliefs about the invisible changes in the soul. It is only after a period of liminality that the dead man is viewed as separating himself from the living and finally settling down among the dead. This is the period when the mourners are separated from the society of ordinary men, are often seen as polluted and have to be slowly reintegrated into the society of ordinary men and women.

In the Indian case, recent works by Kaushik (1976) Das (1976a) and Parry (1981) have demonstrated that the scheme outlined by Hertz could be successfully used to understand the transformation of the dead man from the state of the living to that of *preta* (ghost) who is finally transformed into *pitr* (ancestor) through the proper performance of rituals. Kaushik (1976) showed that the ritual functions of caste specialists who performed the various rituals relating to death could be understood within a triadic structure.

The barber mediates the mourner's relationships with the dead body (*shava*). During the liminal phase when the dead person is conceptualized as having the form of a ghost (*preta*), the caste specialist who guides the mourner into making food offerings to this ghost is the *mahapatra*, a caste of funeral priests who are considered to be Brahmins but who occupy a very low position in the caste hierarchy. The end of mourning rituals when the death impurity of the mourners is terminated corresponds to a change in the conception of the dead person who is seen as finally integrated into the world of ancestors by becoming a *pitr* (ancestor) himself. Rituals directed towards the dead person as ancestor are officiated by the *purohita* or the pure Brahmin priest. Thus the three aspects of death rituals – those dealing with the dead body and directed towards its disposal; those dealing with the intermediate or liminal phase when the dead person is seen as separated from the living but not yet integrated among the dead; and the final phase in which he is incorporated into the society of dead are clearly identified by the different terms – *shava*, *preta*, and *pitr* – as also by the differential functions of the caste specialists.

The importance of certain ideas specific to Hindus was underlined not only by the manner in which the social divisions of caste could be better understood in terms of the tripartite structure analyzed above, but also by the demonstration that death rituals were framed on the model of sacrifice. Death could be viewed as the perfect sacrifice since the individual offered himself as a victim instead of using a substitute. (See Biardeau 1977 and Das 1983.) These studies show how abstract ideas about immortality, danger, and purity are given a concrete form in the lives of the Hindus.

There is one important question, however, to which one cannot find any answer in these studies: how can we locate the subject in all these structures of collective representations? I recognize that this is an extremely difficult question to answer. If we move from the collective to the individual we encounter the problem that the coherence constructed by the anthropologist at the level of the collective may be unconscious, latent, or at the very least not well-articulated at the level of the individual subject. Lévi-Strauss considers it inevitable that in any ethnographic description the subject should tend to disappear (Lévi-Strauss 1969).[3] Ricoeur (1976) asks how can we move from structure to discourse?

If we start at the level of the individual and then try to move to the understanding of the collective, the task is as difficult as the construction of a grammar from the study of vocabulary. Yet death is an event that profoundly involves the individual. However aware one may be of the finitude of life and however well rooted the cultural belief in immortality may be, the individual is faced with the task of severing a relationship yet not erasing it completely. My knowledge of death in general can never adequately prepare me for the trauma of death of a significant other or for my own death. The question of individual meaning in the context of death must, therefore, be addressed, however unsatisfactory our attempts may be, to bridge the hiatus between the individual and the collective.

One of the ways in which we could approach this question is to focus on an intensely personal emotion such as pain or grief and enquire how it is projected in an interpersonal space. In the context of death, I intend to examine the category of mourners to see whether we can discern a structure within which grief and loss are articulated, such that the connections between individual grief and societal patterns of mourning may be laid bare. Whereas Hertz (1960) and Dumont (1970) and others have concentrated upon the pollution of the mourners and their temporary separation from the community, I shall concentrate in this paper on the grief of the mourners and the 'work' of mourning through which a proper sensation between the living and the dead is brought about. In order to address this problem I have drawn my materials from the lives of an urban Punjabi community among whom I conducted fieldwork for the duration of one year 1974–5. Some of this material has been reported in earlier studies (see Das 1976b, 1977 and Das and Nicholas n.d.).

THE COMMUNITY

I do not intend to describe the community in detail but we need to understand some of the salient features of its social organization, so as to lay the framework for the later discussion. I studied a kinship network of fifty families. Selecting the universe in this manner has the disadvantage that one cannot select the families by using sampling procedures, but it has the advantage that the family is studied in the context of a wider kinship system and in important interactional settings. While the core of this kinship network was located in Delhi, there were a few families that lived in other towns. My contact with these families was primarily through marriages and deaths that occurred in the core families.

With the exception of one branch of this network which was settled in Eastern Punjab, all the other families had migrated from the cities of Lahore and Gujranwala on the partition of India. These families were traders by caste and had a long history of urban settlement. There was tremendous variation within this network in terms of income, occupation, level of education and living conditions. There was also a significant variation among the members of this network with regard to their sectarian affiliation.

It is well-known that Hindus in the unpartitioned Punjab were a minority, and lived in close contact with the Punjabi Muslims and Sikhs. Their major languages of communicaton were Punjabi and Urdu. Hence it is not surprising that many local level cults of the Punjabis displayed a syncretism of Muslim and Sikh elements. In the late nineteenth century, an important reform movement began to gain popularity in the Punjab. This movement, started by Swami Dayanand Saraswati and his followers, came to be known as the Arya Samajis.[4] Swami Dayanand Saraswati tried to reform Hinduism by attacking its popular practices such as idol worship, and performance of priestly rituals, which he described as 'superstitions.' He advocated a return to what he considered the pristine purity of Vedic Hinduism. This meant that whereas certain aspects of the Sanskritic tradition were seen as legitimate for the practice of religion, other aspects including those adopted from Sufism and Sikhism came under direct attack and were either abandoned by the Arya Samajis or incorporated at different levels of their practice.

There are two points of relevance in this connection that we need to mention here. The first is that some families belonging to the kinship network that I examined were strict followers of the Arya Samaj. Two of the ancestors in their genealogies had been converted to the Arya Samaj in 1877. In fact they were among the first 300 Punjabis in Lahore to have been converted to this sect. However, marriages between the Arya Samajis and the Sanatan Dharmis (followers of the eternal code of conduct – a name by which traditional Hindus in Punjab who were opposed the the Arya Samajis came to be known) were not forbidden. This meant that within a single kinship network and sometimes within the same family one could find adherents of both sects. Further, the families I studied differed considerably in the degree of strictness with which they followed the norms laid out by the Arya Samaj. Very often, concessions were made to allow traditional customs to be followed in order that one or another set of relatives may not be offended. This pluralism with regard to belief is essential for a comprehension of the variations that are possible within *a single kinship network*, not to speak of variations within and between larger social groups.

The second relevant point regarding the ideology of the Arya Samaj is that its anti-ritualistic orientation shifted the centre of gravity in death rituals from the elaborate priestly rituals and rules of pollution to a simple and ascetic performance of the necessary ceremonies. In his book, *Samskara Vidhi*, Swami Dayannand quoted the Yajurveda to argue that death rituals come to an end with the cremation of the body. He forbade the rituals performed by Brahmin priests and derided the Hindu belief that elaborate food offerings bestow appropriate bodies (e.g. *preta-deha* and *bhoga-deha*) on the dead man for the various transitional stages before he could become an ancestor. Similarly, the elaborate rules regarding purity and pollution came under attack as having no basis in the Vedas. Hence the two favourite topics of the anthropologist – the study of non-verbal, culinary codes, and the study of rules regarding pollution – are found in a very abridged form in this community. It becomes all the more interesting, then, to see other layers of social life which had not received very much attention by the anthropologist surfacing for study. These include the customary laments on death, which have perhaps not been studied because their semi-crystallized forms are difficult to study within a traditional anthropological framework.

Anthropologists have been very successful in studying formal aspects of life when individuals can be shown to be playing roles, or when they are engaged in formal exchanges or when people are acting out rituals whose format is collectively agreed upon. But in the entire mushy area of life when individual emotion seems to confuse the formal pattern or when the context is not formally structured as in Lévi-Strauss' (1969a) example of two strangers sharing a restaurant table in Paris, the models of the anthropologist begin to falter.

In the case of death, a certain embarrassment surrounds the discussion of grief which is quickly passed over in favour of safer subjects such as the nature of death impurity, the food offerings, and the ancestral cult. This silence in the face of grief is a characteristic of modern western sensibility. Hence, demonstrative mourning is alternately admired, seen as evidence of 'honesty' and 'unselfconsciousness' on the one hand and as causing 'astonishment' and 'terror' on the other (cf. McManners 1981: 297–8).

THE FUNERAL OF PYARELAL

During the period of my fieldwork four deaths occurred in these families. The first two were of people who had grown-up children and who had died of disease. The third was of a pregnant woman, who died of a medical complication. The fourth death was of a young man who died in a tragic road accident. The first two deaths were seen as normal, not only in the sense that both persons had discharged many of their obligations as householders, but also because their deaths were not seen as violent. The third death was considered to be a violent one for the death of a woman during pregnancy or in childbirth is considered to be particularly dangerous for the survivors. She is said to become a ghost who will torment pregnant women and new mothers. Similarly the death of the young man was traumatic because it is considered particularly tragic for a parent to witness the death of a grown child and also because deaths resulting from homicide, suicide, and accidents do not allow for an easy transition of the dead person into an ancestor. A contrast between the normal deaths and the violent ones would have been particularly instructive but cannot be taken for further discussion in this paper.

Let me take the two normal deaths for study here. These made me realize that the motif of one mourning may differ subtly from the motif of another although there may be considerable stability in the rituals. While rituals vary in accordance with the role and status of the person who has died, they cannot express the quality of the relationships that have been severed by death. For this we have to turn to the forms of grief and the verbal expressions of the people. Let me begin with the death of Pyarelal before I address the question of variation. Pyarelal died at the age of fifty-four. He had been ailing for a year. When he died people felt that he had died an early death but not an untimely one.

Pyarelal had suffered from a kidney ailment. His disease was characterized as a terminal illness by doctors. He was not informed of the prognosis of his disease. Over the years he slowly became bed-ridden. For almost two months before he died he was unable to perform any bodily functions without aid. He was cared for at home by his wife and children. According to all accounts, he was conscious until the end. It was not known whether he had been conscious that he was dying even at the last moment.

In the last two months of his life, Pyarelal may have suspected that life was ebbing away. He had lost his appetite, was frequently nauseous, felt that his limbs had lost all their strength, but he somehow maintained a stoic silence. The most poignant story that I heard was that his wife had noticed tears in his eyes on the day that he found that he did not have the strength to get up in the morning and offer flowers to his favourite picture of Lord Rama and his divine consort Sita. This particular picture had belonged to him for as long as he remembered. He was not given to frequent visits to temples and did not have the patience to listen to religious discourses. His only gesture towards god was to offer flowers and stand in mute silence before this picture in the morning, and to offer his thanks to god with folded hands before going to bed. The only other event of importance to him used to be an occasional visit to the pilgrimage Hardwar where he loved to take a dip in the Ganga, and to float a tiny flower boat with a lighted lamp in the dark river at night. When he found that he did not even have the strength to get up for this simple gesture of prayer, he requested his daughter to bring that picture to his bed-side in the morning and at night.

For the last two months that he was ill, Pyarelal was visited every evening by an old friend of his who was a *vaid* (practitioner of traditional Ayurvedic medicine). Patient and doctor would sit in a companionable silence sipping tea. The *vaid* had informed Pyarelal's wife that her husband did not have long to live. All the relatives had been informed. The family was visited frequently by the relatives. As his wife said, meeting the sick man was like *darsan mele* – a privileged viewing of the person, the quality of which is as ephemeral and transitory as glimpsing a beloved face in the melee of a carnival – before you have time to greet the person, she said, the face has disappeared.

The last day

Pyarelal died on 31 March. It was only in the last hour that it was realized that he was dying. His son rushed to the *vaid* who arrived at the bedside. Even as his son was rubbing his cold feet with powerful herbal remedies to stop the ebbing of life, Pyarelal shouted at him to go and prepare some tea for the *vaid*, instead of looking so stricken. These were the last words that he spoke. At the last moment the son tried to bring his picture of Rama and Sita to his bedside, but he was gone.

I was told that at first his wife insisted that he was not dead. But the *vaid* was firm that there was no calling him back. They then lowered his body on the floor. Pyarelal had often said to his wife that he did not wish to die on the floor as good Hindus do. This was the reason that no attempt had been made to lower him to the floor in his last hour, a gesture that spells imminent death. According to the *vaid* it was the sight of his lifeless body lying on the floor that finally communicated the irrevocable fact of his death to his wife.

The widow now let out a loud wail and started hitting the wall with her head and breaking the bangles which are the signs of the auspicious state of wifehood. Widows are considered inauspicious and are not allowed to participate in the life – affirming rituals of birth and marriage. The neighbouring women, on hearing the wails, left everything they were doing and rushed to her. They began wailing with her while men began to send appropriate messages and telegrams to the relatives. It is customary to make a little tear on the side of a letter if it carries news of death.

When I arrived, having been informed of the death, the women were sitting around the corpse and were wailing. At this point it may be necessary to explain the structure of certain events in the funeral. I have been told by my informants that it was customary among the

Punjabis for women relatives to surround the body, all the while wailing loudly, beating their breasts, and inflicting wounds upon themselves to the extent that some relatives would faint. This form of mourning, known as *syapa*, was strictly for women. They were greatly aided by the availability of professional mourners. I have not been able to trace the social background or caste affiliation of these women except that the barber's wife always had an important role to play. The special position of the barber and washerman among the servicing castes has been noted by many authors (Dumont 1970; Pocock 1962; Srinivas 1959). In the Punjab the barber's wife mediated on birth, marriage, and death rituals. She acted as midwife on birth and carried invitations and news of weddings. She accompanied a newly married girl to her husband's house. Similarly the barber's wife played an important role in death rituals, washing the body of a female corpse, paring the nails of female mourners, and sometimes removing the signs of the married state such as ornaments, red markings on the hair, from the body of a newly widowed woman (see Gill 1977; Hershman 1981 and Tandon 1961). The professional women would arrive in a house where death had occurred. They would sing ritual laments while moving round and round in a circle, and making frenzied rhythmic movements. They were joined by the female relatives of the dead man.

While women were required by custom to indulge in an orgy of grief and self mutilation, and were encouraged to vocalize the grief for the dead person, men were required to maintain a stoic silence. The Arya Samaj attempted to purge the death ceremonies of the 'undignified' mourning performed by professional mourners. They were successful to the extent that professional mourners are not found in urban centres today. However, this has not eliminated the wailing and self-injury by women relatives.

As Durkheim (1947) observed in his study of piacular rituals, even when mourners seem to be giving themselves up completely to grief and are inflicting horrible injuries upon themselves, one can discern the presence of a certain structure. For example, among the Australian aborigines, the appropriate amount of injury to inflict upon oneself is determined more by kinship distance than by the violence of the grief. Thus, we have to examine carefully the structure behind the spontaneous and often unbearable expressions of personal sorrow.

To return to our description, the women were sitting around the body when I arrived. As each relative arrived, he or she would be greeted by a wail led by one of the women already present, which would identify some aspect of the newcomer's relation with the dead person. If the person arriving was a woman she would sit in front of the widow, hug her, and let out a loud wail addressing the dead man. From the widow she would move to the children, hug them and cry. If the person who had arrived was a man he would sit quietly at the periphery of the circle holding his head in his hand, or wiping his eyes.

All the mourning laments, whatever their particular content, focused on one basic scheme. This was that the dead man had voluntarily chosen death, deserted the living relatives, and thus must be persuaded either to come back or to take the living with him.[5] The following are a few examples:

The oldest woman present there was Pyarelal's aunt who kept saying, 'My son, was this time for you to go? I am still living in the world, and you have gone? Please take me with you if that *darbar* (court) of Yama (the god of death) is so dear to you.'

An elderly distant female relative made an entry – weeping and saying, 'I knew, I knew this would happen. Last night I saw him in a dream. He was dashing, handsome and young and he was riding a bridal horse. His bride is death. The ill omen has come true.'

The dead man's classificatory sister cried, 'Brother, open your eyes just once this time. When we were young and we played hide-and-seek, you would open your eyes the moment I asked you to. Why are you so cruel today that you do not open your eyes even once though I beg and I beg?'

The widow's brother's wife said, 'My children (referring to the dead man's children) have been ruined. From where has this thunderbolt fallen? Whose evil eye burnt the prosperity of my sister's house? Oh, who will care for these orphans now?'

All this was interspersed by the widow's repeated sobs and her saying, 'I want to go where he went. Take me on the same path as you have traversed today.'

As the morning wore off, the laments became more stereotyped. Meanwhile, Pyarelal's elder brother had made the necessary arrangements for the funeral. It was conventional for the dead man's agnates to provide the shroud, the bier, *ghee* (clarified butter), incense, and *havan samagri*, which is a mixture of dry ingredients to be offered to the fire. The new clothes in which the corpse was to be dressed are conventionally provided by the affines. In this case it was the widow's brother who provided these clothes. A priest from the local Arya Samaj had been sent for.

The men were now getting restive. The work of the funeral needed to proceed. The women seemed unable to relinquish the dead body. The priest started urging the men to wash the body and prepare it since it would be very difficult to do so later. The widow's brother signalled to his wife and his adopted brother's wife that they must allow the body to be taken into an inner room and washed.

At this stage I was asked to go with some people to find out if it was necessary to obtain a death certificate. It was felt that my education might help me to negotiate on this intricate problem. The events of the next hour are constructed on the basis of what people told me and not my own observations.

I was told that the body was bathed and dressed by 'relatives.' On enquiring which relatives, I was told that the dead man's sons were considered to be too young to absorb the shock of handling their father's dead body. Hence others, 'classificatory sons' (*rishte vic ladke*) had performed the necessary ablutions and dressed the corpse.

When I came back, the body had been washed, dressed in new clothes, and was lying on a bier in the *gali* (lane), just outside the door. The sons and brother's sons of the dead man lifted the body taking care to first touch it with their left shoulders. Several others came forward to touch the bier with their shoulders. This gesture has great symbolic importance. To give one's *kandha* (shoulder) to the dead man is to support him on his last journey. The Punjabis say that just as the dead man had carried his sons on his shoulders when they were little, so the sons now reciprocate by carrying him on their shoulders. When the corpse was lifted, everyone shouted in a chorus '*Rama rama satya hai!* The name of god is true, it is eternal.'

The widow seemed to have suddenly lost control. She rushed to the bier and said, 'You have tied him too tightly. He hated tight clothes. Don't you know that?' She then clung to her son and said 'Have you assured that the fire is not too hot?' Now her brother's wife came to pull her away. Several people started saying 'Why do you argue so? Is death an adversary against whom one can win? Has anyone ever succeeded in erasing that which has been written? Keep calm, collect yourself, think of your children.' Finally, the widow was calmed enough to let go of her son. The funeral procession proceeded towards the cremation ground, situated on the bank of the river Yamuna.

At the cremation ground

It was customary among the upper caste Punjabis that men carried the dead body to the cremation ground and the women stayed at home, wailing the loss that had been made even more concrete by the disappearance of the body. These days, however, women often accompany the funeral procession. In this case, most of the women assembled in the house went to the cremation ground.

According to the teachings of Arya Samaj, the services of ritual specialists, such as the barber to shave the mourner, the Dom to give the funeral fire, or the Mahabrahmana to make *pinda* offerings, are forbidden. Similarly there are no rituals to remove the signs of auspiciousness from the widow's person. These are considered to be examples of the later corruption of Hinduism by the greedy Brahmins.

At the Nigam Bodh Ghat, where the body was taken for cremation, there is a separate pyre for the funerals of Arya Samajis. This is built as a sacrifical altar (*Yajna kunda*). In deference to the Doms, an untouchable caste which has a monopoly over the sacred fire of the cremation grounds, the elder persons of the family bought the wood from the Doms. The Doms laid out the wood on the pyre. Meanwhile, the mourners carried the body to the river front and immersed it in water accompanied by sacred verses. The eldest son, the chief mourner, was accompanied by some male relatives. He took some water in his hands and performed the necessary ablutions accompanied by verses. This simple ritual has replaced the traditional bath of the mourners.

The body was brought back and laid on the pyre. The face was uncovered for the last privileged viewing (*darsana*). All the mourners circumambulated it with their auspicious right side towards it and saluted it with folded hands. The widow touched Pyarelal's feet for the last time, ending the relationship by the very gesture with which it may have begun some thirty years ago.

The priest covered the face of the corpse and recited some sacred verses. He then urged the eldest son to light the pyre. The son would

191

simply not move. Everyone present seemed to have frozen for that instant. The boys' *mama* (mother's brother) went up to him and urged him to light the pyre. It was the sons' very special responsibility to do so – this responsibility could not be avoided and it could not be entrusted to anyone else. As if in a dream, the son stepped forward and lighted the pyre while the mourners chanted to implore *Agni* (fire), the representative of the gods, to take the dead person through the good path to the abode of gods. They urged Agni to burn more ferociously as he was being fed by the sacred *havi* oblations.

The mourners stood around the pyre, throwing handfuls of oblations and *ghee* to the accompaniment of verses. After the final oblations were offered, everyone stepped down. The Doms had agreed to keep watch and two nephews of the dead man were going to wait with them to see that the fire did not die out so that the body could be completely burnt. Although the rationalist ethics of the Arya Samajis do not allow them to acknowledge the existence of ghosts and demons, I think they considered it necessary to have some family members keep a vigil over the burning body precisely because the soul of the dead person is believed to be especially susceptible to evil influences of ghosts and demons. The Doms were paid for their services and were also given the clothes in which Pyarelal had died, his personal effects such as his spectacles, and the bed linen.

The priest made everyone sit down a little away from the fire and gave a short funeral oration about the indestructibility of the soul, the journey of the dead man towards the god head, and implored everyone to try and bring peace to their ravaged hearts. He recited the prayers for peace (*santipatha*) and then the mourners slowly made their way home.

The subsequent ceremonies

In most discussions of death rituals among the Hindus, the description of ceremonies subsequent to cremation is dominated by rules of pollution and the various food offerings. The ceremonies of *sraddha* (etymologically the offering of *sraddha* or faith) terminate various stages of mourning and signal the invisible changes that the dead man is considered to be undergoing. According to the ideology of the Arya Samaj, as I have indicated, these ceremonies are forbidden. Swami Dayanand was especially opposed to the large scale feasting of Brahmins who are supposed to eat away the sins of the dead person.[6]

The Arya Samajis do not believe that sin is transferable or that one can 'buy' merit by gifts of food. They do observe a number of taboos but these are seen as expressive of piety towards the dead rather than being markers of pollution. The most important taboo is that cooking fires are not lighted for four days and food is provided by neighbours. In the matter of clothes, white is worn by the mourners and all who visit them. The women do not wear ornaments or any auspicious red markings. There is, however, no taboo on combing of hair or shaving as is observed in many other Hindu communities.[7]

The most important obligation of the mourners, subsequent to cremation, is to sit formally for four days and read the texts of sacred scriptures such as the Bhagavad Gita. The Arya Samajis say that they do not believe in the lingering *preta* (ghost) of the dead man as other Hindus do, but they do believe that the soul (*atman*) of the dead man hovers around the house for four days. In this period the major religious duty of the mourners is to read the scriptures. Members of the family and friends take turns in reading the Bhagavad Gita. Hearing Krishna's words about the immortality of the soul and the perishability of the body is said to console the living and to help in severing the links of desire by which the dead man feels himself bound to the living relatives. It is said that the dead man is not yet reconciled to his separation. If his wife and children were to cry for him then he would find it very difficult to leave them. Although I did not hear anyone say that the dead man may possess one of the living, it is clear that some danger to the survivors is envisaged. The apprehensions are not given a definite form.

In accordance with the beliefs mentioned above, the people who came to visit the bereaved family for those four days were expected to listen in silence to the scriptures. They often sat around whispering about the way in which the close members of the family were affected by the death or the manner in which they were bearing up to it. These were also the four days in which relatives from other parts of the country arrived. On each new arrival, the women began to weep and express their grief. However, neither was the wailing loud nor was it allowed to continue for long. There is a quality of silence that marks these four days. It is a silence, however, which is always on the verge of being broken by the violence of the grief. For example, when Pyarelal's widow's sister arrived from Amritsar, the two women hugged each other and sobbed softly. Then in a split second, they were suddenly transformed into hysterically sobbing women who were consoled and separated, while the reading of the texts continued in the background.

On the fourth day (*chautha*) the male relatives went to the cremation ground to collect the bones known euphemistically as 'flowers.' The bones and ashes were collected from the pyre in an earthen pot which was covered by a white cloth and brought home. At the sight of these 'flowers' the women once again gave in to loud weeping. It was the most concrete symbol of the absence and void created by death.

Once the bones have been collected, the members of the family do not have to formally sit in mourning any more. In a very few families mourning is formally terminated on this day after which agnates of the dead man take the bones and the ashes for immersion in a holy river such as the Ganga. For most others there is a final ceremony on the thirteenth day, which ends the period of formal mourning and after which the mourners return to the mundane world.

In this case, Pyarelal's sons and their father's brother took the bones to Hardwar, an important pilgrim centre, where the bones and ashes of the dead man were immersed in the river. I should mention that whereas most ceremonies had been held according to the injunctions of the Arya Samaj in Delhi, in Hardwar the men who had taken the ashes simply followed the local priest. They made the various *pindha* offerings prescribed for these occasions in the Pauranic texts. This is not the place to comment on the significance of this, nor is it sufficient to simply say that this is a departure from the norms of the Arya Samaj. The important point is that a certain kind of pluralism is often permitted and even embraced by the survivors on the occasion of death which may not be encouraged on other occasions such as that of birth and marriage. It is felt that death involves so much that is unknown that it is best to accommodate different points of view rather than display a moral arrogance and offend others.

On the thirteenth day, the final ceremony known as *pagdi* ceremony took place. This is a formal occasion. These days, many families send black bordered cards to invite relatives and friends while others advertise the event in newspapers. Pyarelal's family had simply communicated the date of the *pagdi* ceremony by word of mouth. In any case invitations in the case of death convey only information. They are not signifiers of the family's regard for the invitees. In contrast, marriages are events in which people can easily take offense if they feel that they have not been properly and lovingly invited.[8]

When all the relatives and friends were gathered, the same Arya Samaj priest performed a *yajna* (fire sacrifice). The eldest son was the chief sacrificator accompanied by his brother, his father's brother, and his male agnatic cousin. After the *yajna* was completed the priest made a learned speech. He emphasized that this *yajna* commemorated the dead man, who was a virtuous person and had found release from this world securing a place for himself in heaven. He commented upon the ephemerality of life, emphasizing that everything was a flux and we should not try to hold on to people, places and possessions. We should let go our hold on them. Then a pink *pagdi*[9] (turban) was handed over to him from the *mama* (MB) of the chief mourner. The mother's brothers of the chief mourner also gave gifts of money to his father's brother.

The priest tied the turban round the boy's head. Then he said, 'I pronounce you the successor to your father. I hope that you will fulfill all your obligations. Your sisters and your father's sisters must continue to receive the same welcome and care in your house as they did during your father's lifetime. Learned and religious people, unannounced guests and travellers must share in the prosperity of your house.'

At this stage the son stood up with the elaborate turban tied round his head. He first touched the feet of the priest and gave him *daksina*, the sacrificial fee that terminated the responsibility that each had undertaken towards the other. Then he touched the feet of the elders who were present there, most notably his father's brothers, mother's brothers, and mother. Accompanied by close relatives he then moved towards the door. With folded hands, they stood in silence while all the people who were present filed out quietly folding their hands in salutation to the mourners, sometimes nodding and touching the mourners lightly, at other times saying, 'We come,' for one should not refer to any departures so soon after a death. This signalled the end of mourning and the return to normality although this normality had itself been fractured by the grief of death.

Certain commemorative rituals were to be performed at the end of six months and again at the end of a year, when *yajna* would be performed and the deserving and the poor would be fed. These, however, would involve only the close relatives and were not likely to be such 'public' events. Taboos expressive of piety would be observed for one year by close relatives. These include the taboos on bright colours and ornaments by women, and a taboo on fried and sweet foods. The widow would henceforth wear only white.[10] These taboos, however, display a very different rhythm and it was clear that most dramatic phase of the 'work' of mourning was indeed over.

DISCUSSION

Freud (1915) and Malinowski (1948) have both described the emotional ambivalence towards death. As Malinowski said, the attitude to the dead is constituted by fear and fascination. The living have contradictory impulses to flee in panic as well as to follow the deceased to the grave. Seen from the perspective of the grieving individual, the ceremonies of death should help him make an emotional withdrawal from the dead person. But they must also assure that he does not simply flee away from the scene of death, and deny it completely. Malinowski's formulations inevitably draw one's attention to the category of mourners which Hertz (1960) treated as a homogeneous category. As we shall later explain, he did not pay very great attention to the differential symbolic functions of men and women; kin and affines; family mourners and professional mourners; a differentiation that I consider essential to the understanding of the structure and pattern in mourning. Hertz emphasized the separation of the mourners from the community of ordinary men. Since the dead person is believed to hover between the living and the dead for some time before he is finally accepted in the community of the dead, the mourners are endangered, contaminated and made the subject of stringent taboos for the period of mourning. It goes to the great credit of Hertz that he was able to show that the changes in the visible community of mourners may best be seen as indexing the invisible changes that the dead person is believed to be undergoing. I believe that we could strengthen these insights considerably if we combined them with Malinowski's identification of the type of ambivalence that the living feel towards the dead.

Stated without much preamble, my thesis is the following. It is not the dead who hover between the community of the living and the dead. Rather, these beliefs about the dead mirror the ambivalence of the living towards death – for it is they who hover between a fatal fascination to follow the fate of the dead man and the terrible temptation to deny his very existence. Rituals of mourning have to provide a mediation between these two opposite poles in which life and death are seen to be completely conjoined and which are seen to be in complete disjunction. This mediation becomes possible only if we conceptualize the mourners as having the structure of a heterogeneous rather than a homogeneous totality. The heterogeneity is provided by the sharp distinction in the roles of men and women on the one hand, and kin and affines, on the other. It is their differential symbolic functions which allow the work of mourning to proceed by making it possible for mediation between these two poles to occur.

THE NATURE OF MEDIATION

In the last decade we have learnt much on the structure of mediation from the work of Claude Lévi Strauss (1969). As he has shown, it is best to understand the nature of mediation from the perspective of non-mediation. The two poles of non-mediation, he has argued, are constituted by symbols of excess representing a complete conjoining of the opposites, and symbols of lack representing a complete disjunction of the opposite poles. Thus he has shown how noise and silence may represent excess and lack respectively, at the level of the acoustic code.[11] Both, however, signal the absence of mediation. When mediation occurs we have the emergence of meaningful speech.

In the case of death among the Punjabis, it seems to me that complete conjoining of life and death is represented through symbols of excess which are articulated through the behaviour of women. Loud weeping, wailing, beating of breasts, and fainting mark this behaviour. Their laments basically express two ideas.

First, that the dead man is not really dead but has simply turned away from them and can be persuaded to come back to life. Second, that they will follow the dead man to the nether regions and themselves relinquish life. The two kinds of laments are polar opposites in meaning but point to a single theme. This is the refusal of the women to allow a separation to take place between the living and the dead. It is not that women feel more grief than men. It is rather that the culture allows and even enjoins upon them the obligation to display symbols of excess.

Whatever the personal grief that a man may feel, immobility and silence are the only languages available to men. They act as if they were dumb and deaf and somehow incapable of comprehending that death has occurred and requires them to perform certain ritual and ceremonial roles. I have sometimes seen a father, or a brother or a son (rarely a husband) suddenly break down and cry but he is immediately admonished for his 'womanly' behaviour.

It is to be noted that although I have characterized the behaviour of women as marked by symbols of excess, we are confronted at the level of the acoustic code, not by meaningless noise but meaningful speech. What are the characteristics of this speech? It seems to me that its most important characteristic is the *marked* use of ordinary words to convey the pathos of death. For example, women use such expressions as the departure of the dead man and the journey he has undertaken. They describe him as having been lured by the charms of another kingdom. Expressions such as 'the man has closed his eyes, does not hear us speak and ignores our pleadings' cease being the expressions of everyday life and take on the character of ritualized speech. These activities are now part of a broken rhythm of departures and arrivals, the closing and opening of eyes, ignoring one's loved ones and paying them close attention, and it is this broken rhythm that transforms ordinary speech into metaphoric speech.

The most poignant motif in this culture is the description of death as the reluctant, shy bride who has to be wooed into submission. This description is dwelt upon at length if the person who has died is a young man as I found in the case of the twenty-seven-year-old man who died in a tragic road accident. This description is taken from the motif of a heroic death, for the warrior goes out into the battlefield to embrace death voluntarily as if it were his reluctant bride. In the case of Payarelal, this motif was referred to once, when an old relative related a dream in which she had seen him riding a bridal horse. Such a dream conveys an ill omen, for it is a messenger of death. However, when an elderly person dies the reference to his death as a marriage marks a subtle shift in emphasis. It conveys the *bhakti* notion, popularized by Sufi saints in the Punjab, that for a saintly person death is a welcome event as it unites the soul with its beloved god. The death of a Sufi saint is alluded to as his marriage. Thus the *voluntarism* by which the close women relatives of the dead man conceptualize this event participates in a whole complex of ideas according to which it is only appropriate that a hero or a saint should happily embrace and welcome death.

KIN AND AFFINES: CLOSE AND DISTANT MOURNERS

In the work of mourning, there is a diversification in the symbolic functions performed by men and women as described in the last section. The mourners are further divided along the lines of kin and affines. I now propose to show the role of this diversification in the work of mourning.

It is possible to distinguish the women mourners between the close mourners and the distant ones. Before we examine the genealogical composition of these two types of mourners (for the question is a difficult one), let us first see the role of these two types of mourners.

Among the close mourners we can identify those who mourn on behalf of the dead man and those who mourn on behalf of the widow. All the women identified as 'mothers' of the dead man, his brothers' wives, close sisters and daughters, as well as his own wife express the grief of losing an important and close relative. On the other hand, the close relatives of the widow such as her brother's wife, her sister and her classificator mother's sister mourn on behalf of their daughter or sister who has become widowed and who may have to be provided care and support. These are the women whose language expresses great personal grief at the loss they have encountered. Women whom I have described as distant mourners may be best described by identifying the group of bride-givers to Pyarelal's agnatic group and the bride-givers to their bride-givers. In the former category would be included his brother's son's wife's mother and the latter category of women who are designated collectively as *samdhans*. The term designates those who are related through the marriage of their children. Somewhat at the periphery of kinship relations, this group merges with the category of neighbours. Genealogically distant relatives whose contacts with the family have been peripheral mourn in a manner similar to the relatives mentioned above.

What are the functions of 'distance' in the process of mourning? In general, the women who have been described here as distant mourners perform two functions. In the initial stages of the mourning, they join in the laments of the close mourners but since their memories of the dead man do not have a strong, personal content, their laments tend to be general in character. These laments include references to ill omens, chants on their ill-luck at not having been able to see the dead man in the last few days, and reference to culturally valued traits such as generosity, hospitality, love etc. which they attribute to the dead man regardless of whether he had demonstrated these qualities in his life or not. One realizes this by simply contrasting the general nature of their comments – 'Oh, he was such a good man, he never turned away a poor man or a suffering man from his door, etc.' – with the comments of the close mourners which capture the individuality and specificity of the life that the dead man had lived. For instance, when the men were about to take the bier away, the widow rushed to her son and implored him to loosen the strings with which his body had been tied for 'he hated tight clothes.' Similarly she asked him if he had assured that the fire was not too hot as Pyarelal had never liked the heat of summer.

The distant mourners seem to have a great ability to be wailing loudly and beating their breasts one minute and then turning around to discuss the most trivial matter such as a child's school admission at the next moment. This often gives their performance a very theatrical appearance. One is tempted to characterize them as showing false emotion. Yet having watched this process closely, I am persuaded that they provide the language in which grief can be presented and expressed. Because of the participation of the distant mourners in this fashion, the close mourners are not allowed to relapse into silence. When grief seems to become inexpressible and the close mourners are too dazed to say anything, the distant mourners step in to wail loudly and thus nudge the close mourners to join in. Earlier the most distant mourners might have been the professional mourners. We may view them as providing the structural code or the mould through which individual grief found expression and received validation from the collective conscience.

The second important function of distant mourners was to provide consolation to the close mourners and this came to the fore in the ceremonies subsequent to cremation. Until the *chautha* was held when the ashes were collected, the mourners had to formally sit in mourning and read or hear appropriate scriptural texts, as described earlier. On these four days, the *samdhans* would often put forward views that may be described as *fatalist*. For instance, at one occasion the widow of Pyarelal suddenly remarked that if they were rich they could have saved her husband for she had heard that a minister in the government had suffered from a similar ailment and had been sent abroad for treatment. Her husband's brother's son's wife's mother, who had played an active role in the mourning immediately consoled her by saying that she should not grieve so – disease was simply a pretext that death found in order to fulfill its appointed task. At this stage, the diverse roles of men and women also become less sharply differentiated, and one can find people consoling each other in similar terms.

The distinction between close and distant mourners does not correspond strictly to the distinction between kind and affines, at least in the case of women. This is because women in North Indian kinship are Janus-faced creatures as noted by Dumont (1975). The in-coming wives are slowly incorporated into the husband's group and thus lose their characteristic of being affines. Hence time enters into kinship relations significantly. A man's mother, his brother's wife as well as his sons' wives are 'brides' of the family in structural terms. In temporal terms the sons' wives have a more affinal character than the mother. Considerations of time are important not in terms of reckoning generational distance but also as clock time. For instance, the widow's classificatory sister had two married sons. One of the sons' wives mourned as a close mourner while the other did not participate much since she had been married for a short time only and would take time to be incorporated into the family. Distance which is a function of time, however, is different from structural distance. Unlike the latter the former will be transformed into closeness in the future.

The structural position of out-going sisters and daughters is the inverse of in-coming wives. Whereas genealogically close daughters mourned as close mourners identifying themselves completely with their natal groups, genealogically distant daughters and sisters had the choice of identifying either with their natal groups or affinal ones. Genealogical nearness always signals closeness in the case of daughters and sisters. Genealogical distance has to be mediated by other factors such as close residence, friendship etc. to preserve nearness of the relationship.

The distinction between kin and affines is clearer in the case of men and is best articulated in the structure of gift-giving as shown by Vatuk (1975) and Dumont (1975). Gifts of money came from bride-givers to bride-receivers, the major recipient being the dead man's brother. The major gift-giver was the brother of the widow. Her second brother played a subsidiary role since he was an adopted brother and chose for himself a low-keyed role. It is the structural position of affines who mediate nearness and remoteness, that allows them to signal the termination of mourning by gifts. Kinsmen, by virtue of being too close to the dead man, and strangers by virtue of being too remote, could not play these roles.

This particular role of the affines is also expressed in less crystallized forms It is they who persuaded the women to relinquish the body when the latter seemed unable to do so. Similarly, it was the chief mourners' mother's brother who urged him to light the pyre. It is as if society intervenes through the affines to mediate the two poles of conjunction and disjunction between life and death.

One final point needs to be mentioned here. The Arya Samajis do not employ members of the lower castes to perform the 'polluting' and dangerous tasks of washing the body, or preparing the mourners. Instead, the handling of pollution becomes an index of intimacy. Thus the washing of the body which may be entrusted to members of lower castes because of its polluting nature in other parts of the country, is entrusted to close relatives here – younger male agnates in the case of a man and women who are 'wives' to the agnates' group in case of women. By participating in these 'polluting' and 'dangerous' tasks they show their love for the dead person.

THE COMPARATIVE PERSPECTIVE

One may ask whether the conclusions arrived at in the paper have any general validity. It seems to me that there are two important points in this paper which could be examined in a cross-cultural perspective. First of all, the attitude to death cannot be characterized in terms of an essence, such as 'romantic,' 'macabre' or 'distant' as was done by Aries (1981) in his study. Rather the societal attitude to death is best described in the form of a dialogue. In my own study it appears that the dialogue is between a point of view which may be described as *voluntarist* for it sees death as voluntarily embraced even as one embraces a beautiful bride. The second point of view may be described as *fatalist* for it represents death as a violent, forcible, and inevitable seizure of life. It was the close women mourners in the case studied above who represented Pyarelal as having voluntarily chosen death. In contrast, the affines and neighbours who had to undertake the task of consoling the mourners represented death as a formidable adversary, as a thief who steals in unaware. According to them, the so-called causes of death such as disease and accident were only the pretexts (*bahane*) for death to perform its appointed task. Thus the arrangement of roles in a funeral gives an institutional locus to this dialogue. It is interesting to ask whether the attitudes to death within a single culture that have often been characterized as contradictory may not be part of a dialogue representing the two poles on which the work of mourning rituals oscillates.

Second, the mediation provided by death ceremonies in our study has the structure of a series of oscillations. The process of mourning proceeds by moving between the opposite poles constituted by the noise and excess of women and the silence and immobility of men. This is not to suggest that women are always identified with symbols of excess. We have only to shift to other codes (e.g. culinary) and other events modelled on the analogy of death (e.g. equinox) to see that even in Punjab these roles can be exchanged between men and women. The point is that the binary distinction of gender is used to articulate the opposition between complete conjunction and complete disjunction of life and death.

Apart from the oscillation between men and women, the mourning process is also constituted by the diverse functions of distant and close female mourners. The former provide the collective code, or the structural mould which can give form to the grief. Finally the opposition of kin and affines among the male relatives provides the momentum and the punctuation to the process of mourning.

What happens when mediation fails? Geertz (1973) has provided us with a very interesting case study of precisely such a failure of the ritual process. He describes how ritual faltered in providing a secure world of meaning in the case of a sudden death of a young boy in the city of Modjokotu in Java. In that case religious meaning and political meaning became so jumbled that for a long time the mourners were unable to decide which were the proper ritual procedures and proper ritual functionaries to perform the cere- monies of death. Geertz traces the disruption of the funeral to a single source, viz., 'an incongruity between the cultural framework of meaning and the patterning of social interaction: an incongruity due to the persistence in an urban environment of a religious symbol system adjusted to peasant social structure' (Geertz 1973: 169).

On reading the careful account of this disruption provided by Geertz, one wonders whether it is adequate to characterize the failure of ritual in this case as the failure to provide a 'secure world of meaning.' Would the disruption of ritual hold a different mean- ing if the ritual disrupted had been that of marriage rather than that of death? Geertz seems to feel, at least implicitly, that the two could be treated at par. Yet his powerful description tells us the exact consequences of the disruption of a funeral, and helps to give content to this otherwise vacuous expression about meaning. There are two episodes of importance in his account. The first when the mother lost her composure and insisted on seeing the body of the child before it was wrapped. In the words of Geertz:

> The father at first forbade it, angrily ordering her to stop crying
> – didn't she know that such behaviour would darken the boy's
> pathway to the other world. But she persisted and so they
> brought her, stumbling, to where he lay in Karman's house. The
> women tried to keep her from stumbling too close, but she
> broke loose and began to kiss the boy about the genitals. She
> was snatched away almost immediately by her husband and the
> women, though she screamed that she had not yet finished; and
> they pulled her into the dark room where she subsided into a
> daze (Geertz 1973: 159).

Later, people admonished the mother, saying 'Calm yourself, think of your other children – do you want to follow your son to the grave?'

The other point of tremendous tension was when a bystander suggested that they just take the body out and bury it and forget about the whole ritual. The failure of mediation, then, was expressed by the mother's handling of the body and kissing it in a way that was not permitted and also the bystander's suggestion that one may simply dispense with ritual. Both suggest that a specific content can be given to the task of mourning rituals rather than describing them vaguely as providing a secure world of meaning. On the occasion of a death it is precisely the too close conjunction and the complete disjunction between life and death that ritual mediates. When death is politicized as in this case (but we have many other examples ranging from the death of political leaders, death in famines, riots, to death in a revolution or a war) we inevitably have a shift of level signalled either by too close a conjunction or complete disjunction. However, ritual can also mask the absence of mediation as our final example will show.

A FINAL EXAMPLE

I should like to conclude this paper with an example of a death that shows how ritual can provide a means of dealing with problems created by modern urban environments.

Suvira was a seventy-year-old widow and had been struck by paralysis which had left her immobile and unable to care for herself. She had two sons who were married and well-settled. She also had three daughters, all of whom were married and had children. When Suvira was stricken by paralysis she was living with her eldest son. The younger son lived in a different city and provided financial help but was unable to take her to live with him. Hence all the responsibility of caring for the old lady fell on the eldest daughter-in-law. One has to appreciate the sorry situation in which the family found itself. Domestic help was not easily available. Suvira had become very difficult to please and seemed to hold many grudges against all her relatives. Her daughters were completely absorbed in their conjugal families and had little time to spare. Many discussions were held among the close relatives but no solution could be found to the problem. This seemed to have left all the relatives with feelings of guilt.

One week before her death, Suvira fell in a semicoma and was moved to hospital. For the seven days that she was in the hospital she could not recognize anyone. Once when she regained consciousness she instructed her son that her brother should not be allowed to touch her body for he had not been regular in visiting her and Suvira felt betrayed by his indifference. She clearly knew that she was dying and that none of her children or siblings had cared for her in accordance with her wishes.

When Suvira died, her youngest daughter was by her bedside. The daughter claimed that she knew that the moment of death had arrived for her mother's knees jerked due to the violent encounter with death. At the final moment, her mouth had opened wide to allow the soul to escape. I was told that life escapes from one of the orifices. It is a sign of the purity of the dying person when life departs from an upper orifice rather than a lower one. Her death had occurred in the morning at 4 a.m. The relatives, who had been expecting to hear news of the death, gathered in the hospital by 5 a.m. It was decided to take the body directly to the cremation ground. Normally the body is first brought home, but there was great tension among the relatives and the best course appeared to be an abridgement of normal wailing and mourning that usually takes place at home. No one was sure what that might bring to the surface.

There was relative silence surrounding the body. It was washed and prepared in the hospital morgue. Whereas it was Payarelal's agnatic nephews who had washed the body, Suvira's body was washed by her daughters-in-law and her brother's wife. They insisted that daughters were not permitted to touch the body, since they belonged to other families.

While the body was being washed, the women discussed the pure and saintly nature of Suvira. This was demonstrated, they said, in the fact that there had been no bodily emissions. Her soul was pure and it was good that god had taken her away for she had suffered a lot. There were no wails or rhythmic chants of the kind that were described in the case of Pyarelal's death. I have heard such chants even in hospitals. In this case, however, the women either did not seem to need that form for the expression of grief or else there was a fear that wailing might turn into accusations and counter-accusations. Her elder daughter-in-law seemed to be smitten by guilt. She kept crying and saying that she had performed no service (*seva*) for her husband's mother. She was consoled by the other women.

A controversy arose as to who was to provide new clothes for the corpse. Customarily it is the woman's brother who provides the clothes. Suvira's sons, however, wanted to make an issue of this since he felt that his maternal uncle had given very little help in the care of his mother. Hence he insisted that the new clothes would be provided by him since his mother was not in need of 'charity.' Some relatives who wanted to intervene on behalf of Suvira's brother were reminded by her son that Suvira had said that her brother should not even touch her body. The boy was told, however, that dying persons often expressed wishes which were mysterious or tabooed and the living should learn to ignore these. Those who intervened on behalf of Suvira's brother were also insistent that death was not the occasion on which divisions should be expressed. In the face of death it was important to be united and solidary.

The son gave in when these arguments were made. I felt, however, that he succeeded in giving a voice to his frustration since the strained nature of the relations between brother and sister had been expressed before the assembled relatives.

The rituals at the *ghat* followed much the pattern described earlier. If anything, there was meticulous attention to detail. The very best *ghee* and wood were used. All the discussion on the cremation ground were on the general relation between life and death. On the subsequent ceremonies also people talked of the kindness that death had shown in extending its friendly hand and how the survivors had shown their piety by performing the rituals in such a meticulous fashion.

Pyarelal had been at the apex of kinship relations. In contrast, Suvira's life had become something of an embarrassment. The tensions among the relatives which had arisen in the process of caring for her had threatened to disrupt the funeral. Ritual and clever arbitration, however, stepped in and allowed everyone to express their piety to Suvira in her death; something they had been unable to do in her life. Grief had found no expression but one suspects that the sons and daughters of Suvira would have to find ways of expressing it unaided by the interpersonal space of a funeral ceremony.

NOTES

1 This paper was first presented in a seminar of the Sociological Research Colloquium of the University of Delhi on 16 December 1983. I wish to thank all members of the seminar who commented on the paper. I would particularly like to mention M.S.A. Rao, A.M. Shah, Patricia Uberoi, and Rajendra Pradhan for their insightful comments and to express my gratitude to J.P.S. Uberoi for a lengthy discussion on every point of significance that arose from the paper.

2 I have found it necessary to coin the term *irrealities* to refer to the combination of the irrational and the unreal.

3 It may be worth quoting Lévi-Strauss on this point. He says:

> I am perfectly aware that it is this aspect of my work that Ricoeur is referring to when he rightly describes it as 'Kantism without a transcendental subject.' But far from considering this reservation as indicating some deficiency, I see it as the inevitable consequence of the ethnographic approach I have chosen, since, my ambition being to discover the conditions in which systems of truths become mutually convertible and therefore simultaneously acceptable to several different subjects, the pattern of those conditions takes on the character of an autonomous object, independent of any subject. (Lévi-Strauss 1975:11).

4 For a detailed account of the Arya Samaj in Punjab, see Jones (1976).

5 This pattern of laments may have a cross-cultural character which may be seen from the following quotation in McManners (1981: 297–8):

> Indeed, savages, by their honesty in facing the reality of death and their unselfconscious respect for their dead kinsmen, have a certain superiority to civilized men. . . . Their funerals are marked by forceful and highly personal expressions of grief. 'They respect their dead' wrote Buffon, 'They adorn them, they speak to them; they recite their great deeds, they praise their virtues; and we, who pride ourselves on our sensitivity, we do not even show ordinary human sympathy; we flee, we abandon them, we do not wish to see them, we have neither the courage nor the will to speak of them; we even avoid going to places which could recall their memory, we are either too indifferent or too weak-spirited. . . .

> In the Arab women of the Barbary coast who tear their hair and address all sorts of pleas and reproaches to the corpse, the abbé Poiret saw 'une éloquence naturelle et pathétique.' In Greece, Madame Chenier reported, there were similar lamentations from the women – 'You are but sleeping,' they say, 'Do not abandon me,' 'I will revive you in my embrace,' 'I am dragged down to the grave with you.'

> . . . 'Among a people enslaved by the decencies of fashion', says

208

Nicandre, 'sorrow has to be still and silent, but with us it is eloquent and sublime.'

6   For an excellent description of a case of funeral priests in Banaras who can absorb the sins of the dead person, see Parry (1980).

7   For details of these taboos, see Das (1982) and Nicholas (1981).

8   The ideas surrounding an 'invitation' are extremely complex. Marriage and death can be seen as completely contrasting events from this perspective. In the case of a marriage, the family of the bride or groom have to visit each relative and hand over the invitation card personally, impressing upon them the importance of their participation in the event. In earlier days, the family barber would be sent with sweets to invite relatives who did not live in the city. These days the invitation card when sent to another city may contain a line seeking forgiveness for the inability of the members of the family to visit personally. Often it is considered necessary to write a personal letter, thereby giving a personal touch to the impersonal card and establishing the importance of the relationship in its individuality.

In the case of death, no one expects an invitation. As people hear of a death they come to express their grief (*afsos karna*). Someone who heard of a death in a known family and did not go to mourn would be considered as violating the norms of humanity, not just those of caste and kinship.

9   In some families it is customary to tie a white turban. Pink is a colour of auspiciousness and festivity and its use on this occasion is a rather loved announcement of the termination of mourning.

10 The shift to white saris in the case of widows is not as dramatic in Punjab as in some other parts of the country. This is because as women grow older they shift to white clothes which do not necessarily have coloured borders.

11 Lévi-Strauss uses the linguistic concept of a code to refer to the system of sounds. He points to the significatory and communicative function of sounds in human societies and takes the systematic character of these signs as the object of his studies.

REFERENCES

Aries, Philippe, *The Hour of our Death*. New York: Alfred Knopf, 1981.

Biardeau, M. and Malamoud, C., *Le Sacrifice dans L'Inde Ancienne*. Presses Universitaires de Paris, 1976.

Das, Veena, 'The Uses of Liminality: Society and Cosmos in Hinduism', *Contributions to Indian Sociology* (n.s.) 10,2:244–64, 1976a.

Das, Veena, 'Masks and Faces: An Essay on Punjabi Kinship,' *Contributions to Indian Sociology* (n.s.) 10:1–30. 1976b.

Das, Veena, 'Reflections on the Social construction of Adulthood,' in *Identity and Adulthood* (ed. Sudhir Kakar). Delhi: Oxford University Press, 1979.

Das, Veena, *Structure and Cognition: Aspects of Hindu Caste and Ritual*. Delhi: Oxford University Press, second edition, 1982.

Das, Veena, 'The Language of Sacrifice', *Man*, September 1983, 18,3: 445–62.

Das, Veena and Ralph, W. Nicholas, 'Family' and 'Household': Difference and Division in South Asian Domestic Life in *Welfare and Well-being in South Asian Society* (eds. Veena Das *et al.*). Delhi: Oxford University Press (forthcoming).

Dumont, L., *Homo Hierarchicus: The Caste System and its Implications*. London: Weidenfeld & Nicholson, 1970.

Durkheim, Emile, *The Elementary Forms of Religious Life*. Illinois: Glencoe, 1947.

Freud, S., 'Mourning and Melancholia' in *General Works*: 10, 1915.

Geertz, C., *The Interpretation of Cultures*. New York: Basic Books, (pp. 142–70), 1973.

Gill, H.S., *A Phulkar from Bhatinda*, Patiala: Punjabi University, 1977.

Hershman, Paul, *Punjabi Kinship and Marriage*, Delhi Hindustan Publishing Corporation, 1981.

Hertz, R., *Death and the Right Hand*. London: Cohen and West, 1960.

Jones, Kenneth, *The Arya Samaj*. Berkeley: University of California Press, 1976.

Kaushik, Meena, 'The Symbolic Representation of Death,' *Contributions to Indian Sociology* (n.s.) 10:2, 1976.

Lévi-Strauss, Claude, *The Raw and the Cooked*. New York: Harper and Row (paperback edition 1975, Basic Books), 1969.

Malinowski, B., *Magic, Science, and Religion*. Garden City, N.Y.: Doubleday 1954.

McManners, John, *Death and the Enlightenment; Changing Attitudes to Death*, Oxford: Clarendon Press, 1981.

Nicholas, R., Sraddha, 'Impurity, and Relations between the Living and the Dead', *Contributions to Indian Sociology*, (n.s.) 15, 1 and 2: 367–79), 1981.

Nozick, R., *Philosophical Explanations*. Cambridge: Harvard University Press, 1981.

Parry, J.P., 'Ghosts, Greed and Sin: The Occupational Identity of the Banaras Funeral Priests'. *Man* (n.s.) 15, 1:88–111, 1980.

Parry, J.P., 'Death and Cosmogony in Kashi', *Contributions to Indian Sociology*, (n.s.) 15, 1 and 2: 337–36, 1981.

Pocock, David, 'Notes on *Jajmani* Relationships', *Contributions to Indian Sociology*, VI: 78–95, 1962.

Ricoeur, Paul, *Interpretation Theory: Discourse and the Surplus of Meaning*. Texas: Texas Christian University Press, 1976.

Srinivas, M.N., *Religion and Society among the Coorgs of South India*, Oxford: Clarendon Press, 1952.

Tandon, P., *Punjabi Century, 1857–1947*. London: Chatto & Windus, 1961.

Vatuk, Sylvia. 'Gifts and Affines in North India,' *Contributions to Indian Sociology*, (n.s.) 9:155–96, 1975.

Vatuk, Sylvia, 'Terminology and Prestations Revisited,' *Contributions to Indian Sociology* (n.s.) 9: 197–216, 1975.

IX

'HEART' AND SELF IN OLD AGE: A CHINESE MODEL[1]

Julia Shiang

ABSTRACT

In this essay, Julia Shiang discusses the meaning of family transactions in the Chinese family, in the context of the concept of 'heart.' This concept, basic to the pattern of relationships, is especially key in the analysis of the dynamics of inter-generational balance. Through a detailed study of several Chinese families living in the US, Shiang's essay outlines and analyzes the meaning of reciprocity and obligation, as well as sensitivity and affection, in the parent–child relationship.

The Chinese word 'heart' expresses a concept central to the dynamics of family transactions. This essay will explore the meanings of this term and suggest how these affect the self-images of both parents and children, and ultimately, the meaning of intimate relationships in Chinese culture. We will examine the dynamics of how the generations attempt to achieve a satisfactory balance between being close to each other and being separate from one another. This will help us explain, for example, why parents would give one child a loan and not another, why a son would suddenly get married when his mother developed cancer, or why a child would absolutely refuse to ask his parents for a loan.

We will examine the meanings attached to transactions between parents and children. When a parent gives her child a sofa for their new house, the sofa is the object being transferred. But there can be

211

a message associated with the object; this is a meaning connected to the transfer. The message might be 'I am giving you something so you will remember me,' or it might be 'If you accept this, you will owe me something later.' The impact of these messages on parent–child relations is the focus of study.

The present study focuses on relationships between elderly parents (average age of parents was sixty-five years) and their adult children in twenty-two Chinese families living in Greater Boston and its suburbs.[2] In this essay I will speak about a 'median' level of interaction, behaviour, or belief – around which there is rich and subtle variation. Sixteen of the families had lived in the US for more than twenty years. All parents, with the exception of two, were born in China, presently the People's Republic of China. The total number of parents, adult children, and grandchildren in the sample was 117. The present essay stems from earlier work (Shiang, 1984) conducted on the analysis of the content, direction, frequency, and quantity of transactions between parents and children over an eighteen-month period.

I TRANSACTIONS AS A WAY OF EXPRESSING FEELINGS AND BINDING FAMILIES TOGETHER

It is necessary to make clear the impact transactions have for the population under study. In general Americans express their feelings both through actions and words. A gift is given. One says, 'I like you.' In love relationships great emphasis is placed on getting the lover to acknowledge feelings through words, to say out loud that 'four letter word,' LOVE (Bob Dylan). But most of the elderly Chinese in the sample do not talk openly about their feelings; the appropriate medium for the expression of feelings is through presentations. An elderly widow explained it this way:

> Of course, you love your own daughter. It doesn't show much – it's not something we talk about. But a parent has love for their children. I suppose you could say we did little things like [giving] birthday presents.

A young Chinese woman, Deborah, raised in the US, concurred:

> I remember every time I left home [on a long trip] I would give

my mother a peck. She didn't exactly force me away, but she didn't really encourage me either. . . . In our family love was based more on respect and understanding . . . we don't have any great demonstrations of affection or talks between us. It is all low-key. You read a lot through actions.

Most of the parents do not say 'I love you' directly to a child; affection is implied when the parent gives 'a little something' special, sews a jacket, or remembers that the grandchildren need new slippers.

But not all children understand the absence of the verbal expression of affections and the meaning attributed to 'gifts.' One young man wasn't clear about reconciling the differences between his parents' behaviours and what he saw as appropriate American parental behaviour. They gave him gifts but he felt something was lacking. His sister described it,

He came to me and said, 'Deborah, I think there's something wrong with our family.' Of course, he didn't state it in such a direct way. He really hemmed and hawed. He said, 'We don't touch or kiss or anything as a family.'

He wonders about his parents' affections. Yet his parents, from their point of view, have been appropriately expressing their desire to have him emotionally close by providing appropriate gifts.

The concept of 'heart': the sentiment that binds

Transactions symbolize the sentiment that binds together parents and children. The Chinese expression, having 'heart' was used by the elderly in speaking about the quality of the relationship they wanted with their adult children. 'Heart' is, xin, a Chinese character that literally means heart, the organ in the body. The heart is seen as the center of emotions as evidenced by the use of the radical in many words denoting emotional states.

In the specific context of parent–child relations, the elderly interviewed used the expression having 'heart' in two ways:

a) 'ni hao xin' (Mandarin) or 'neih hou yauh sam' (Cantonese) you have very much heart, you are very thoughtful, very kind.

213

b) 'you xin' or 'yauh sam' showing heart, expressing kindness, thoughtfulness, to be kindhearted in deed.

For example, one elderly woman said she had done enough for all her children including seeing them all married, living in houses, and having their own families with good earnings. Now that she was older, she said,

> What I want is their heart and recognition of me and my husband. My son told me to really enjoy myself. If I want to gamble, I can gamble. I need not be worried with money. If I lose everything, I can come live with him and his wife. I felt very comforted and touched by what he said despite the fact that he may not be able to live up to his promises. He has the heart for me.

'Heart' is to be thinking about the other person and to be willing to provide. It is expressed when her children tell her that now it is time for her to enjoy herself; she has worked hard enough. After many years of running a laundry business and raising her children, she now expects them to be connected to her by actively thinking of her and meeting some of her needs.

How do people show 'heart'?

An earlier quantitative analysis of transactions (Shiang, 1984) between family members showed that of all the transactions that took place between family members, the transfer of money occurred most frequently. Twenty-one of the twenty-two families in the sample reported at least one transfer of money. Most were engaged in multiple transfers of money that involved actual cash flow both from parent to child and from child to parent. Money was also given by parents to children specifically earmarked as downpayments for buying a house. I looked at reasons people gave for engaging in such transactions. What meanings did the individuals attribute to their money transactions?

One of the primary reasons was need. In one family, a daughter and her husband realized that her parents had lost a great deal of money in the stock market.

. . . we knew that they had bought stocks and lost heavily. So we

knew that they needed money . . . no they didn't ask [us] . . .
we initially sent them about $100 a month and by the time my
father died, it was close to $450 a month . . . they were
grateful . . .

One elderly man and his wife, now living in government subsidized
housing, gave all five of his children money for downpayments.

Altogether I gave about $80,000 to the children. The pension
money is all spread out, we don't want the money. If they [the
children] have a difficult situation, I want to help. Last year my
youngest daughter wanted to buy a second house to rent [out],
so I loaned them $5000, no interest. If they don't want to
refund, then forget it, it doesn't matter.

This father clearly states the attitude of many parents. Parents have
made money and 'giving [money] to children is what it is for. . . '
But even as these informants speak about the economic aspects of
money transactions, they see such transactions as a way to show
care and concern toward others. One elderly widow said,

One can give money to one's parents anytime. When [the child]
gets a job, she can give money to her mother on her birthday.

The woman then advised the interviewer to:

find excuses to give money to your mother. You should buy a
piece of chicken leg and Chinese fried dumplings on your
mother's birthday. In China, you could include money as part of
gifts to parents. You could put money in red bags[3] that were
considered as lucky money. . .

The transaction of money was also seen as a way of maintaining
communication between the generations. Children in the sample
paid back their parents when they could. As one father said,

I didn't ask them (to return the money) but now (my youngest
daughter) is giving $500 each month. It is good for them, to like
to help!

He sees this interchange as a vehicle through which the children can
learn about parental needs. Frequent phone calls and letters allow
him to mention casually his needs and the urgency of the situation.
It is important to remember the historical fact that many parents

215

have maintained monetary transactions for many years with their own parents in China, Taiwan, or Hong Kong. Many of these relations spanned more than thirty years. In some cases it was the grandparents in the US sending money back to their sons in Taiwan or Hong Kong to be used for investments. For most, however, it was the parents who sent monthly allowances to their own parents. In any case, money was often the vehicle through which contact between the generations was made. While this was seen as an obligation for some, others saw money transactions as a symbol of the 'heart' and concern that should exist between the generations. This aspect was emphasized most often when young adults spoke about their perception of the meaning attached to money. One college educated daughter said,

> I sent some [money] back [to my parents] not because they need it but because I think they're happier knowing that I'm thinking about them. . . I sent some on Chinese New Year and my mother was really pleased. She wrote me a note saying how pleased she was, and how she had sent money to her mother, and now we were continuing the tradition.

One woman described her older sister's method of giving money to her parents.

> We are expected not only to spend time with them [parents], but also to contribute financially once we are working. This is true even of my older sister who is married and living somewhere else . . . she helps out . . . she disguises it . . . by sending several tens of dollars on their birthdays and other special occasions. My mother is not a tyrant who can compel a child to give a specific amount each month.

Another young woman, an assistant professor in a Massachusetts college, was asked whether her parents had ever talked about being taken care of in old age. She replied that they didn't expect to live together but they had made clear their expectation of support.

> My parents think we are awful, especially me. I'm the worst. My parents already expect financial support saying, 'It's not that we really want your money. It's just a measure of how much you care.' . . . When I finished college and worked for five months . . . I sent them my very first paycheck. It was sort of symbolic.

216

Besides the transfer of money, the giving of services was also seen as an appropriate way of expressing 'heart.' Parents and children gave each other help in the areas of companionship, cooking and housekeeping, transportation, child care, home maintenance. Families exchanged store-bought items, handmade gifts, and advice concerning business, health, and home buying. One young woman bought a house in the same neighborhood as her mother and 'checked in' with her on a regular basis.

> That way we can serve them better. I don't mean to serve them all day long, but just be available. They know if something happens, we can be there right away.

Analysis of the concept of 'heart'

A review of all the interviews revealed four aspects of having 'heart' as most important to the informants; each is an area where a problem in communication of a misunderstanding between the generations can cause a breakdown in relations. The likelihood that heart is expressed properly is greatly increased when the children have been explicitly taught the proper conduct or when the family is surrounded by others who can admonish and correct improper behaviour.

1 Heart involves the anticipation of needs. Since actions count more than words (see above), the anticipation of needs also carries extra weight. One should not just provide a gift of service but one should be able to anticipate the need without being told. To be told explicitly what is needed is to cheapen the relationship. A number of parent–child conflicts centered around the adult child's failure to anticipate or thoroughly consider his or her parents' needs appropriately. While it may be that the child merely did not know of the need, the parent's view is that the child is neglectful, unsympathetic, and uncaring. Parents expect their children to be thinking about them and to know beforehand what they might want. She counts on her second daughter and her youngest son to anticipate her needs.

2 Children should initiate acts that show heart. Children are

Julia Shiang

responsible for contacting parents, inviting them out, giving parents the option of joining them for holiday celebrations. Parents should not have to initiate. The child who has heart finds ways of 'checking in' with parents so that parents can then let the child know about their specific needs. In one family the children were paying more than a thousand dollars each month for their mother to stay in a nursing home. But the elderly woman didn't have any pocket money to buy a book or a gift. Because of this, she was unhappy. From her point of view, the children should have been able to anticipate what she needed; they certainly had enough money. Because children are supposed to initiate this kind of giving, she felt that she could not directly ask for a few extra dollars. The children wondered why she complained about little things each time they met. They were left at an impasse, in a situation satisfactory to none. In the eyes of her elderly friend, the children were not meeting their responsibility to their parent.

3 Awareness of need must be expressed by appropriate actions. It is not enough for an adult child to express sympathy; showing heart involves action and not just 'empty talk.' Knowledge of a need must be expressed through doing or giving something, however small. Small 'tokens' such as gifts, money, or a small service on a special occasion convey the idea that one is thinking and concerned about the person. The tokens are symbolic of a readiness or willingness on the part of the other person to be available if needed. Furthermore, actions must take place in an appropriate manner. Children must be able to discriminate between proper and improper actions. As we have seen, gifts of money are most frequently used to convey heart. Obviously, services given in appropriate form may also convey concern and caring.

4 Children's appropriate actions play a critical role in both the elder's self-image and in the adult child's self-image. The presentation of oneself to others outside the family plays a central role in determining self-image. Signs of children's care and concern are more readily apparent when relatives and friends can 'see' such acts taking place. Everyone understands the positive implications for one's self-image when a daughter-in-law serves tea during a mah-jong game with friends. Weekly dinners in Chinatown with all the family present are a sign to others of family harmony. Telling one's friends that

218

children are home for the holidays can boost a parent's image, but there is less concrete evidence of concerned children since there is no presentation in a public setting. When children understand the various forms of heart and the appropriate manner in which it is to be expressed, then both parents and children gain in several ways. They reinforce their own images of themselves as responsible, mature adults – in the parenting role and in the caring child role. They may also garner the respect and admiration of others in the presentation of their public selves.

We now turn to a family case study to illustrate the various and subtle ways in which family members do and do not express 'heart'.

II THE JENS

Mrs Jen specifically said that what she wanted from her children in old age is 'their heart and recognition.' Mr and Mrs Jen, in their early seventies, live in the suburbs of Boston surrounded by their four adult children. In fact, their two sons live above and below them in separate apartments in the Jens' house. Their daughters live with their families in two houses only ten minutes away. Mr and Mrs Jen have a high number of transactions with their children.

I will discuss some of the differences among the children in their interactions with their parents to illustrate the various ways parents and children express 'heart.'

When she was nine years old the oldest daughter, Mary, was left in China by her mother (her father was already in the US) to live with her grandparents. When the Japanese entered their area, she and her maternal grandmother fled to Hong Kong where she grew up. Her parents sent her $600 a year for support – quite a lot of money in those days. She was able to go to school and later met her husband through a cousin. Once she was married, her parents stopped sending her money. For ten years, Mary took care of her father's mother in Hong Kong. Later the grandmother was brought to the US by the Jens and cared for in their home until her death. Mary and her family emigrated to the US five years ago, and now live in a house owned by her father. All the other Jen children were born and brought up in the US.

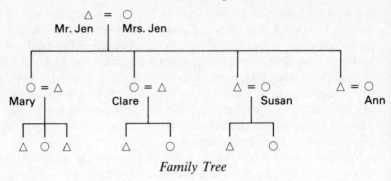

Julia Shiang

Family Tree

Parents' view of family loyalty

Every Tuesday night, Mrs Jen has the whole family for dinner. She cooks a huge meal for her eight children and seven grandchildren – they have to set out two tables to seat everyone. For fourteen years, Mrs Jen 'has insisted [they] have this dinner for the sake of family unity and contact with one another.' In their living room hangs an embroidered tapestry of five pairs of birds. Mr Jen pointed out that each symbolized a different aspect of the unity and harmony which one hopes characterize family relationships. One bird symbolizes loyalty; another symbolizes long life. Mr and Mrs Jen sold their laundry business and are now retired. They spend their days shopping, playing mah-jong, reading the newspaper, sewing clothes, and visiting with friends. Although their schedules are not the same, both Mr and Mrs Jen accommodate and support each other. Their marriage is an example of how well a 'blind' marriage[4] can work out. When the interviewer asked about old age and when a person could be considered old, they spoke in animated tones and with such excitement they couldn't wait for the other to stop talking.

People in the village didn't mind the fact that they were getting old. As a matter of fact, people didn't mind being called 'louh minh' (old lady) because other people would give more respect to them. Their social status would be higher. When young people had problems, they would be advised to ask the 'old' ones. The old people are supposed to have more living experience. In the village, people would value the experience one has rather than the amount of education one has. The old people do have more experience than the young people

Traditionally, the oldest son's wife would assume the responsibilities of taking care of the aging parents. It was assumed that one's daughters would shift their loyalty to their husband's family after marriage. And when the interviewer asked how this attitude had changed, Mrs Jen answered,

> I know at least half the Chinese families [in the U.S.] are not living with their elderly parents. . .I know many cases where the mother-in-law was kicked out of their children's house.

But she blamed this discord not only on the children but also on the mother in law.

> The mother-in-law still thinks her son is still hers whether he is married or not. Little do they know that women [in the US] have more authority than they had in China. Men listen to their wives more.

Mrs Jen realizes she cannot control her children and even though she obviously wishes for the 'old days', she understands her role must be more circumspect. Yet she insists on holding Tuesday night dinners so the whole family can get together regularly.

Variations in family transactions

Mr and Mrs Jen's different relations with their children can be seen in the varying transaction patterns they have with each. In the following section I focus on transactions with their daughters and daughters-in-law as a way to illustrate the various ways these can vary within one family.

When the interviewer praised Mr and Mrs Jen for all they have provided for their children, Mrs Jen was quick to reply that her oldest daughter, Mary, did not appreciate what they had given her. After all, they had provided $600 a year for more than ten years, and a house when she arrived in the US. Her daughter still thought that the house she received was 'an old and worn-out one.' When Mary and her husband went to China, they didn't tell the parents until a few days before they left. In contrast, their second daughter asked her mother to accompany them on their trip to China. Even if Mrs Jen didn't want to go with Mary and her family, she still expected that it should have been her choice to refuse. Another incident reinforced Mrs Jen's view that in spite of the fact she has given Mary a lot, her daughter does not show her the proper respect. Mary's teenage daughter came to do some house-cleaning for her. After completing some of the chores, the girl started complaining about being tired. In order to urge her granddaughter to finish the tasks, Mrs Jen told her that when her second daughter was young she had started cooking at the age of twelve and ironed clothes even earlier. Mrs Jen later told Mary how her daughter hadn't completed the tasks. Mary's reply was, 'Each person has a different fate. Some people are born to suffer all their life and some people are born to enjoy.' The implication was that Mrs Jen was born to suffer and it was just too bad because that was her fate. Mary was not going to make her daughter behave in the way Mrs Jen thought she should. While Mrs Jen related this information to the interviewer, Mr Jen was silent, and appeared to agree with his wife.

Over the years, tensions between the oldest daughter and her mother have developed; Mrs Jen feels her daughter doesn't appreciate and respect her. Perhaps Mary feels she was abandoned in Hong Kong and that no amount of money could make up for what she had to suffer. She sees herself as having endured more than her mother, and that her daughter will not, if she can help it, suffer in the same way. She had already taken care of her grandmother for ten years; she doesn't need to continue proving that she is a caring daughter. Perhaps Mrs Jen gave her daughter a 'torn and worn-out' house with the hopes that Mary would take the responsibility to fix it up herself, but without saying so explicitly. So when no improvements are made on the house, the mother silently despairs. Using Clare, her second daughter, as a model of proper behavior in admonishing her granddaughter only serves to reinforce the differences between mother and daughter. While mother and daughter have transactions with each other (the weekly dinner, the house the daughter lives in) most probably neither derives satisfaction from these interactions, and as more incidents reveal this tension, the distance between them is reinforced. Mrs Jen feels her image of herself as a 'responsible' mother to Mary is not enhanced. Mary feels her efforts are not appreciated; she is not reinforced in her own self-image as a 'responsible' daughter.

In contrast, Mrs Jen's relationship with her second daughter, Clare, is supportive and mutually enhancing. Clare works in China-

town in a community support program and both parents are proud
of her accomplishments. Mr Jen said, 'she is doing something good
for Chinese people and is getting to be an important person. She is
getting greater as she does more.' He beamed as Mrs Jen talked
about this daughter; she confirms the image they have of themselves
as responsible parents. When Mr Jen turned sixty years old, Clare
gave her parents $2000. They put the money in a joint bank account
that they and Clare have shared ever since she was young – they will
use it 'if there is an emergency.' She offered her father a monthly
allotment of money saying she wanted to pay him a nominal rent
even though she doesn't live in a house he owns. He waved his hand,
'I did not let her.' On her parents' fiftieth wedding anniversary,
Clare gave them two plane tickets to LA and accompanied them.
Besides providing these tokens of concern, she and her mother also
share a passion for recreational gambling. Mrs Jen feels that she
should be able to gamble now that she is retired and every week she
plays mah-jong. Clare also likes to gamble and invited her mother
down to the horse races in New Jersey. Mrs Jen said, 'My husband
does not like to be adventurous. . . . I was very excited to go to this
place. . . '. But not all social events work out; Clare asked her to go
to a Mandarin opera, but Mrs Jen said 'it was boring and I could not
understand what it was all about.' There is warmth and room for
disagreements between the two women. Mrs Jen says with pride,
'Clare refuses to buy jackets at the department store because she
says I make warmer ones.' Mrs Jen feels that her efforts are
unconditionally appreciated.

Yet another pattern has evolved with her oldest son's wife,
Susan. The son had reached his thirties without marrying, and
according to his father, was 'unable to find someone in Boston that
fitted what he wanted.' Mrs Jen activated her network of relatives
and friends and took her son to Hong Kong to meet prospective
spouses. Mrs Jen was instrumental in choosing Susan as her son's
spouse and Susan is most probably grateful for having the opportunity to come to the US. But it also appears that Susan would like to
maintain some distance from her parents-in-law. For example, even
though the couple live in an apartment just above his parents, Susan
made it clear to her mother-in-law that she would not accept any
clothes made by the grandmother. Mr Jen said, 'She prefers to buy
things from the store.' Whether this was the real reason was hard to
tell, but Susan's refusal places a distance between herself and her

mother-in-law, a woman who takes pride in the fact that she makes most of her own clothes by hand. Susan may have given her mother-in-law the message that she is not willing to assume the traditional role, as oldest son's wife, of caring for her aging parents-in-law in their last years of life.

The second son's wife, Ann, was born in the US. Mrs Jen referred to her as the 'siu sam pouh' (small daughter-in-law), an affectionate term. The Jens' second son is the 'baby' of the family'; both parents hold a special sort of affection for him. With obvious pleasure, they told the interviewer about the series of events that led their son to be quite content to live surrounded by family. At age eighteen he tried living apart from his parents by getting an apartment with friends. It didn't work; he loaned money to unreliable friends and his apartment mates never paid their share of the rent. In the end, his parents bailed him out and 'since then he never wanted to live outside [the parents' home] again.' Mrs Jen and her son also share the same love for gambling – and now that he is making a sizable profit on his restaurant, he told his mother that she should gamble. He says he will take care of her if she has any problems. His wife, Ann, agrees fully. 'He has the heart for me,' said Mrs Jen, expressing her feeling of closeness to this son and daughter-in-law.

Forms of 'heart' expressed through transaction

Mrs Jen's second daughter, Clare, and her second son are tightly bound to the mother through appropriate transactions which symbolize 'heart'. By offering gifts, Clare continually demonstrates to her mother that she is thinking about her parents. Physical proximity obviously serves to support an emotional closeness but living nearby does not necessarily mean that parent and child will be emotionally close: such is the case with Mrs Jen and her first daughter.

Mrs Jen feels that her own image of herself as a responsible mother is enhanced through her transactions with her second daughter and her youngest daughter-in-law. This is a mutual process; each person's self-image is enhanced as their actual transaction pattern closely approximates their idea of how transactions should take place within the family. The two young women get positive satisfaction from their part in giving to the parents. On the other hand, the oldest daughter feels excluded and finds transactions with the family only a reminder of how she doesn't measure up to family expectations. But the fact that she is willing to continue engaging with her mother suggests that she is still attempting to work out their relationship. When Mrs Jen's first daughter-in-law distances herself by refusing to carry out certain transactions, she is reinforcing her separateness.

III THE TRADITIONAL MODEL IN CONTEMPORARY PERSPECTIVE

What standard for behavior in relationships is used by family members in determining what constitutes proper and appropriate transactions? The fact that all the families in the sample have experienced migration leads us to consider two factors that affect family functioning: (a) the traditional Chinese ideal of parent–child relations in parents' old age that these parents brought with them from the old country, and (b) the way these ideals have changed as expressed by present-day examples of 'good' and 'bad' models of behavior used by parents to educate their children about proper and improper behavior. It is then possible to contrast these two factors with actual patterns of care as illustrated by the transactions that occurred between parents and children in the sample.

The traditional Chinese ideal

The traditional Confucian ideal of family relations made explicit the nature of the reciprocal relations between parents and children. Parents give to children when they are young and receive in old age. The force of this obligation to parents was particularly strong due to the cultural practice of linking it to keeping one's ancestors happy (Hsu, 1948). Second, the relation between caring for one's parents and the definition of the 'good' person was clearly defined in the concept of 'jen'; or 'humanness, reciprocity in desirable act, fellow feeling' (Richards, 1932: 69). One aspect of 'jen' lies in 'serving the parents and with every effort to strive for mutuality and so act. . . ' (Mencius, 1895: 353). The specific word, 'xiao' is used to define the obligation that children should show their parents in old age. One shows filial piety towards parents with 'heart.' One of the stories from The Twenty-Four Examples of Filial Piety from China illustrates the strength of the tie between parents and children.

A boy, Wu Meng, lived with his parents during the Chin Dynasty (4th century A.D.). They were so poor they could not afford to furnish their beds with mosquito nets. Every night mosquitos attacked them without restraint feasting upon their flesh and blood. Seeing his parents thus annoyed in their sleep, the boy felt a great grief in his heart. He took off his clothes to attract the mosquitos. Even though he felt the pain from their attacks, he would not drive them away for fear they might go attack his parents instead. He would rather endure the suffering for the sake of his parents.

While this and other stories in the Twenty-Four Examples are extreme in their caricature of parent–child relations, they were effectively used for centuries to inculcate proper relations between parents and children. They indicate the importance of serving one's parents for as long as one lived. Chinese parents could plan for retirement and old age with certainty that one of their children, usually a son, would provide for them as they withdrew from the more productive sphere of society. Daughters did not take on this responsibility for their own parents, but once in their husband's household, they assumed major roles in caring for their parents-in-law.

Filial piety demands absolute obedience and complete devotion to the parents. . . . In traditional society an individual from childhood to the end of his life was completely immersed in an atmosphere which compelled the observation of filial piety (Yang, 1959: 86).

Numerous studies of Chinese families (Freedman, 1970, Lang) point to the force of this reciprocal relationship; parents give to children when they are young and receive in old age.

It is this ideal that the Chinese brought with them as they settled in the US. Of course, the way in which the ideal was worked out by each family, even in China, deviated from the ideal. A study of these differences is found in the work of Ikels (1980). Ikels contrasts rural and urban solutions to old age using a number of factors important in determining the position of the elderly in a culture. For

China, she suggests that 'practical economic considerations, super-natural sanctions, structural factors, the force of public opinion, . . . and self-interest . . . all combined to ensure that the village elderly were granted their due' (1980:88). The norm of reciprocity was held intact in the village setting. In contrast, the population of urban elderly pre-1949 was actually very small and the relatively greater instability of personal relationships contributed to a much less sure existence for the elderly in the last years of their lives. The ideal of parent–child reciprocity was not as easily achieved. How-ever, the ideal was clear and attaining a close approximation to the ideal meant that parents could then view themselves as having fulfilled parental responsibilities and children could view them-selves as filial children.

Present-day 'good' and 'bad' models

We now turn to consider present-day examples of 'good' and 'bad' parent–child interactions. These are particularly interesting in that they are a powerful force in the setting of a standard and the teaching of proper and improper behaviors. Many elderly have heard of these models and soon they become the model 'to emulate' or the model 'to avoid becoming at all costs.'

Models to emulate   Several informants spoke about a woman, Mrs Wang, who was 'an excellent example of taking care of her hus-band's mother for a long period of time.' The whole extended family deserved merit for the care they took of the aging grand-mother, but this woman deserved special credit because it was she who really maintained the day-to-day care. Everyone in her circle of friends knew of her devotion and spoke about her in glowing terms concerning her filial behavior. When Mrs Wang was interviewed, she minimized her burden:

> Grandmother rotated among her four children in the US.
> Everyone expressed enthusiasm that she should stay with them
> even though I think she really preferred to stay with her oldest
> son – she thought her place was here. In our house,
> grandmother was mobile and wanted to try to help cook a dish.
> But that would be too much and she would get tired. She was

fairly easy to get along with – she was not an emotional type, but very logical. About a year before she died, the whole Chinese community [friends around Boston and New York] had a party with 150 people to celebrate her 80th birthday.

Grandmother lived with her daughter-in-law for fifteen years. She did live with the other children for extended periods of time. In fact, a daughter and son-in-law also took care of the grandmother despite the fact that the daughter, herself, had been 'given away', to another family as a young child for five or more years. 'There were just too many girls in the family.'

Mrs Wang spoke about the experience of having grandmother in the household while she was still having children.

It was good for them [the children] when they were really young to have a grandmother play with them. They grew up with her. In fact my youngest daughter was born after grandmother came to the United States and the third child was only seventeen months old. It was natural.

Her youngest daughter, concurred, and spoke with obvious warmth about her grandmother.

I remember grandmother very well and I also have fond memories when I see the old pictures. She would make things. I was intrigued by her bound feet – she would make her own shoes with a pattern using vises to hold the material together. It was very clever. I drank Pepsi and she could open the bottle with her own hands – she was very strong. I tried to do it but couldn't. She made origami animals and tried to teach us.

She would sit in her bedroom . . . and we would visit her, sit with her and talk with her. She would teach us things – she was a part of my life. She tried to learn English – just a few words but soon would forget them. She couldn't absorb them. But I would teach her words – the younger teaching the older – and this made me feel good. [Grandmother] being there definitely was not negative! It was taken for granted that she was supposed to be there.

Later in the interview series, the young woman spoke about what she would do for her own parents.

I have felt very strongly that my parents would live with me. The

228

thought of putting my parents in a nursing home is very repulsive to me. When I said this to my mother, I also said that this would not be a burden on me.

Negative models We now turn to examine the families that were cited as having problems. Much discussion and gossip surrounded the 'stories' of these families; it was clear that the informants felt they must avoid 'ending up like this.' Some of the examples centered around being put in nursing homes:

Mrs Wong lived far away from her children; they had all moved away. Now she was getting old and the children wanted to put her in a nursing home, but she fought it. She didn't want to and resisted.

Other examples focused on the loss of friends and familiar surroundings.

One old man had a heart problem, he was already eighty-six years old. His daughter convinced him to move to California to be with her, but he lost his friends. He didn't have a place to read – he used to go to the [Asian] library at Harvard . . .

The old man seemed just to fade away. He died less than a year after his move.

The following example of a 'bad' model focuses on troubled relations and their effect on family transactions.

Mrs Wu took care of her mother for nearly sixteen years in Hong Kong before she came to the US. During those years she said she had 'done her duty' by helping her mother in many ways. Her mother said she didn't want to be a burden and offered Mrs Wu $50 (Hong Kong currency) a month but she did not take the money,

I would feel shameful to accept my mother's money. It is my duty to take care of my mother.

At the same time, her brother, already living in the US., was sending the mother about 40 US dollars each month. Even though Mrs Wu left Hong Kong to live with her husband in the US, she still continued to send money to her mother by sending it through friends and requesting them to buy her mother food and clothes. After a while, she began to realize that the relatives taking care of her mother were abusing her by locking her out of the house and giving her little to eat.

Another relative saw my mother one day sitting in front of the house of the relative where she was supposed to be staying. Mu asked how she was doing. She said she was locked out again . . . she did not dare go outside because the relative would not let her in the house . . . she wished she had a chicken leg to eat.

Mrs Wu had already tried to bring her mother over to the US but her own limited financial resources prohibited this. She contacted her brother and sister who lived with their families on the West Coast only a block apart from each other. Eventually, Mrs Wu's own son applied for the old mother to come to the US. Arrangements were made so that she would spend the weekdays with the sister and weekends with the brother.

When everything was ready, we contacted my oldest brother to confirm his commitment. He said he needed to talk with his wife and would call back. When he called back, he sounded unsure. His wife had talked to my sister . . . and said something to upset my sister . . . they had an argument. I found out that my brother did not want to be responsible for all the expenses my mother might impose on him such as medical and funeral expenses . . . unfortunately, the brother did not want mother to come. He felt it would be too much for him. My sister was upset with him and his wife because he is the oldest son and is responsible for taking care of mother in her old age. She is the daughter and would not take the responsibility that should be his. She was so upset that she never had any contact with his family any more though they live only a few streets apart.

Mrs Wu was also upset,

My brother owns a chicken farm. He owns a house and a car. . . . My sister married a business man from the Philippines. All her children have been able to attend universities and have good jobs. She has a house and several cars. Besides, she is not working and travels to different cities in the US. If she has the money to travel, she must have enough to support mother. After all, how much can an old person eat?

While her mother was alive, Mrs Wu received $200 designated for her daughter. She complained, 'What nice jewelry can $200 buy?' She asked her mother to leave a ring to her son; it had been passed from generation to generation and was quite valuable. But the woman refused, saying that the ring would be given to her son's wife. 'Even though my brother did not treat her nicely, my mother favored the son more than anybody else.' When Mrs Wu's mother died, it was discovered that she had squirreled away nearly $10,000 in her bank account in Hong Kong. No one had been aware of the money. In her will, Mrs Wu's mother gave the bulk of it to her son, his wife, and children. She even took care of the son's adopted son. But to Mrs Wu and her children she only left a small amount; Mrs Wu complained that 'it was unfair'. After all, Mrs Wu had tried as hard as she could to help her mother over all those years and her brother had refused. The favoritism her mother showed to her brother was an important factor in coloring Mrs Wu's relationship with her brother and sister. Mrs Wu felt bitter; she had been cheated but what could she do?

A family with troubled relations is not merely seen as lacking in something; it is seen as failing. The parents cannot be seen as responsible parents and their children are not filial.

Actual patterns of transactions

What models did parents provide their children in caring for their grandparents? Of the sample of twenty-two families, eleven (50 per cent) parents provided a 'live' model of daily care for aging grandparents to younger, growing children. In this process, children are made more thoughtful about what is required in the care of an older person. Learning is casual, a part of everyday life. When the time comes for that grown child to decide whether to care for his or her aging parent, the inclination to care is based on past experience. This is shown in the following results: Of the eleven parents who provided a 'live' model, five (45 per cent) parents showed a present pattern of co-residency with adult children. Of these same eleven families, three (27 per cent) parents had spent a short period of time 'trying out' living with children in the children's household. The hope is that by living together for a period of time, both generations will learn whether co-residence is feasible in the future. Eight families showed a pattern where the parents provided no 'live' model because of physical distance and only sent money back to grandparents in China. Of these eight families, none (0 per cent)

Julia Shiang

showed a pattern of co-residency with adult children and only one (12 per cent) had spent an extended period of time living with children. The presence of a 'live' is associated with co-residency and the willingness to try living with adult children. (See Shiang, 1984 for statistical analysis).

While it is also apparent from the 'models' discussed above that many parents still look to their sons to provide 'heart' in the traditional vein, there is evidence that more and more parents in the US setting look to their daughters, rather than their sons to provide 'heart' in their old age. This is particularly true for those elderly who do not require financial assistance after retirement as shown in the following chart.

Proximity of elderly to geographically closest adult child (N = 15)

	Transaction Patterns			
	Middle Income Families		Upper–Middle Income Families	
	son	*daughter*	*son*	*daughter*
Proximity of closest child				
co-resident or same building	4	1*	0	0
close by	0	1	2	1
more than 50 miles away	0	0	3	3
Total	4	2	5	4

* Living with daughter, but explicitly stated that the target child is a son.

The chart shows that children of middle income parents are living closer to parents than children of upper-middle income parents. Transactions that occurred with parents of the middle income group generally took place with the most proximate *sons* whereas transactions for the upper-middle income group took place with both *daughters* and *sons*. Thus, while the traditional norm exerts a strong influence in the choice of which child is most proximate and carrying on transactions with parents, the data suggest that in higher socio-economic groups the expression of 'heart' can now be more easily cultivated with a daughter.

The consequences of showing and not showing 'heart'

As family members judge their behaviors according to these standards, is 'heart' expressed in a satisfying manner? How do parents and children negotiate a closeness that is satisfactory to both generations? Parents in the sample were quite active in their attempts to influence their children, especially in the areas of marital choice, career choice, and cultivating relations with one child who is most 'sympathetic' to their situation (Shiang, 1984). Not surprisingly, family members sometimes don't see eye to eye in negotiating this closeness. This happened in at least two ways: in some families it is the parents who don't meet the image that children have of family closeness; in some families, children maintain greater distance than parents desire. For the most part, parents and children both engage in a process of delicate balancing; on one hand, they try to preserve a separateness from the family and on the other hand, they try to achieve a satisfactory closeness.

For example, not all parents want to make themselves available to their children. Some parents would rather not babysit, to the chagrin of their children. Parents feel they have their own lives to live. Some parents say they have 'to rely on no one but themselves' and stress their own independence from children. Some parents may insist on being independent to avoid the onus of not meeting the parental goal of raising concerned children. Their statements may also reflect the fact that the daily lives of elderly people simply do not revolve around children. In one family, the daughter said she realized that since her parents had moved away from Boston, she had to be more active in trying to preserve ties with her parents. When it was clear that her parents weren't coming to see their second newborn child, she and her husband packed up and flew to where the parents lived. She said,

> My mother said she couldn't come because she had been sick but I knew that they were also very busy with their own lives. So we went there. Even though it was a lot of trouble for us, I wanted the three generations to be together. I really wanted my mother to have a chance to see her granddaughter when she was just born – to have a sort of bonding between them.

At the same time, she also realized that if her parents were to live

233

with her right now, it wouldn't be so easy.

> My mother and I were talking – we sort of agreed that she got along better right now with my brother's wife – she's from Hong Kong and – she has less conflict with my mother . . . my mother's values and mine just aren't the same right now . . . she wants things for me that I don't want right now – like getting a dining room table. Those small things make it pretty difficult to live together on a day-by-day basis. Probably someday it will be important to me to have a dining room table . . . but not right now.

Another forty year-old woman had the same opinion. Both mother and daughter have a stake in trying to 'convince' each other of her own point of view, sometimes leading to conflict.

> I think all mothers and daughters have some conflict. My difference with my mother is in the religious area. I don't agree with the way she approaches God. This is a real area of friction – at times I cannot talk about it in a calm way [with her]. I get upset and speak my mind and she withdraws from confrontation. The more she withdraws, the more I want to talk and convince her. I should be more tolerant.

One woman, Mrs Tong, spoke about the need to 'separate' the mother and son. As a social worker she saw many cases of

> passive-aggressive behavior on the part of children who could not separate from the mother . . . the kids do not like their situation but they do not know how to break away.

This had already happened with her husband's younger brother. She and her husband had already moved away from the parental household in Boston when they realized that the husband's younger brother was skipping school and getting away with it.

> He didn't finish high school. He would just go out and play ball with his friends. Mother would just accept this behavior, so we had them come down to New York. He did his high school equivalency in New York, tried several jobs, and then went to the university for a year . . . we really had to help him, and he is very grateful. He is happy with his marriage, his family, and his job. . . . Once mother wanted him to have a car and told each

son a different story as to why he had to have a new car. I think she came up with the money herself. The brothers would say, 'Don't indulge him.' We worked on the separation of the mother and the son. Otherwise he would have never gotten away.

During the course of the interview, it appeared that Mrs Tong's own son, twenty-four years old, was facing the same issue. Mrs Tong, herself, seemed to be unaware of a parallel in the behavior of the two men. After graduation from college, her son returned home to live and found a job nearby. Mrs Tong said he was 'wrestling with the decision of going out to get his own apartment.' Eight months later he moved out to a separate place about ten miles away. She explained, 'This is closer to where he works.' But it was also clear that he could see his parents as often as he or they wished.

In some cases, the price one has to pay in order to distance oneself from parents is very high. In one family, the elderly mother was admitted to the hospital with terminal cancer; she was given only a short time to live. The father was clearly in despair; he began to turn to his children to determine which one would be available to come and live with him. Suddenly two of the sons married. Their choice of marriage partners made it clear that they could not be counted on as target children to provide care for their needy father.

The focus on negotiating a satisfactory closeness also illuminated some of the atypical behavior in some families. In all families except one, children reached or exceeded the educational level of their parents. In the one exception, the father had a college degree from China, but the sons had only high school degrees. The sons entered the restaurant business; the mother appeared to discourage further education and supported their decisions. Perhaps she realized that if they continued working in Chinatown, they would continue to stay nearby. Indeed, when the mother became widowed, this proximity ensured the daily availability of her sons, and more importantly, their wives.

In some families the parents were still attempting to bind the children through acts of giving; in some cases the children refused such offers – refused to take and refused to ask even when in need.

One daughter-in-law was about to give birth to her first child. The husband's mother asked if she could make a sweater for the baby and the daughter-in-law agreed, but added a stipulation. She 'hoped' the mother wouldn't use the color green. She didn't phrase it diplomatically by saying, for example, that she liked the colors red and white. These interchanges were carried out over the telephone, so there was less opportunity to make sure of what message was intended. Was the daughter-in-law saying that she really didn't want such a gift from her husband's mother? Or was she just stuck on some color scheme for her first baby? The mother-in-law had offered generously, but now a qualification had been placed on the gift. The baby arrived, the sweater did not. The daughter-in-law learned that if she wanted to continue having these interchanges, she could not express her own personal likes and dislikes in this fashion. Her mother-in-law saw them as a rejection of her handi-work and of herself. Voicing individual preferences at this level of interchange carried too high a price.

Other children chose not to involve their parents even when in need. A thirty-year-old son and his wife were planning to buy a home but found that he did not have enough money for the downpayment. He called his older brother and asked to borrow $5000 with the specific request that the brother not tell his parents about the arrangement. He felt that their father had been too critical of him in the past; he wanted to act without his father's help. Perhaps he wanted to give his father the impression that he could do it on his own. Anyway, the older brother was sworn to silence. Over the course of a number of years, the older brother was paid back, with interest. When the older brother then bought a house, he borrowed $10,000 from his parents. Interestingly enough, he ex-plained it as borrowing only $5000 from his parents since he had loaned $5000 to his brother earlier. In his mind, the responsibility for giving out loans rested with his parents.

Later, another younger brother asked him if he could loan him money so he could buy a house. The older brother said it would be fine but added that their father would just love to lend him something. In fact, the older brother and his father had discussed this the previous Christmas; it would give the father positive pleasure to loan the younger son money. But the son refused to ask, saying, 'Even though they got away pretty cheaply on me since they didn't have to pay for my schooling. And after all they bought you [the older brother] a car and he promised me but didn't.' He didn't want to tie himself to his father in this fashion but the fierceness of his conviction also indicated his uncomfortableness with the situation. Although he tried to deny it, he was still very much connected to his father. In the process he was also denying his father a certain pleasure in the proof that they had the proper 'heart' for each other. As the brother said,

> You want to feel close to your parents – after all they are your parents and always will be. You won't have another set, um? But it's often difficult.

As one thirty-two-year-old woman put it,

> Of course, you are the child and you have been getting things from your parents all your life. But now [as an adult] it's time to say I am my own person. I can't be forever depending on parents. but it always seems to be a struggle between being and doing what makes me happy and what makes them happy. And I always wonder if what it is that makes them happy, strangely enough, also makes me happy. But their idea of me isn't always the same as my idea of me. And when you take [something], it gives them the message that you're willing to be everything they want you to be. But when you say no, then you know that you've hurt them.

These adult children are struggling to find a balance between being separate from their parents and yet acting responsibly towards their parents. They experience a 'filial anxiety', worrying about whether they can appropriately and adequately pay back their parents. They struggle with the desire to be independent of feeling obligated to parents and the knowledge that they do 'owe' something to their parents. They also realize, at some level, the harm they do to their parents by denying them the appropriate expression of concern. Unfortunately, it is the parents faced with the most uncertainty who experience greater 'parental anxiety' and to some degree, shame. As one elderly woman said, 'You know that friends would not make you lose face when you see them, but you also know that they are talking behind your back about the shameful situation.' They are the parents who feel they have failed to live up to their parental goal of raising children who reciprocate in meaningful ways in their old age.

Family ties and the cultural ideology which supports them are an important factor in the definition of the individual's life goals and responsibilities. Clearly, the emphasis placed upon the importance of family ties varies across societies: western observers of Asian (especially Confucian) models of family have tended to stress the constraints on the individual represented by intergenerational responsibility, or 'filial piety'. By seeing this aspect of relationships only through a 'cost-benefit' perspective on the individual, they have often ignored cultural dispositions felt and experienced by people in these societies. This examination of relationships in Chinese families, caught in a trans-cultural environment, reveals both the centrality of intergenerational relationships as a benefit and goal for one's life in traditional Chinese conceptualizations, as well as the areas of ambiguity introduced by a very different western perspective in the younger generation.

NOTES

1 I would like to thank Dr R.A. LeVine, Dr C. Ikels, and Dr M. Katz for discussions on earlier versions of this work. I would also like to thank F. Shiang, S. T. Shiang, Y.Y. Tsien, H.C. Tsien, N. Li, Y.T. Li, and R.W. Tsien for helpful discussion on the concept of Heart.
2 Ten families were Mandarin-speaking and twelve families were Cantonese-speaking. Differences emerged between these two subgroups in the types of transactions that took place between family members as well as in the frequency and direction of transactions. Unfortunately, the richness of this data cannot be detailed in this short essay.
3 Money given in red envelopes was considered 'lucky money'; traditionally the money was given at Chinese New Year.
4 'Blind' marriage: Neither party is introduced to the other before the actual marriage ceremony. Baker states, 'the family . . . controlled the individual, for marriage was arranged for the individual, not left to his own free choice dependent on the vagaries of 'love'. . . . No matter that the husband found he did not like his wife much – he and she were there to continue the family. . . ' (1979: 33–4).

REFERENCES

Baker, H.D.R. 1979. *Chinese Family and Kinship*. New York: Columbia University Press.
Dylan, B. 1968. 'Love is a Four Letter Word' sung by Joan Baez on *Any Day Now*. New York: Vanguard Recordings.
Freedman, M. 1970. *Lineage Organization in Southeastern China*. London: The Athlone Press.

Hsu, F.L.K. 1948. *Under the Ancestor's Shadow: Chinese Culture and Personality*. New York: Columbia University Press.

Ikels, C. 1980. 'The Coming of Age in Chinese Society: Traditional Patterns in Contemporary Hong Kong.' In C.L. Fry (ed.) *Aging in Culture and Society*. New York: J.F. Bergin.

Lang, O. 1946. *Chinese Family and Society*. New Haven: Yale University Press.

Makara,M.L. translation of *The Book of Filial Piety*, New York: St. John's University Press.

Mencius, 1895. *The Book of Mencius*. trans. by James Legge. *The Chinese Classics*, vol. 2. Oxford: Clarendon Press.

Richards, I.A. 1932. *Mencius on the Mind*. London: Routledge & Kegan Paul.

Shiang, J. 1984. *The Significance of Transactions: Reciprocity Between Chinese Elderly and Their Adult Children Living in Boston and Its Suburbs*. Unpublished Dissertation.

Yang, C.K. 1959. *The Chinese Family in the Communist Revolution*. Cambridge: MIT Press.

X

SKILLS AND LIFE STRATEGIES OF JAPANESE BUSINESS WOMEN

Sumiko Iwao

ABSTRACT

In 'Skills and life strategies of Japanese business women,' Sumiko Iwao examines the lives of two successful business women. Iwao focusses her analysis on the importance of 'attention to minute detail' in interpersonal relations, and illustrates how this sensitivity has helped these women thrive in the traditionally male world of business. While Iwao acknowledges basic differences in the lives and personalities of these women, she sees them as having in common a desire to please 'by means of high quality and service,' which they have placed above their desire for high profit. Iwao concludes from her case studies that women are more attentive to details and interpersonal relations, have a higher propensity to save and are more likely to retain the status quo. While in American culture, Iwao argues, achievement and affiliation are seen as antagonistic needs, in Japan the two are joined, as achievement needs are 'fulfilled only through close personal relationships.'

INTRODUCTION

Different cultures provide different opportunities and conditions for the development of human potential. And the way people express their potential is the product of the historical, cultural and natural conditions surrounding them. Japanese women are not exceptions. Therefore, it is necessary to look into their historical and cultural background to have better understanding of the following two cases of women in small businesses.

A century ago, at the time of the Meiji Restoration (1868), 80 per cent of Japan's population was involved in agriculture; since that time the country has moved rapidly toward industrialization. But even in its agrarian stage, Japanese society was significantly different from other contemporary agrarian societies for the following reasons: Given the large proportion of mountainous terrain, a high percentage of the population lived in the coastal areas of arable land where the soil is not very rich; this resulted in small scale labor intensive farming with maximum utilization of all available land. It is a common sight in rural Japan to see very precisely laid out, small terraced rice fields. It was thus originally out of necessity that Japanese paid a great deal of attention to minute details which we find today in contemporary Japanese arts, cookery, the making of industrial products, as well as in human relations. The latter can be clearly seen in both of the following cases: in Mrs Edo's high level of sensitivity to interpersonal relations and in Mrs Tanaka's precision in her choice of gifts and training of her employees.

There were neither multiple nor abundant rice crops in old Japan and the barely sufficient crops depended upon the conditions of weather, on the amount of rain and on the temperature. Japan not only has four distinct seasons but the weather is also extremely variable from day to day. Therefore farmers have to plan each day's work very carefully, anticipating the weather. Neglecting to do the appropriate things at the right time could mean complete destruction of the crop. Attention has to be paid to the subtle indications of on-coming change in the natural world. Additionally, the frequent typhoons which ravage Japan at harvest time sometimes wipe out crops completely. The sensitivity to subtle differences or minute detail, which came out of agricultural necessity, has persisted well after Japan urbanized.

In subsistence farming under conditions of unpredictability, a high value was placed on industriousness. Men and women worked side by side in the fields from very early in the morning till late into the night. In addition to their work as laborers, women's most significant role was that of distributor of food. Women were responsible for stretching a limited amount of food among a large number of mouths and for making it last through scarce times between harvests. They had to make the best use of whatever little

Sumiko Iwao

they had and this was where their ingenuity was highly valued. This role and its concomitant abilities have made women the pivotal members of the family. Women were required to be extremely diligent, ingenious in planning, thrifty, capable of exercising a strong sense of justice, and needed to have a talent for averting conflict within the family.

Their additional role in controlling the supply of *sake*, although they themselves did not usually drink it, increased their power over men as managers of the household.

The second significant function in the woman's role was responsibility for clothing the family. This required the development of further skills and ingenuity which greatly enhanced their managerial role in the family. Women were also traditionally the weavers and tailors for the family.

The transition from an agrarian to an urban society was accompanied by the transition from an autarchic to a monetary economy in which men were the breadwinners earning income in work outside the family while women remained in charge of the family budget in keeping with their historical role as family managers. Their ingenuity and creativity in controlling and husbanding the family's resources gave women a sense of responsibility, freedom and self-expression which was unique to their situation.

The historic context of scarcity of resources has left a long lasting impact upon the Japanese and it can be seen in the behavior of contemporary Japanese women. As we shall see, both Mrs Edo and Mrs Tanaka's reluctance to expand their business and to engage in risk-taking is one example. This is also seen in the Japanese propensity to save for rainy days. Yet, there is a strong bias against miserliness. Money 'circulates around in the world' [kane wa tenka no mawarimono] and therefore, one should not try to monopolize it or hope to keep it forever; just as typhoons destroy rich harvests leaving almost nothing, we cannot depend on money. This sort of distrust in the power of money has made the Japanese place more value in other things, such as good human relations based on trust.

If even hard work cannot make life easy, where do people find compensatory satisfaction? One way is in the belief that one is doing one's best and that therefore there is no need to blame oneself if one's expectations have not been realized. If you keep high moral standards, you should not be ashamed of yourself even if things do not go well and people will accept you as you are. Another way is to be grateful for whatever little one has or to convince oneself that one finds pleasure in work itself. This is particularly strong in the case of Mrs Edo. Another is to expect the worst. While in America, people are motivated by maintaining positive expectations, Japanese are motivated by the comfort which comes from being prepared for possible failure. This may lead to reluctance in taking risks.

WOMEN IN SMALL BUSINESSES

Though men are responsible for the legal and developmental aspects of their business enterprises, women as shopkeepers and managers of small businesses also exhibit talents for managing personnel. Goals of harmony and avoidance of conflict are cultivated in women in the home and their abilities to achieve these are carried naturally in the work arena. Very often women provide the real power behind the scenes in the running of businesses [*shikkari mono no okamisan*]. A highly developed sense of empathy with the customer lay at the foundation of a relationship of trust which takes priority over the profit-making incentive among these women. The long lasting scene of trust and the constant desire to please the customers are factors responsible for a stability in market relations and the endurance of small family businesses; these skills are carried on today just as they have been in the past. They denote relationships between the buyer and the seller entirely different from those found in other cultures, one manifestation of this can be seen in the tradition of not tipping. Service is inherent and given freely by the seller, rather than something to be purchased or earned by the buyer.

I The traditional model

Mrs Edo is a dainty woman with fair skin who dresses elegantly in kimonos of good taste. She is quiet and always modest to the point of being self-demeaning. Her manners and movement are graceful and she has great self-control. She 'wraps up' people with her sincerity and warmth. She repeatedly asked how a story of somebody like her who has no special talent could be of use to an

243

interviewer. Her question was asked out of politeness but said in all sincerity.

Mrs Edo, now seventy, was the fifth-generation owner of a renowned Asakusa Japanese restaurant, 'Ichinao,' which has been in operation for 250 years. Mrs Edo has handed ownership of the restaurant to her second son, but was exclusively responsible for its post-World War II restoration and success.

Her restaurant is in Asakusa, the older section of downtown Tokyo on the bank of the river Sumida. This place is particularly famous for its grand fireworks during summer. The neighborhood developed around the Asakusa Kannon Temple which dates back to the seventh century. There are many small shops along the way to the Temple which are always crowded with visitors looking for colorful souvenirs. Because of the temple, there are many stores which specialize in Buddhist ornaments and ceremonial goods. As many visitors wanted to have a good time in Asakusa after paying their respects to the temple, many restaurants and theaters appeared, making this a traditional entertainment center. Asakusa is representative of old Tokyo in many ways, especially with regard to interpersonal relations. There are closely knit ties within the community.

Ichinao is a *ryotei*. Although the word ryotei is translated as 'restaurant' in English, ryotei are quite different from regular restaurants with big dining rooms. Ryotei are high class Japanese style restaurants. They are housed in traditional Japanese buildings with separate rooms for dining. You never share a room with another group and usually one room is completely reserved for the whole evening for one party of customers. Therefore, customers are not accepted without a reservation. After the customers are shown into a room, the sliding door is closed and, therefore, completely private dining is guaranteed.

The Japanese style room is decorated with a flower arrangement and a hanging scroll and the esthetic quality of the room is highly valued. The room and its objects, the garden and dishes are meant to be appreciated for their elegance and beauty, as is the food itself. Full course dinners are served course by course, and a great deal of attention is paid to the dishes being used and details of arrangement of food on the dishes.

Okami, the female owner, usually appears once during the evening to welcome customers and thank them for coming and also

244

to see them off as the guests are leaving. It is the role of the female owner to see to it that every need of the customers, even the unspoken ones, are met, and that they go home satisfied with the excellent service and good food. Enjoying the atmosphere of the room is an important part of the evening at a ryotei.

Mrs Edo learned her trade by a natural apprenticeship to her mother- and father-in-law. Mrs Edo's mother-in-law, former female owner of Ichinao, played a key role in running Ichinao in the past and Mrs Edo acquired the necessary skills by observing her. The role of her father-in-law was that of master chef. He represented the Asakusa Ryotei Association. He was highly respected by other members of the association because of his good judgment, and people used to come for his advice whenever problems occurred. He seemed to know the importance of the role of the female owner as the manager of the restaurant and Mrs Edo thinks that it was because of this that he was very demanding and strict. She was only seventeen when she got married and used to miss her own home, her loving parents and her many sisters and brothers, thus his high standards occasionally seemed oppressive to her. Mrs Edo's father-in-law was especially strict about manners and all his daughters were sent to other families for *gyogi minari* (mastering of social graces and proper manners through observation by living with a good family).

At ryotei, prices are not listed nor is there such a thing as a menu; the customers expect the food to be expensive and in return to be guaranteed an evening of good food and impeccable care. Usually, customers are either introduced or are regular guests and are known to the restaurant. They do not pay immediately after dining; a bill is sent later. There thus has to be a relationship of trust between the restaurant and the customers.

The daughter of a family of five sons and five daughters who owned a Buddhist religious artifact store in Asakusa, Mrs Edo was discovered by her future parents-in-law, the owners of the Ichinao Restaurant, when she was seventeen years old. The future parents-in-law happened to be shopping at the store of her parents when she was minding the store. Because of her beauty, personality, kindness and willingness to serve and please the customers, they regarded her as the ideal wife for their son, although her own parents initially opposed the match on the grounds that the restaurant business (as part of the 'water trades' [mizushobai]) was neither stable nor

245

sufficiently respectable for the daughter of a stable merchant family. Usually, women brought up in *karyukai* [flower and willow world], another euphemism for the entertainment industry, are considered to be suited to the role of female owner of a restaurant because they know how to deal with customers who have had drinks, especially when they are a little worse for alcohol. The marriage was the choice and the decision of the parents of her future husband rather than by his own free will. Therefore, she felt sorry for her husband who had to put up with her even when she was obliged to respect his parents' wishes above those of her husband She was hesitant about the marriage but the Edos persisted because they regarded her as especially suitable since she had been brought up in a stable family. The marriage took place with little consideration for her future husband's opinion. It was obvious that the marriage was an arrangement to benefit the whole family, rather than the individuals involved. Because of the way the marriage took place, Mrs Edo has always felt indebted to her parents-in-law and tried to live up to their expectations. This has made her husband jealous and unhappy.

The early years of her marriage were extremely difficult due to the fact that her husband's mother died when he was young, leaving him with a demanding step-mother and strict father who ruled the family with an iron hand. Since Mrs Edo's two sisters-in-law had been sent off to receive instruction in social graces among prominent families, one of which was the family of the founding president of Waseda University, she found herself obliged to attend to her parents-in-law conscientiously. Every night she would wait on them until they retired late in the evening and then she would rise early in the morning to serve her father-in-law tea before he went off to the wholesale market for the restaurant, which was usually before six o'clock. While her husband was out on such business as attending restaurant association's gatherings, she was required to look after the business and all the workers, fifty altogether, and, therefore, she never went out alone with her husband. Much demand was placed upon her as the wife of the heir of a famous old restaurant. Her responsibilities were heavy under the family system in which emphasis was placed on the family line rather than the interests and desire of the individual.

Her young husband was sent to Osaka for training at two very prestigious restaurants for three years, leaving her alone to look after the house, restaurant and parents. The birth of a small and sickly baby added to her troubles. The practice of receiving training under a master other than one's own parents was considered to provide a better opportunity to learn. One is expected to be more patient, and to learn better, under a master who is not a blood relative. Her husband became a very able chef and those working under him respected him and obeyed him completely. But after his death it was at times difficult to control the chefs employed at the restaurant and Mrs Edo was often sorry that she herself had had no professional training as a chef.

She bore five children before her husband died, placing her in charge of the Ichinao Restaurant. It was only for the two-and-a-half years between her father's retirement and his early death that her husband was in charge of the restaurant. When Mrs Edo was first faced with the responsibility of running the restaurant alone because of her husband's death and her father-in-law's infirmity, she had had no formal experience at all. Only a highly developed sense of empathy for the customers – her primary motivation in running the restaurant came from a compelling desire to please – helped her manage. Under her direction, the restaurant rapidly gained a reputation for excellence. It is clear that her motive to maintain good relations with those around her is stronger than her motive to achieve. Perhaps, it is more accurate to say that these two motives are not in conflict, but rather that satisfactory human relations mean achievement and success to her.

When the war broke out, all luxury businesses were frowned upon, and as an act of patriotism, her father-in-law decided to turn over most of his accumulated wealth to the government to aid the war efforts. The money her father-in-law had put aside for the entire family to live comfortably on for the rest of their lives lost its value due to extremely high inflation. The site of the original restaurant was in the Asakusa Park, and the property, six times as large as the present one with a beautiful garden, was turned over to the government. Her father-in-law closed the restaurant saying that serving food bought at the black market would ruin the name of the restaurant and he would not be able to 'hold his head up' before his ancestors.

Thus, when the war ended, the family found themselves in extreme penury, without capital or resources to start over. They did not even own a house. Mrs Edo was living in a small rented house on the outskirts of Tokyo. One day, a former customer passed by the house and was surprised to see her playing with her children in front of the house. He asked her what she was doing there and urged her to return to Asakusa by saying that it was a great loss for the community that such a renowned restaurant with such a long history had disappeared. He scolded her for not telling her former customers about the difficult situation her family was in.

Remembering her outstanding reputation, a group of former customers rallied around to encourage her to re-open the restaurant, and raised money to acquire new premises and to set her on her feet. The restaurant was re-opened but the taxes were very high and she found herself with mounting debts. She thought then that it would not be long before she had to close the restaurant again. She sold everything of value she had including her jewelry and her best kimonos. As her natal family ties were very close she held a meeting with her brothers to discuss her difficult situation and they decided to let her borrow a certain amount of money from a small credit union with their endorsement. It turned out that the man who used to supply Ikeda with vegetables had made a lot of money and by that time had risen to be the president of the credit union. He remembered how very kind Mrs Edo used to be and wanted to be of some help so that he could pay her back for her generosity. He set up credit on his own property necessary for the loan so that she could borrow money from the union.

Mrs Edo, in her overriding desire to please the customers, made no profit whatsoever during the first years. Though food supplies were bought at inflated prices on the black market she did not charge the customers expensive bills. She recalls that in these first several years after the war, her business consistently ran a monthly deficit of 200,000 yen.

She wrote a letter to a former customer asking for advice. This customer, the president of Mitsui Construction Company, offered her a space in his office building to run a lunch/coffee shop; at the same time she worked in the Fuji Television Broadcasting Company cafeteria in the evenings making bento (lunch boxes) for employees. She worked hard, harder than anybody else, thinking that if she did so her children and employees would try as hard as they could too. She worked until her 'bones were ground into powder.' Her reputation for preparing lunch boxes became so widely spread that Sankei Newspapers asked her to provide lunch box services for their company cafeteria, too. During this time her primary concerns were to repay her debts and to maintain her high standards of service to customers; her own personal comfort and living conditions were secondary to these. Nevertheless, this attitude of empathy and servitude to the customers proved to be the key to her success; doing so she has gained their trust. This was also critical in her family life since she had to provide strong and empathetic guidance to her five children in the absence of their father. It was also comforting to her that her brothers all extended support and help to her.

In accordance with her Buddhist religious upbringing, she also had a strong sense of obligation to her ancestors as to the task of restoring the Ichinao Restaurant to its previously unchallenged standards of excellence. Because of her commitment to perfection, her customers frequently offered to help her extend her operations, but she refused to compromise either on quality or detail through expansion. Today, the restaurant has ten chefs and eight maids and operates on a much smaller scale than that of the time when her father-in-law and her husband were in charge.

Because her first son was sickly, it fell to her second son to take over the business even though this meant his sacrificing a college education for fear that it would jeopardize his commitment to the family restaurant. The second son was a very good student and was eager to go on to a university with his teacher's encouragement. Mrs Edo still feels badly that she could not let him receive the college education which he wanted so badly. Instead, as part of his training, he accompanied the Japanese ambassador – her late husband's classmate at a private grammar school – to Austria as the official embassy chef. Upon his return to Japan his mother arranged his marriage to the daughter of a Kyoto sushi-restaurateur, a girl from the 'water trades.' Mrs Edo does not approve of some of the attitudes her daughter-in-law holds, while she calls her a 'good business woman' but denigrating the fact that she 'likes to make money too much.'

Mrs Edo's major concern was not to ruin the name of Ichinao, a restaurant with such a long history and tradition, and carry on the business until the next heir was ready to take over. Therefore, her approach to business is more passive or defensive, and therefore, she does not want to expand. She is not assertive verbally but wins respect from those working under her by quietly working very hard and sets herself up as a model that people working under her would be proud to follow.

Mrs Edo is a classic example of a traditional Japanese business woman attaining success through placing greater emphasis on good quality and service than on profit-making.

II. The modern model

Making a striking contrast to Mrs Edo is the model offered by Mrs Tanaka, president of an importing company for veterinary pharmaceuticals. Mrs Tanaka, who is now fifty-nine, is quite attractive with big almond shaped eyes. She dresses elegantly in fashionable clothes and is extremely confident and impressive. Her cheerfulness and sense of humour soften her strict approach to her workers.

She was born in Seoul, Korea in 1922 to a family of five children. Her father was conducting a medicine distribution business, which distributed medicines to all over Korea and Manchuria. There was a dormitory attached to their home for those young men working for her father. They were mostly people who had come to Seoul from Japan seeking better opportunities than what was available for them in Japan. There were always about thirty people living there.

Her mother looked after the dormitory and also played the role of mother to the boarders – taking care of their food, clothing and shelter. She supervised both the Korean and the Japanese servants, cooked meals for almost forty people three times a day, did the laundry, and sewed all clothing and bedding. She cooked various dishes of the boarders' home-land for the people who were away from their parents, and special dishes during festivals and New Year. She tried very hard to make everyone happy and ease their homesickness by making various delicious foods. All the boarders liked Mrs Tanaka's mother, and from the boarders her mother would learn a great deal of things related to her husband's job. She would give serious thought to these things and sometimes she would give valuable advice to her father. Therefore, Mrs Tanaka thinks that her father's business success owes a great deal to her mother. Mrs Tanaka, by observing what her mother did and how she helped her husband, learned a lot which became useful in her later years when she started her own business.

According to Mrs Tanaka, her mother's life was not unusual but the normal way of life for a merchant's wife. Women in those days never took a leading role but instead, bore and brought up a lot of healthy children, made every effort to assist their husband's job, had good relations with many people, worked actively, and tried hard to learn new things.

Mrs Tanaka was brought up in such an environment. Her parents expected and hoped that she would become a 'good wife and wise mother' which was thought to be the ideal type of woman to be, and they educated and prepared her according to their ideal. Her parents found a husband for her and she married him when she was twenty years old. Even though both her brother and herself had learnt their father's trade and became licensed to practice pharmacy, her parents did not expect her to work and even opposed her taking up a job.

A year after Japan entered the Second World War, her husband was drafted after three months of married life. At that time she was already pregnant. Three years later, when the war ended and Korea became independent, she came back to Japan with a three-year-old son, a small amount of money, enough for four or five months living costs for two of them, and all the luggage she could carry besides her baby. Everything else had to be left behind. A year after her return to Japan, the government notified her that her husband with whom she had lived only three months, had died on the battlefield, three days before the end of the war. Without adequate shelter, food and money, she and her family had to go through much difficulty as did many other Japanese at that time. A year after the notice of her husband's death, her son died from malnutrition. This too made her plunge into her work.

In Seoul, her life was quite comfortable as a daughter of a big pharmaceutical distributor and later as the wife of an officer. But the life back in Japan was very miserable and it was obviously necessary for her to work if she wanted to survive. When it became necessary for her to work, she said to herself that she would never work in a business where she had to be seen primarily as a woman such as becoming a hostess, nor engage in a business whose customers were only limited to women. When starting to work, pharmaceutical business seemed the natural thing to choose as she was brought up observing her father, and also, both she and her brother had licenses as pharmacists. Her older brother had returned from the war and started a pharmaceutical distributing business in Kyoto.

251

She first worked for a wholesale pharmacist for three years or so but then left and began to help her brother. She did not have much warm feeling toward her brother nor his wife. It was apparent that her brother's home was not a place where she could stay long. She worked with her brother for a year and a half and accumulated a small amount of money as a broker. But about that time, she was swindled out of all she had except for a small piece of property in Tokyo which is where her company is today. So she left Kyoto and moved to Tokyo.

Now in her late twenties, she had to start over once again. She was interested in regular pharmaceutical drugs but she knew that they were too expensive a proposition for her to engage in given her lack of financial resources. But dealing in drugs for household pets and small livestock was financially more possible, and even though at that time only the American Occupation army and their families could afford to have pets, she could already foresee that Japan's growing post-war prosperity meant that Japanese families would soon enjoy the luxury of having pets. Furthermore, she had a friend who suggested that distemper vaccinations would be a good thing to start with and they started an importing business together as partners. But soon her partner wanted to monopolize this business and its profits so they parted, and Mrs Tanaka found herself on her own again. She started her own business. She anticipated that a market for household pets and small livestock would develop and began importing high-quality drugs from abroad. She conducted a preliminary survey among Dutch, British and American companies to identify the most promising products. She settled on the Phillips Company from the Netherlands which manufactured veterinary pharmaceuticals as well as electric products on the grounds that the Netherlands was a comparably small country producing high quality products at competitive prices. This was the beginning of the Kyoritsu Shoji Company which she started with three or four employees but has now grown to be a company with three hundred employees.

After starting with distemper vaccinations for dogs, she ventured into drugs for chickens. She thought that she should eventually establish a research institute where she could test new drugs before applying to the Japanese government for permission to import and sell. Only a week after she mentioned her plan of acquiring a piece of property on which she could build an institute to a mentor, she was notified of a 6000 *tsubo* property which had been placed on the market because the owner was moving to Brazil and needed to get rid of it quickly. She had only five million yen but the owner was willing to sell it to her for that amount of money so the property came into her possession. A year later, the area was designated as Tsukuba University town and Research Centers, and all the research institutes with which she had dealings moved to that site from Tokyo. The value of the property today is phenomenal. It was there she started working on obtaining data on chickens using vaccinations which she had imported experimentally. She consulted frequently with her mentor, Dr Kawashima, who was considered to be the top man in the field.

Though she began by importing distemper vaccinations for sale to American Occupation families she gradually extended her business to Japanese middle-class families whose affluence had increased as she had predicted. She expanded her business to include drugs for larger farm animals – cows, horses, pigs, etc. Furthermore, she kept abreast of the latest developments in the veterinary medical field by going abroad every couple of years. Simultaneously she instituted the practice of bringing leading American and European veterinarians every year to lecture in regular seminars in four major cities in Japan to their Japanese counterparts. This served the multiple purposes of establishing herself in the Japanese veterinary community, of rendering the practitioners a service for which they were indebted to her, of maintaining her in a position of 'gatekeeper' of new information on animal drugs, and of legitimizing and enhancing her role as supplier of imported products to the Japanese market.

Besides inviting noted lecturers from abroad, and holding seminars, she puts out two different journals, one for scholars in the field, and the other for the general public, twice a year which includes translated information on the care and treatment of small animals. Because such information in Japanese is scarce, her efforts have been very much appreciated. This has not only helped her establish herself in Japan but also to establish herself abroad.

She went on to forecast that with the advent of jet travel Japan would move into the mass importation of chickens from abroad, and she proceeded to develop vaccinations for the various diseases, especially Newcastle's disease, which she thought would be imported as well. Shortly after, Newcastle's disease was brought into

Japan with imported chickens and it became so widely spread that it proved to be the most serious problem for those farmers in the chicken business. The Japanese government decided to import vaccination drugs for chickens from abroad on an emergency basis then, and the data her research institute had obtained four years before became extremely useful. It was the only research institute with the data necessary for obtaining government permits for imports. The whole situation was written up widely in newspapers and she 'made money without even the need to advertise.' Surely, she was very lucky but it was not only luck which brought her great success. It has always been her policy to import only high quality drugs even though the price was high. Only by doing so could she establish her reputation as a very reliable importer.

She has been very clever in forecasting which diseases are likely to spread and consequently, which vaccinations will be needed. She duplicated her results with the chickens by such foresight and practical preparation when mink and racehorses were imported as Japan's prosperity increased.

Mrs Tanaka's emphasis on quality is reflected in her thorough laboratory testing of all her products. This is yet another aspect of her long-term planning. Her testing has usually preceded by a considerable length of time the Ministry of Agriculture's decision to approve the drugs in question. She maintains that she values the superior quality of imported European drugs over domestic products and that she has been vindicated by the fact that people did not mind paying more for proven quality. She does not forget to sharpen her sensitivity by going abroad every two years to see not only drug-related businesses but also to see what people are interested, and what kind of fashions are popular, etc. She frequently visits users of the vaccinations to see their needs herself so that she will be a step ahead of others in the field, and she also spends time in the places where many people gather so that she will be able to forecast accurately how the world is turning.

Her policy is also reflected in her dealing with banks. She does not borrow more money from the bank than is absolutely necessary, nor try to expand her business much. But she seems to know how to make the largest profit out of whatever she does. She has adopted her elder sister's son and hopes he will succeed her in the business eventually. Rather than train him herself, she sent him to England to be trained and let him start a new business other than pharmaceutical import. The business he came up with is connected with disinfectants for men's rooms. In order to break into this totally new field, she successfully surveyed only the first class places – the Imperial Hotel, Ministry of Finance, the Bank of Japan, Mitsukoshi Department Store, Tokyo International Airport. She thinks this method is as effective as other types of advertisements. She then has pamphlets made showing those prestigious places listed as users.

Her business acumen shines forth in countless other ways; she entertains infrequently, but in memorable fashion when she does – she does not go out with businessmen to restaurants and bars because she feels they are used to going to good ones already. Instead she breaks tradition by hosting them in grand style once a year at her home. Instead of giving gifts at the traditional seasons (July and December in Japan), Mrs Tanaka does it at times when she will be more highly appreciated and remembered, during the *nippachi*, the months of February and August when all the gifts sent during the regular seasons have already been consumed.

In training her personnel, she attends to an array of minute detail and maintains an atmosphere of sparseness and thrift. She tries to present her business as smaller than it actually is. The office, still in the same small building she acquired after the war, is small and modest, encouraging an ethic of economy among the workers, and her employees reflect her attention to quality in their service. When I was interviewing her, her secretary served us tea and cake and fruit in such an elegant manner I almost forgot that I was interviewing her in her office.

She knows the different personalities and abilities of each of her employees and treats them with the same care and difference that a mother might show to her children. She tries to correct the manners of her workers because unless she does so, they embarrass themselves when they are dealing with outsiders, she says.

She firmly believes that unless users are pleased with the drugs they buy from her and unless she is of genuine use to them, her business cannot be expected to develop and prosper. She tries very hard to please her customers, and this in turn has become a source of satisfaction and joy to her.

She has one particular mentor, the above-mentioned professor of veterinary science from the University of Tokyo who gives her advice about, among other things, laboratory sites and installations. She considers that two or three other professionals in the field have been crucial to her success, but she has received little family help or guidance. On the contrary, she supported her mother and a younger brother for many years. She is very good at getting information and advice from professionals whenever she has questions. She values this sort of learning even more than monetary gains. She values interpersonal relations highly even in the business world.

Mrs Tanaka's talent lies in her unique sense of timing and anticipation, her long-range planning ability, her desire to please the buyer, her attention to detail at all levels and in all aspects of the business, and in her step-by-step advancement through increasingly refined stages of business development.

After twenty years, her company now imports from various countries in Europe medicines for chickens, pigs, cows, minks, dogs and cats, and sells them all over Japan. They also have a laboratory for producing and conducting research on vaccines for animals, and have subsidiary companies, such as Nippon Calmic Company which is a joint company with Burroughs Wellcome of England, and Aesop Pharmaceuticals which is a specialist company of medicines for pets. The total number of employees is more than three hundred and the business is still developing.

CONCLUSION

While being cautious not to overgeneralize the similarities between these two case studies and Japanese businesswomen in general, it is true that they share many characteristics in common with other Japanese women in business. These two women were interviewed as part of a much larger sample (fifty-six) for a study on Japanese businesswomen. Due to limitations of space, I have restricted myself to these two women, but they are representative of the larger sample.

It must first be noted that when talking about women in business in Japan it is more reasonable and appropriate to focus on women in small and medium sized organizations (where the power and presence of women have a long tradition), as represented by Mrs Edo and Mrs Tanaka, rather than big corporations where women have only recently entered and where the number of women in managerial posts is still quite small due to short tenures and unequal treatment.

There are both close similarities and great differences between these two women. Mrs Edo's business is traditional and labor-intensive, whereas Mrs Tanaka's is modern and knowledge-intensive. However, both share the common factor of wanting to please by means of high quality and service, and both have placed this value high above the profit-making incentive. Both believe that long-range success and profit are derived from the ethic of hard work, trust and attention to detail in all areas of their respective businesses.

In both cases, they do not seem to think that their being a woman is in any way a disadvantage or hindrance in their business careers. They both appear to have taken advantage of being a woman by obtaining help and information from men, where men would have had greater difficulties. The lack of discrimination against Mrs Edo is understandable as her business entails a specifically prescribed role for a woman, but Mrs Tanaka, who is in a traditionally male sphere of business, has never experienced any discrimination because she was a woman.

I should point out here that there are many similarities between male and female managerial skills within Japanese culture. If, however, we compare male and female managers, we find that women tend to pay more attention to details and interpersonal relations, have a higher propensity to save and are more likely to retain the status quo than expand. The long tradition women have of being the keeper of the purse, distributor of food and clothing and general manager within the family has established their reputation as sound business managers with good solid judgment and is expressed in the phrase *shikkari mono no okamisan*. Most of the Japanese women managers interviewed had few difficulties in obtaining bank loans (contrary to our expectations) because bank managers think male managers spend money much more unnecessarily and extravagantly as compared to female managers.

The kinds of abilities valued in women in the workplace are those that are also valued in the home, i.e., nurturing, pleasing, serving others, attending to detail, and giving satisfaction from facilitating the promotion of others. And this is exactly what we have observed in these two women. It is not really surprising that it has not been difficult for these women who were brought up to be 'good wives and wise mothers' to enter into the business world and be successful. As a matter of fact, both Mrs Edo and Mrs Tanaka's management style can be called 'maternalistic,' in that it pays attention to minute details, which they both seem to recognize as possible pitfalls. In addition, skills have been derived from a traditional background of thrift, management and planning combined with an inclination toward stability and low risk-taking. Where men are more apt to gamble and take larger risks in order to gain larger profits, women tend to stick to smaller risks and more stable profits. Therefore, while missing the chance for windfall profits, they instead gain credibility in the eyes of bankers which facilitates the bank's willingness to make loans to women in general. As one banker commented, bank notes do not have any sex and it is irrational to take the sex of the person doing business into consideration. They both seem to have a strong belief that the relationship between the client and business person must be based upon trust and should extend beyond business dealings. It is clearly exemplified by the way Mrs Edo sought advice from the president of Mitsui Construction Corporation.

Clearly, human relations are important in Japanese society, especially in the business world, even more so than managerial ability. This trait is even more prominent in female managers than in male managers. In motivational theory, as it has been applied to behavior in American and European culture, achievement and affiliation are seen as antagonistic needs given the competition inherent in the former and the need for close personal relationships in the latter. In Japan, however, it seems that achievement needs are fulfilled only through close personal relationships, thereby joining both achievement and affiliation.

Both come from a large family. Mrs Edo must have learned the importance of equal and fair treatment among people by being one of five sons and daughters. And this must have helped her smooth running of a big restaurant with many in-laws and live-in employees. Mrs Tanaka's family is not as large as that of Mrs Edo's, but those young workers in her father's dormitory were like extended family members and she must have observed her mother's management and equal treatment of everyone in the extended family. They both must have learned the importance of interpersonal relations and harmony within a group. Such family background and childhood experience provided a valuable place for training and learning by observation. Qualities such as empathy and personal care were highly developed in such a family environment.

Neither of them has professional or formal training in business or business degrees, but learned the trade by observing their elders –the mother-in-law in the case of Mrs Edo and her father in the case of Mrs Tanaka. But because they have no professional business training, they have had to rely on their own efforts, sincerity and industriousness. These qualities have become their assets in business dealings.

This has also determined their conviction in the value of learning from observation, 'a deed is more eloquent a teacher than words.' They work harder than anybody else at the workplace and set high standards of conduct for others to model. This is in line with the traditional Japanese method of teaching, i.e., learning from observation rather than the teaching of skills through verbal transmission of knowledge. I believe that learning from observation requires a great deal of involvement and initiative on the part of the learner and is often an easier way to learn because of its concreteness. I think that what has been learned through observation learning 'sinks' deeper into the learner and therefore, lasts longer.

One striking contrast between Mrs Edo and Mrs Tanaka is that the former is passive in her business dealings as well as in her outlook toward life whereas the latter is active and quite broad and international in her outlook. I would assume that it is partly due to the fact that Mrs Tanaka was born and raised in Korea where she must have met people other than Japanese in her everyday life. Therefore, it is rather natural for Mrs Tanaka to think internationally and to have a broad perspective. This has helped Mrs. Tanaka in her importing business. Mrs. Tanaka is extremely independent while Mrs Edo is not. Mrs Tanaka does not have a husband or child to tie her down. Mrs Tanaka has been free, and at times forced to make business judgments by herself while Mrs Edo has to uphold the history and tradition inherent in the good name of the restaurant.

There is a common saying in Japan, 'to eat from non blood-related people's rice cooker [Tanin no kama no meshi o kuu].' This implies that receiving training from other similar organizations would be a much better way for developing potential even when you can train your successor right at home or at your own organizations. Sending the successor away from a well-protected home into the 'cold world' is expected to make him/her strong and, therefore, he/she will be better prepared to succeed. This is exactly what these two women have done with respect to their successors.

What we have observed in these two women are the products of intricate interactions among persons, culture and natural conditions. It is interesting to see how both Japanese women's and men's skills, life strategies and practices will change with the gradual increase of women with managerial power in the Japanese business world and society at large.

XI

SELFHOOD IN CONTEXT:
SOME INDIAN SOLUTIONS
Prakash Desai and Alfred Collins

'Now I am all alone – all alone,' he thought, 'In all India is no one so alone as I! If I die today who shall bring news – and to whom?' 'Who is Kim – Kim – Kim?'

Rudyard Kipling

ABSTRACT

In 'Selfhood and context: some Indian solutions,' Alfred Collins and Prakash Desai examine the Indian concepts of atman and ahamkara, translated as 'transcendent self' and 'ego self.' They trace the evolution of the concept of self in the Vedas and Upanishads, and focus on the image of the Cosmic Man, Prajapati. The chapter attempts to bring together psycho-analytic and object relations theories about the self with the Indian conceptions. The authors also point out that the Indian formulations of self exist in contemporary life, not just in the ancient texts.

Surely no culture has been more preoccupied with the experiences and concepts of a 'self' than India. At least since around 1000 BC (during the earliest or Vedic period of Indian culture) no subject has been more central to Indian thought. Solutions to India's self-questions have been extremely diverse, ranging from the orthodox Hindu attempts to assert the absoluteness and indestructibility of an inner self (*atman*), which develop from the earlier idea of a world-encompassing cosmic man, to the denial of that self's reality or importance in the *anatman* ('no self') doctrine of Buddhism, to various sorts of immanent and transcendent selves (Yoga and theistic Vedanta) and highly social practices of life stages (in the *Dharmasastras*) which provide places for a special kind of self-realization. In a way, however, a certain consensus does prevail: concepts of self in India bifurcate early on, and consistently in the classical and modern traditions two sorts of self are opposed to one another. Although there are other concepts, and wide differences of meaning for these two selves in different schools of thought, the opposition of these two is almost universal, and it may be helpful to view them under the rubrics *atman* and *ahamkara*, more or less adequately translated as 'transcendent self' and 'ego self.' Both terms are present and developing in the Upanisads (around 700 BC), and have long and rich histories after this time. *Atman*, although always also a general term for all kinds of selves as we shall see in more detail later, comes to refer to a sense of '*I-ness*' supposed to be independent of, prior to, and transcendent of the flux of temporal change ('*samsara*') and the particulars of personality and world. It is also ultimately interior, being for instance compared to a thumb-sized man within the heart. *Ahamkara*, literally the 'utterance of the word "*I*",' became closely related to pride and an inflated sense of personal worth which was thought to result from ignorance of one's true nature. Two words often used with *ahamkara* suggest its narcissistic dimensions: *gaurva*, 'swollen and heavy with a sense of self importance,' and *smaya*, 'the smile of pride of one who receives a compliment or views himself in a mirror, etc.' (definitions from Hulin, 1978). Needless to say, *atman* is one of the most (if not *the* most) positively valenced of Indian philosophical terms, while *ahamkara* is one of the deadliest (if not *the* deadliest) of 'sins.'

Full discussions of the early development of the two terms will be found in Renou (1951) for *atman*, and van Buitenen (1957) and Biardeau (1965) for *ahamkara*, while both words have been treated in Hulin's recent book on the Indian self. Briefly, *atman* (cognate with ancient Greek *atmos*, 'breath') began as both a reflexive term ('myself,' etc.) and a name for that part of a person which acts as the center for a set of otherwise discrete parts. Thus, in very early literature, *atman* is used to describe the breathing, pulmonary trunk of the body which unites the arms and legs. In general, it was the unity, totality or inner life principle or soul of a person, and even later, in the classical tradition, *atman* retains an implicit reference to the unity of the body and its psychological faculties. From a name for a person's wholeness, *atman* came to designate a profoundly spiritual 'numinous' sense of conscious selfhood, very close to many western definitions of the self.

Ahamkara was a word invented by the priestly authors of the Upanisads. It was used primarily to denote the sense of '*I*-ness' or 'mine-ness' which arises in a child at a certain age, or by extension in a creator god or creative principle at a certain moment in cosmogenesis, the moment after which individuation or separation of particular entities is an issue or fact. In different ways both *atman* and *ahamkara* named a sense of *I*-ness, while this became understood as positive for non-bodily and transcendent *atman* and negative for bodily and worldly *ahamkara*. There is an easy, effortless quality to many descriptions of *atman*, whereas *ahamkara* is typically filled with struggle to claim, assert or become a self. One could view much of Indian philosophy as an attempt to separate 'true' (positive, *atman*-like) from 'false' (negative, *ahamkara*-like) selfhood.

In this chapter, we shall attempt to look more deeply into these ideas, tracing the evolution of the concepts of 'self' by a review of the early Indian literature of the Vedas and Upanisads, focusing on the career of the Cosmic Man, Prajapati. Our purpose is to bring together psychoanalytic and ancient Indian theories about the self. We will also try to show that the Indian concerns and formulations are not simply ancient or textual. The parallels in contemporary Indian life are remarkable in their continuity with the ancient tradition. We will further attempt to use psychoanalytic thought to uncover common theoretical grounds for understanding India's diverse views of the self, and will show that *atman* and *ahamkara* can be reconciled by a deeper understanding of their implicit natures and functions.

The Indian concern with selves (especially of the *atman*-type) is notorious in the west, and has been debated there for the past 200 years or more by various romantic apologists and tough-minded detractors. These include, respectively, Romain Rolland and Sigmund Freud whose correspondence on the 'oceanic feeling' is well known (Freud, 1930).[1] Some of the most sensitive (and positive) western views of the Indian sense of an *atman*-self have been those of literary artists – Forster, Hesse, Kipling and Eliot come to mind. Anthropologists, psychologists and psychoanalysts who have recently begun studying the personalities of actual Indians and their social relations have in general been more negative, and have not discovered a stable and definite self, individuality or ego boundaries in India. Dumont (1970), working from historical texts, locates individual selfhood only at the level of society as an organic whole, or in the king or brahman ('priest') who are its center and source respectively, although he recognizes a second sort of individuality in the world renouncer (*sannyasin*). Marriott interprets Indian understandings of persons as concerning open 'dividuals' (Inden and Marriott 1977) whose physical and social skins designate only moments in indefinitely ongoing, substantial liquid processes, a dynamic of particulate exchanges (called 'mixing' to the extent that they are irreflexive, that is, externally related; 'marking' when asymmetrical; and 'unmatching' insofar as they lack affinity and are unstable or intransitive (Marriott, 1980).

Roland (1980) identifies a 'familial self' characterized by partial mergers, as of fathers and son (called 'idealizing self object' relationships following Kohut, 1971), but like Dumont also allows for an immanent and transcendent self apart from the familial one. Kakar (1981) from an Eriksonian perspective, identifies an unstable alternation of self-regard between grandiosity and self-devaluation as characteristic of the Indian personality. B.K. Ramanujan (1980), in a lucid essay, acknowledges a reality behind the notorious Hindu 'confusion' of what westerners distinguish as inside/outside, self/other, etc., but considers that an actual Indian cognitive style analogous to what linguists call 'context sensitivity,' has been misinterpreted as a psychological defect by western observers. This linguistic metaphor asserts that what is said, thought, done or felt need not be a result of an ideally stable interior self 'expressing its needs,' as it were, but rather the more or less appropriate response of an *Ahamkara*-self to the environment of the moment. Like Dumont and Roland, Ramanujan recognizes a necessary concern with universals or entities which need not correspond to any particular contexts, but such invariable, 'context-free' ideas (*moksa*, *atman*, etc.) he takes to be of clearly secondary interest and emphasis for ordinary Indian thought. This distinction between two kinds of self (contextual *v.* transcendent, etc.) has been called 'split-level consciousness' (Desai, 1980; Desai and Coelho, 1981). This concept indicates a frequent split between public and private selves, i.e., what one expresses outwardly (or pretends) and what one *really* feels or believes.

Ramanujan observes a key fact about the emergence of 'universals' in Indian thought. In each of the cases he cites (the explosive experience of linguistic meaning – *sphota*, the transcendent esthetic experience – *rasa*, and spiritual release – *moksa* – 'the pattern is the same: a necessary sequence in time with strict rules of phase and context ending in a free state.' For each of his examples, interestingly, the traditions abound with controversy about the same central dilemma: does or does not (and if so *how* does) the context-sensitive flow preceding the moment of 'freedom' bring the latter about? In what way is this flow even relevant to freedom? (cf. Biardeau, 1964; Masson and Patwardhan, 1969). In the Vedanta school of thought, for example, Sankara concludes that the only 'context' which brings about enlightenment (realization of absolute *atman*-self) is the hearing of certain sentences from the Upanisads ('I am *brahman*, [the absolute reality]' etc.) from the spiritual preceptor or guru by a disciple with a properly prepared, receptive mind (Lacombe, 1939). Meditation, yoga, etc., cannot *create* the experience of enlightenment (*moksa*). All they can do is help to remove obstacles and peel away the sense of *ahamkara* which has been superimposed on the eternally free and unique *atman*.

Nevertheless, a 'context' *is* always there, even in Vedanta. Indeed, *in practice*, receiving truth from a Vedantic guru is an exceedingly contextual business. One eats with him, sits with him, is praised and insulted by him for one's subtly appropriate or inappropriate responses. At a certain moment one's mind is ripe and can receive the guru's message: then arises that profound sort of mutual appropriation of guru and disciple about which the Gita says, 'I am in him and he is in me' (*Bhagavad Gita*, IX-29). Again in practice it is not just the repetition of the great Upanisadic sentences which occurs at these moments. Indeed, the folklore of discipleship holds that every moment of contact with the guru, however humble, is potentially a moment of enlightenment, if the disciple's mind is ready.[2] The lesson is important, and is also exemplified in Indian theories of meaning and esthetics: moments of context-free self-feeling, esthetic appreciation and linguistic meaning arise when there is a perfect matching and therefore the possibility of union or merging of inside and outside, subject and predicate, agent and context, guru and disciple. In the Ayurvedic Indian medical literature, as Zimmerman (1975) points out, 'appropriateness' (*satmya*), the key to health, is defined as 'that which is pleasing to the self.' We could paraphase both the Vedantic and Ayurvedic positions in this way – moments of appropriateness give rise to a sense of self.

Notions of the 'self' in psychoanalysis and related depth-psychological traditions have a long and still-expanding history. Freud's concept of 'ego,' as has been noted by LaPlanche and Pontalis (1973), was never intended to designate a purely structural entity. The essential ambiguity of ego as the representative of reality, source of defence, etc., and ego as also a libidinal or narcissistic object (and hence really a *self* image) has been one of the greatest sources of creativity within psychoanalysis. Hartmann's (1964) attempts to clarify the concepts of ego and self were basic to the development of ego psychology, but may have separated these concepts too sharply (cf. Kohut, 1968).

It is widely recognized that Freud's interest in intrapsychic processes sometimes led him to put less emphasis on the environment and its appropriateness to the person than on conflicts within the psyche. In spite of this, however, there are abundant indications of his ongoing, always-implicit concern with the self-environment relationship. This concern is quite evident in the 'metapsychology' papers written around 1915. One telling example is the idea of the 'purified pleasure ego' (Freud 1915). This entity was thought to include the environment as part of the (fantasied) self, in so far as that was pleasurable. In other words, the appropriate part of the environment was included within the sense of self, while the inappropriate part became the 'other,' along with the pain it induced. An understanding of a part of the self as outside is implicit in this formulation. Even more significant was Freud's (1917) dictum that 'the shadow of the object has fallen on the ego' which led to the idea that aspects of the ego are based on the relationship between self and object images. Perhaps the most telling instance of Freud's concern with the self's environment, and the infantile feeling of unity between self and world that sometimes lives on into adulthood 'side by side' with what the modern west thinks of as a more normal sense of separateness from the world, is found in *Civilization and its Discontents* (Freud 1930, p. 68).

266

Selfhood in context

Our preliminary overview of the Indian literature on selfhood suggests that inner experiences of selfhood were always correlated with a certain environmental 'appropriateness,' although this was consciously denied by some Indian philosophic traditions. At this moment we simply note the parallel with psychoanalysis, and suggest that some of the same perplexities are present both in Indian thought and psychoanalytic object relations theories. Perhaps the most important of these is this: *Is the self located wholly within the person, or is it partly located (or felt to be located) outside, among objects? Conversely, is the world entirely outside the self, or has it somehow come to reside within?* These are clearly questions to which psychoanalytic ideas concerning internalization are relevant, and these ideas will be considered later in the discussion.

The earliest self-experience has been imaginatively reconstructed by Erikson (1981) and Kohut (1978) as something prior to any clear sense of oneself as separate and different from the 'other.' They suggest that a sort of self-awareness, or perhaps better a sense of selfhood, arises epigenetically in all babies fortunate enough to have responsive mothering. The experience may be marked by the selective smiling response to the mother, an ecstatic moment when the mother's and infant's mutual delight in the other's existence lays the groundwork for the narcissistic development line of self regard. The heart of narcissistic development seems to be in this highly emotional, 'numinous' experience of '*I*-ness,' Erikson (1968, 1981) hypothesizes that this I-ness quickly becomes associated with sources of pleasure and effectiveness (sex organs, musculature, cognitive faculties), and shortly thereafter is constrained by social considerations of shame and guilt, and becomes 'ritualized' in identification with a social self acceptable to parents and society.[3]

Like Erikson, Kohut wrestled with the question of the relationship between the self as such and its specific abilities, self-images, goals, etc. In Kohut's terminology the question becomes: what is the relationship between the 'whole self' and the parts which seem to comprise it, or even between this whole self and the 'nuclear self' in which self-parts are organized through more or less well-developed narcissistic configurations?[4] Kohut's most developed thoughts on this subject are contained in a lengthy letter written in 1974 and revised subsequently as part of his collected writings (1978). These 'Remarks about the Formation of the Self' record Kohut's movement from the position that 'self nuclei'

267

('body-mind fragments') coalesce into a total self to the idea (which he never abandoned) that 'the developmental path of the experience of (the child's) self is separate from that followed by his experience of the single body parts and single bodily and mental functions.' Again, 'The child's self experience arises separately, increasing in importance as it develops next to and, more and more, above his experience of body parts and single functions. . . . The parts, in other words, do not build up the self, they become built into it.' The primary evidence for the view of developmental lines for the whole self and part selves is Kohut's observation that the environment (mother) responds to the child 'with two sets of responses: one is attuned to his experience of single parts of his body . . . and another is attuned to his beginning experience of himself as a . . . coherent and enduring organization, i.e., to him as a self.' Kohut (1977) also speaks of this primal self as a 'self in *statu nascendi*,' 'a virtual self,' 'primed,' as it were, to respond to the mother's treating it *as* a whole self by becoming one.

There is an ambiguity of the '*I*-sense' or self in the theories just described. The I-sense is considered by Erikson and Kohut to be a primary fact of existence, and only secondarily identified with sources of pleasure, abilities, goals, rules of conscience, etc. And yet it apparently always arises in a moment of intimate interaction with a 'context' (usually the mother and her emotional responsiveness to the young child).

Kohut's paradigmatic situation is the 'mirroring' relationship between the mother and infant, where the child's nascent selfhood is conveyed to it by the 'gleam in the mother's eye.' The mother's attention is a necessary context for the baby's self-experience. But clearly this situation is *also* one where the baby rests in the mother's arms, or in bed (an extension of her body), and just after or shortly before the intimate sharing with her in nursing. Libidinal and narcissistic relatedness are inseparable, and classical psychoanalysts have properly criticized Kohut for minimizing the emotionally charged libidinal aspects of the relationship out of which the self experience arises.

But note the parallel with the Indian situation described earlier. There, too, we hypothesized that the experience of selfhood, analogous to Kohut's *I*-ness, arises only in a context of warm emotional relatedness. If the ultimately private, interior sense of the *I* occurs only in the context of effective relationships, we have a natural paradox, one not generated by culture-specific choices, but rather which people of all cultures must face. Hence another purpose of this essay is to explore how Indians have dealt with the paradox, and compare this with several western depth-psychological solutions, showing how this paradox can be over-come.

'I' THEORY IN THE WEST

Let us examine some recent psychoanalytic theories a little further. Erik Erikson (1981), writing of the *I*-experience in Jesus' Galilean sayings, lists several essential ingredients of perceiving oneself as an '*I*'. First, and most central, is *numinosity*: 'The *I*, after all, is the ground for the . . . assurance that each person is a center of awareness . . . a center so numinous that it amounts to a sense of being alive, and more, of being the vital condition of existence' (p. 323). A second essential feature is the *I*'s '*luminosity*,' its consciousness. It was this aspect of the self that William James (1890) called the 'I' or 'pure ego' in opposition to the 'me' or objective self. Third, Erikson finds essential to the emergence of the *I*-sense an interplay with a maternal Other who in some sense is perceived as a primal *You*. From the beginning, according to Erikson, there is a sense of 'binary' relatedness inherent in the *I*; and the *I* and the *You* are different, though intimately joined. Erikson (1981, p. 330) makes it clear that the child contributes to the mother's *I*-sense as well as gaining his *I*-sense from her: 'it seems of vital importance that this Other [the mother] and, indeed, related others, in turn experience the new being as a *presence* that heightens *their* sense of *I*.' To translate Erikson's idea in Kohutian terms, we may say that the child is a self object for the mother as much as she is for him, and their interaction has the mutuality of a field in which both participate. A fourth necessary ingredient of *I*-ness is a sense of 'centrality,' related to which is a feeling of *inner autonomy*, amounting to a sense of being able *to act effectively*.

Much of Erikson's essay discusses how the *I*-sense could maintain itself in the daily life of some Jews of ancient times who were subjected to an environment that negated in one way or another almost all of its essential conditions. According to Erikson, the solutions arrived at formed the basis of the Jewish and Christian religions; in both cases, though more strongly in Judaism, the *I* was preserved by being lodged in a God who is the transcendent center of the life of the community and of the individual. Hence, Jehovah said to Moses, '*I* am that *I* am.' Religion compensates for a threatened *I* by transcending the need for a supportive context, but also itself supports the *I*-sense of the believing community, becoming a *new* context. One of the most important ways that the Jewish God does this, Erikson suggests, is by strengthening the father-son, or 'patrilineal' identification of the *I*-sense (by stressing the relationship of selfhood to the 'fathers': Moses, etc.) and ultimately connecting it with the idea of the *nation* Israel as a historical entity transcending actual geographic boundaries and to some extent, cultures. This illustrates a fifth essential quality of the *I*: its continuity. We shall find a similar phenomenon in India, where the *ahamkara*-self is sometimes defined through a continuous father-son lineality stretching back through the ancestors to the gods.

In Kohut's (1977) epigenetic theory, the 'spark in the mother's eye' as she looks at him awakens a virtually pre-existent self-experience in the young infant; similarly Erikson speaks of 'the early feeding situation of the human infant, including that meeting of eye to eye which, it is increasingly clear, is an important source of the sense of *I* and of a primal *we*.' But for Kohut a second and equally important source of the *I* is an 'idealizing merger' with the parent (usually the father for the boy). The child's still-shaky *I*-sense is included and participates in the much more glorious *I*-sense and personal effectiveness of the parent, thus strengthening itself. Both this idealizing sort of relationship and the mirroring relationship with the mother Kohut calls 'self-object' relations. In normal development they become partially internalized as ambitions and ideals out of which develop a relatively permanent 'cohesive self,' but no one ever becomes able wholly to do without a contextual contribution to his sense of *I*.

Explicit in Kohut's work is a model of the self that embeds it essentially (although less and less with psychological development) in its mirroring and idealized environment. It is the partial and optimal failure of this environment to meet the person's efforts to view it through the rosy spectacles of the two self-object configurations that brings about internalization, the process whereby mirroring and idealizing become aspects of inner structure, partially independent of the environment. Kohut, however, does not consider the possibility of a culturally-defined environment that *does* live up to the person's self-object informed expectations, or of a self that is more capable of altering itself to find the world an appropriate context for its selfhood. Would internalization occur in such a case? Is it possible for a culture to provide a responsive self-object context which could endure in healthy individuals for a lifetime? Conversely, could persons in that culture learn to transform their selves in order to make the environment more appropriate to them? We will suggest that India approaches such a culture.

THE INDIAN SELF IN THE VEDIC PERIOD: A CASE HISTORY

Self-feeling, so far as it can be discerned in the older Indian texts (*Rig Veda* primarily), was essentially an event closely connected with moments of creation, especially as manifested in the ecstacy of poetic inspiration, and in the gods' magnificent sense of effectiveness in the act of cosmogenesis religious sacrifice and poetic thought participated in and assisted at the opening of the world. Simon and Weiner (1966) have noted a similar function of poetry in Homeric Greece; in both Greece and the *Rig Veda* poetic inspiration magnifies a man's sense of aliveness and agency by uniting him experientially with the cosmic environment; in neither case is any concept of self an explicit object of reflection, but we see here several of the essential qualities of selfhood identified by Erikson (1981) – numinosity, mutuality of self and object, a search for continuity, and a powerful sense of effectiveness.

In the *Purusasukta* hymn which occurs late in the *Rig Veda* (X.90), cosmic sacrificial celebrations (exchanges between poetic man and the cosmos) were interpreted as acts of a single giant figure, a Cosmic Man (*Purusa*) whose body was found to contain the whole cosmos through identification of his articulated parts with those of the cosmic regions (his breath was the wind, his eye the sun, etc.). The Cosmic Man, and his human counterpart the Sacrificer (the man who paid for the rite), were symbolically reborn from a pre-cosmic state of things, a sort of undifferentiated matrix, called *brahman*. The complement of his birth was, however, the Cosmic Man's death through dissection or fragmentation, and various means were sought to ward this off or deny it. These led to subsequent efforts to internalize the sacrifice within the bodily, mental or spiritual self of the human person, so that nothing remained outside to threaten the cohesiveness of this self (cf. Collins, 1976).

Thus arose the Upanisadic doctrine of an homunculus-self called *atman*, not yet equivalent to the transcendent *atman* but on the way to it. This thumb-sized version of the Cosmic Man within the heart (*angustha-matra-purusa*) served to allay some of the fear of dissolution that was widespread at this time, but was not completely successful. For example, the quest of the Buddha was motivated by his perception of both the futility of the communal sacrifice of the Cosmic Man and the fragility and transcience of the sacrificer's body, and led to a total rejection of attachment to any kind of *ahamkara* or bodily self, even of the subtle kind represented by the humunculus self.

We may speculate, as a result of this disquiet, some Upanisadic thought moved towards interpreting the Cosmic Man, and even the humunculus self, as resting on a yet more subtle and interior self, the nonbodily and indestructible, transcendent *atman*. Thus the fear of death (understood as a narcissistic fear of bodily-mental self dissolution) which the earlier ritual-mythical thought had not removed, was at least temporarily and for some people overcome.

We will attempt to explore this development in more detail, using the device of treating the Cosmic Man as a case history. We will call him Prajapati, literally the 'Father of Offspring' or 'Lord of Creatures,' although he takes on many names and personalities. Our approach will treat Prajapati as a model of the life cycle of the ancient Indian self. We will begin with his birth.

Prajapati's birth is repeatedly described in physical terms in the texts. But typically he is not born of a mother or other singular person; often he arises from the pre-cosmic Waters, an image also very common in the *Rig Veda*.

> In the beginning this world was nothing but a sea of water. The Waters desired to be born (propagate themselves). They worked at inward brooding (*tapas*), became heated and produced a golden egg. The egg floated for one year, and Prajapati was born from it. That is why women, cows and mares give birth after one year. *Sathpatha Brahmana* XI.I.6.1–2

Prajapati's birth usually results, as here, from a *desire* on his 'mothers' part to 'be born'. The verb for 'be born' (*prajayemahi*) occurring in the present text (from *pra-ja/jan* in the optative middle voice) expresses parents' desires for an act of 'birth' in which the distinction between parent and infant is not sharply drawn, a nondistinction which permits the parents' existence to continue in the child.

A very common Vedic expression is *prajabhih prayayemhai*, 'May we be born through progeny!' This is a prayer for the speaker's lineage to be 'extended' through the birth of offspring (*praja*). The idea of *extending* a man's lineage is even more explicit in the expression *tanayebhih tanute*, 'He extends (*tan-,*' to extend, hold out') himself through offspring.' The idea of a selfhood uniting a man and his son is omnipresent in the Vedic literature, for example, in the expression, 'You are the *atman* (self) called Son' addressed to the newborn male child by the father (*Paraskara Grhya Sutra* I.16.18 and *Satapatha Brahmana* XIV.9.4.26). When the father dies, he transfers his vital breaths (*prana*-s) into the son, and gives him the sacred knowledge of transcendent *brahman*, which is itself often spoken of as a man's true self.[5] The waters in our story desire to have offspring; but at the same time (part of the same idea) they desire to extend or prolong themselves, or cause themselves to ripen or mature, or become widely disseminated. Prajapati *is* the ripened or extended state of the Waters. All of these ideas are present in the *Rig Veda* at the very beginning of Indian culture, and derive from a basic conception of the parent–child relationship which stresses generational continuity over separation. Simon and Weiner (1966, p. 312) find a similar conception in Homeric Greece, where 'poetry links previous generations with the present generation,' thus blurring 'the lines of individual identity.'

The connection of the father–son unity with the world of the gods (similar to what Erikson finds in Judaism) is clear at *Aitareya Aranyaka* II.1.8.

This world was water: This (water) was the root, that (world) was the shoot, this the father, those the sons. Whatever is the son's is the father's and whatever is the father's is the son's. Mahidasa Aitareya who knew this said, 'I know myself as reaching to the gods, and the gods as reaching to me.'

'Birth' extends the self in (the form of) a person's offspring. It causes a preceding formless, fluid state to become more definite, in something like an act of self-ripening (expressed also by the idea of *tapas*, 'inward brooding').

Equally fundamental to Prajapati's birth is the requirement of self unification.

> In the beginning were the seven Breaths (*prana-s*). They were indefinite and formless (*asat*). They made themselves into seven Persons, but realizing that they could not be born (propagate themselves) in this condition made the seven Persons into one Person. This Person became Prajapati. *Satapatha Brahmana*, VI.1.1.

This story expresses the multiplicity of Prajapati's origins, rather like Melanie Klein's 'part objects,' or Kohut's early idea of multiple 'self nuclei' (Kohut, 1978; also see Gedo, 1979). Implicitly, a determinate, cohesive world arises out of a preceding state of indeterminacy or disorder. The self of Prajapati completes him 'as the whole completes the parts' (Renou, 1951): it is a principle by which cohesion is constructed. In summary, the self is made firm and cohesive through its lineal descent and continuity into future generations; the movement is in both directions, as self-definition increases with time but also with recognition of the self's inherence in earlier states of being (the gods and ancestors).

While Prajapti's birth is discussed repeatedly, the theme of his infancy is given little attention. It does appear frequently enough, however, to suggest that Prajapati's status as archetypal Man extended to all stages of the human life cycle.

> When Prajapati was born from the golden egg he floated on the egg-shell for one year. At the end of the year he spoke the one and two syllable words, 'Bhuh, Bhuvah, Svah,' and each word became the division of the cosmos which it named (earth, atmosphere, sky). Therefore, a child speaks words of one and two syllables at one year of age. Prajapati's words also became the five seasons. Also after one year Prajapati stood up, on the three parts of the cosmos. This is why a child stands at one year. *Satapatha Brahmana*, XI.1.6.1-6.

Here we have a record of two of Prajapati's 'developmental milestones,' the age of speaking his first words and of standing upright. As we saw before, Prajapati's actions are taken as paradigmatic for humans.

Our record of Prajapati's life takes a jump from age one year to the time of his own parenthood; the texts are concerned almost exclusively, it would seem, with issues of reproduction and their implication for the self of parent and child. Prajapati, like the Waters, etc., 'desires' to reproduce himself (the verbs are *ja/jan*, as before, and *srj-* 'to emit, release, emanate, let flow out'). Prajapati's motives are various, but one of the most important seems to be *hunger. Ub ibe stirtm Orahaoatu* (or Hunger personified) was hungry and made other beings in order to eat them.

> Prajapati, called Death and Hunger, creates offspring in order to eat them. Thus, he is called Aditi (a form of the Mother goddess; a play on words is present: *ad* means 'eat'). In the beginning was only Hunger or Death. He thought, 'Let me have a self.' He sang and water flowed out of him. Whatever he created out of the water he desired to eat. After many preliminary creations, Death produced the Sacrificial Horse and sacrificed it to himself (i.e., he ate it). Whoever knows this avoids death, for he becomes the very self (*atman*)of death. *Brhadaranyaka Upanisad*, I.2

Most of the time, however, Prajapati does not, like an Indian Kronos, eat up his offspring. Most texts celebrate the tremendous extent of his procreativity, giving long lists of his issue. A good example is the cosmogenic story which begins Manu'd Dharmasastra. Three other examples from the *satapatha Brahmana* follow:

> Prajapati emitted the Waters, which evolved into foam that became in succession clay, sand, pebbles, stones, ore and gold. *Satapatha Brahmana*, VI.1.3.1-6.

> Prajapati desired to reproduce himself and practice *tapas* (inward brooding, concentration). He released the waters, which flowed out of his body. Then he entered the waters in the form of an egg which evolved into the cosmos, including the earth and the plants and animals which live on it. *Satapatha Brahmana* VI.1.1.1-15.

> When Prajapti had produced living beings he looked about and from delight his semen flowed. Semen is life-sap (*rasa*), and as

far as life-step reaches so far extends Prajapati's self. *Satapatha Brahmana*, VI.2.2.6.

We see here again the fluidity of the initial stages of self-emanation, and in the first story the progression from softer to harder materials (water, foam, clay, sand, pebbles, stones, ore, gold).

A sad, but for the authors of the Brahmanas, overwhelmingly significant result of Prajapati's grandiose self-extension was his *falling apart* into the entities he emitted. Often these are cosmic elements (as above); equally often ritual elements or parts of the body are mentioned.

Prajapati produced creatures, and having 'run the whole race' (image of a complete cycle of existence) fell asunder. The Breath (*prana*) went out of him, and then vigor (*tegas*) departed. He fell down and food poured out of his eye. *Satapatha Brahmana*, VII1.2.1.

Having produced creatures Prajapati fell apart, and the Breath (*prana*) went out of him. The five bodily parts into which he fell were: hair, skin, flesh, bone and marrow. He also fell apart into the five seasons and five regions of space. *Satapatha Brahmana*, VI.1.2.17-19.

Prajapati's disintegration into his world is a central theme of the earlier texts, and solutions to this apparently distressing event are at the heart of those texts and also the *Upanisads*. Various solutions are already present in the early texts, many making use of the father–son unity to reintegrate the father by emphasizing the inherence of the father in the son, by the son's action to save the father, or more darkly, by reabsorbing the son into our father's bodily self.

When Prajapati had fallen apart and all the food flowed out of his eye, Agni ('Fire') ate all of it up. Prajapati's Breath (*prana*) became the wind, and his vigor became the sun. When these were heated, all Prajapati's Breath, vigor and food came back into him. Thus, in the Sacrifice, when the Sacrificer heats the offering, puts it on a golden plate and adds kindling sticks, he puts Breath, vigor and food back into himself and reintegrates himself. *Satapatha Brahmana*, VII.1.1.4-10.

The personified fire god, Agni, has here become an alter ego for

Prajapati – he eats up the products of his father's self-extension, thereby reintegrating them into his (which is also to say his father's) self, Prajapati is reunited through being eaten: since father and son are one and identical, there is no difference between eating and being eaten, and this is the point. The tactic of the son reconstructing the father leads at times to a reversal of their status. This is illustrated in the following episode where the son gives his name to the father rather than the reverse (as is usual).

> Prajapati had created everything and fell apart. He said to Agni, 'Restore me.' Agni replied, 'What will I get for doing it?' Prajapati said, 'People will call me after you, for whichever of the sons is successful in life, after him they call the father, grandfather, great-grandfather, son and grandson.' Saying, 'So be it,' Agni restored his father. Therefore, while being Prajapati, people call him Agni. *Satapatha Brahmana* VI.1.1.10–13.

The idea of the son reconstituting and reintegrating the old, decrepit father by eating him ('incorporating,' as we might say using a psychoanalytic term with oral connotations) is similarly inverted in the Sraddhas, or memorial offerings for the dead 'fathers' (father, grandfather and great-grandfather). These offerings have the aim of reconstructing the departed ancestors' bodies (Knipe, 1977; O'Flaherty, 1980) by feeding them balls of food (*pinda-s*) that represent their bodies. The balls are prescribed to be eaten by Brahmans or cows who represent the 'fathers,' or thrown into fire or water (Kane, 1973, p. 480), evidently so that they can be returned to a fluid condition in order to be reconstituted and the fathers reborn and maintained in heaven. The underlying oneness of father and son is clearly visible in the fertilizing effects of the *pinda* offerings for the *son*: the ceremony is repeatedly said to produce offspring for him. For example, it is explicitly stated that if the wife of the son offering the *Sraddha* eats a *pinda* while repeating the sentence, 'Place an embryo (in me), O Fathers!', she will give birth to a son endowed with various auspicious qualities (Kane, 1973, p.480). Again, it appears that the son can save the father either by eating him or feeding (i.e., being eaten by) him. In either case, both father and son benefit. As the *Aitareya Aranyaka*, II.5 says, 'when the father supports the child before its birth and thereafter he really supports himself,' since father and son are one self.

277

An earlier instance where the father 'eats' the son in order to reconstruct himself is the following.

Prajapati had emitted creatures and entered them in the form of his son, Agni. Then he searched for that boy, desiring the forms which Agni had taken on. Aware of this, Agni entered even more animal forms. Prajapati found him, and again desired to 'fit Agni's forms to his own self.' He cut off the heads and put them on himself, thinking that the animal's essence lay in the heads, and that by putting them on himself he would prevent the Sacrifice (himself) from falling apart. But he was mistaken: the *bodies*, which he had not assimilated to himself, had gone into water and clay. He took these and made a brick, baked it, and took it to himself also. Then he was complete. *Satapatha Brahmana*, VI.2.1.

Prajapati, in effect, kills his own son in order to reintegrate his creative energies and re-establish a cohesive self. This refusal of the father to give his body and powers to the son is a common theme, and seems to be the meaning of the famous Sunahsepa story of the *Aitareya Brahmana* (Gonda, 1975, 394–5). The Indian father's animus towards his son has been called the 'Laius Complex' by A.K. Ramanujan (1972).

Sometimes Father Prajapati is saved from disintegration through his identity with the son who reintegrates him into his (the son's) body, or is himself reintegrated into the father's self or body. At other times, we are told that Prajapati preserves his cohesiveness by separating his own good and bad parts, and defeating or in other ways getting rid of the bad parts. The image is usually that of a struggle between the gods and demons (Asuras), both of which are sons of Prajapati. The bad side of the father is identified as the cause of Prajapati's disintegration, and by defeating or abandoning it he makes himself purely good and thereby immortal.

Desirous of offspring, Prajapati continued his inward brooding (tapas). He put the power of reproduction into himself and made the gods from the breath of his mouth. They entered the sky and were his daylight. By breathing downward he created the Asuras. They entered the earth and were his darkness. He knew that he had created evil (*papman*) since there was darkness for him then. Hence, he put the evil into the Asuras and cast them aside. *Satapatha Brahmana*, XI.1.6.1-10.

On attaining the earth which they had sought through the Sacrifice, the gods saw only darkness. They made a special offering to Nirrti, the goddess of Destruction, to dispel the darkness. Prajapati had fallen apart, and the gods placed him as seed into the fire-pan to be reborn. All his evil parts, the mucus and embryonic coverings, they removed and sent to Nirrti. Thus, Prajapati and the sacrificer tread evil and destruction underfoot. Evil is whatever is nonspecific 'not (yet) a thing' into nothings, lacking quality, undifferentiated, (*alaksana, asat*)' thus, Prajapati makes evil and corruption (*asat*). The sacrificer is instructed to leave Nirrti's place without looking back, and not to touch her offering or place during the rite. Thus, he separates himself from evil and corruption, and 'unbinds' his own life-force (*ayus*). *Satapatha Brahmana*, VII.2.1.

During the Royal Consecration (Rajasuya) an offering is made to Nirrti to separate Prajapati's evil (*papman*) from him. The evil is represented by a portion of rice which is placed in an ant hill, and apparently represents the embryonic coverings which must be removed (Heesterman, 1957).

Perhaps even more important than the tactic of getting rid of evil, putting it out of sight and mind, is the pushing of Prajapati's disintegration to the limit, to the point of his 'having run his course' and being 'consumed and useless' (*Satapatha Brahmana*, VI.8.2.6.); at this moment of maximal disintegration (a predominant symbol of this ultra-chaotic – in Sanskrit, *tamasika* – state is ashes), Prajapati's remains are returned to his Mothers, often the Waters, to be reborn and reconstructed. For example, Prajapati's evil parts are offered to Nirrti in the Royal Consecration and placed in an ant hill, a container which often functions as a symbolic womb out of which life is reborn. (References in Heesterman, 1957.)

After the ashes have been removed from the fire-pan in the Agnicayana rite, they are placed in a bag and thrown into the water. As they float, a small portion is taken back and put into the fire-pan, which represents Agni's body. The text explains this procedure with a story: The gods reflected on what to do with the ashes: 'If we make these ashes, such as they are, part of our own self we shall become mortal bodies, not freed from evil (*papman*); and if we cast it away we shall put outside of Agni what is of Agni's nature. (In other words, to assimilate the 'dead' ashes would make the self *mortal*, while to exclude them would make it *incomplete*.) After considering this dilemma, they decided to put the ashes into the water, 'for the water is the foundation of this universe.' They say, 'O divine waters, receive these ashes and put them in a soft and fragrant place. Matter that is consumed has run its course and is useless.' By being placed in the waters the ashes can be reborn as part of Agni's self. The waters are therefore called Agni's mothers. The ashes settle in the waters which are his womb; having united with his mother, Agni is said to shine brightly again, and to have returned home. He lies most happily in his mother's lap. Thus renewed, he is asked to come again to men with food and new life: 'With wealth return, O Agni, overflow with the all-feeding stream on every side.' *Satapatha Brahmana*, VI.8.2.1-8.

It is interesting that Prajapati's disintegration is associated with a goddess, Nirrti (whose name means Decay or Dissolution), since it is through another feminine power (the Waters, *brahman*, etc.) that he is reborn. But the key fact is that it is his 'evil' which is reborn as nourishment. This theme can be summarized in the rubric, '*papman* becomes *sri*', 'evil becomes auspiciousness.' The same theme is found in contemporary South India, where the function of transforming death into nurturant substance is a property of *women* (Reynolds, 1980).

Prajapati's career, like the seasonal nature that he impersonates, is endlessly circular, moving from formlessness or emerging from the primeval, maternal waters, to the creatures of this world who decoy into, and then again into the waters. Prajapati 'extends' himself in a circle back to his original state, and is then ready to create anew. To express the matter in Marriott's (1976) terms, he moves from his cool ('unmixed'), also whole and integrated ('matched') state of being, in which he lacks specific form (is 'unmarked') to a state of being manifest in many specific forms ('marked' and 'mixed') but disarticulated ('unmatched'); thence he travels back again to his unmarked, unmixed and matched beginnings. One may compare the similarly mobile god Visnu, who alternates along a straight path between a latent, sleeping (unmixed, matched) state during dark periods of cosmic dissolution and an active, reproductive wakefulness during times of his bright cosmic manifestation, when he mixes with and marks the world to restore it to an appropriately marked and matched state of order.

In summary, Prajapati's wholeness is restored, and his disintegration reversed by the following strategies:

1 Prajapati eats or otherwise assimilates his offspring, thus reconstituting himself by reintegrating his dispersed substance.
2 Prajapati is eaten by his son, and participates in his son's wholeness. This strategy is nearly the same as the first, but involves a reversal of father–son status.
3 Prajapati gets rid of his bad parts, which represent his disintegration and identifies with the good or cohesive side.
4 After falling apart, Prajapati's parts are reintroduced into his mother's womb, and he is reborn whole.

One can view of these attempts to redeem Prajapati in terms of self-environment 'appropriateness,' or in the language of the texts, making the world Prajapati's *own*. As Heesterman (1964) says, the ideal sacrificer, Prajapati's human representative, 'is born into a world he has made himself.' This is one significance of the doctrine of *karma* (that actions always have results) for the actor's selfhood: through his self-sacrificial activity of making a world of creatures from his own substance the world is made *appropriate* to his cohesive selfhood, rather than destructive of it.

> The initiant (Diksita) pours out his own self into the firepan, the womb. As he becomes initiated, he makes a world for himself, and when he has become fully initiated, he is born into that world.
> *Satapathan Brahmana*, VI.2.2.27.

It is not difficult to see the issue of self-environment appropriateness operating in each of the four strategies noted above. Prajapati's eating of his offspring and being eaten by his son Agni both united Prajapati with what he has produced out of himself. But Prajapati's offspring also constitute the environment in which he exists, the whole world. The underlying idea apparently is that man produces his world by tearing himself apart. That is, the sense of a whole self is attached by environmental experiences which pull apart its wholeness, demanding responses from the parts only (cf.

Kohut, 1978). For example, the necessity to use the visual faculty to see objects in the environment must have seemed to separate vision from the whole self. Indeed, the Indian theory of perception implicit here (and explicit elsewhere) is that the world outside is created through being experienced. Perception is the process by which an 'environment' is created. Thus, the faculty of sight, and the eye, precede and cause visual objects; for example, Prajapati's sight creates the sun. This means, however, that the destructive, incohesiveness-tending nature of the environment can be redeemed through the coherence of the self from which that environment emanated; thus Prajapati 'eats' his offspring, or is 'eaten' and given a newly cohesive birth by his mother. The strategy of identifying incohesiveness as a 'bad' part of Prajapati and disposing of that incohesiveness attempts to prevent disintegration from proceeding indefinitely.

The second strategy mentioned above, that of Prajapati participating in his son's new cohesiveness, may be slightly harder to understand in terms of self-environment appropriateness, since it is collective or successive cohesiveness. In this solution the self is projected into the environment, and continues a lineage of selves that are identified as a part also of that environment. Since they extend beyond the emanating person, such new selves are sometimes thought to be assumed only after death. Generational continuity affords a protection against disintegration; one's progeny are one's self-objects, extending the 'self' beyond one's own mortal body. The part of the environment which most naturally lends itself to this projection in India is the son, although the implications of locating the father's self in the son were a source of some ambivalence for the Vedic thinkers: the son's life, once separated from the father's life, seemed to weaken the father's.[6]

THE SELF IN THE UPANISADS

After the *Brahmanas*, when thought had been focused on redeeming Prajapati from his periods of disintegration, the *Upanisads* discovered another approach to the problem of achieving a cohesive self. Rather than stressing substantial organization and articulation as the nature of selfhood, the *Upanisads* focus on an identification of the *I* with the inner unmanifest, subtle, liquid *source* of Prajapati's self organization. This can be understood as a development of the fourth strategy discussed above, that of returning Prajapati to his mother's womb. *Atman* becomes the inner, originating life-sap (*rasa*) of things rather than the structures evolved out of that liquid. The central insight seems to have been this: if one's self is the source of everything, decay and incoherence cease to be fearful, since as the *Brhadaranyaka Upanisad* has it, 'one becomes the self of death'.

> In the beginning this world was only the self (*atman*) in the shape of a person (*urusa*). Looking around, he saw nothing other than himself. He said first, 'I am;' thus arose the name 'I'. Therefore, even now when addressed one first says, 'This is I,' and then gives his other name. Because he is a person (*pursua*) existing before all other things, he burns evil. One who knows this burns up any who wants to be 'before' him. He became afraid because he was alone, but realized that he need not fear, since 'fear comes from a second.' He has no delight because he was alone, and made himself into the shape of a man and woman embracing. Thus, as the sage Yajnavalkya used to say, this body is only half of oneself, like half of a split pea. The wife fills the space of the other half.
> *Brhadaranyaka Upanisad*, I.4.1-3.

The *I*-experience here is the source of everything else, and because it is the source it can destroy ('burn up') anything in the environment which tries to oppose it. Even so, reality intrudes in the form of fear – apparently a fear akin to loneliness, or a fear of being unresponded to. The *atman*'s decision to make itself into an embracing couple seems to be a solution to this problem, after an initial attempt at denial ('Fear arises only from a second.').

The aim is to become identified with (to 'know') a self beyond the various parts and aspects of the person (body parts, perceptual faculties, etc.). This self is sometimes understood as their principle of cohesiveness. Thus, he is the one who 'connects' and 'disconnects' (*uh-* and *nir-uh-*) the parts of the person (*Brhadaranyaka Upanisad*, III.9.26). The *atman*-self appears as the 'Breath' (*prana*) which connects the parts in a cohesive whole.

> Prajapati created (manifested out of himself) the faculties of action. Each went about practicing its own specific task (Speech spoke, etc.). Death entered them, but could not enter Breath

which was in the middle. The other faculties took refuge in Breath and became 'forms' of it, thus eluding Death. *Brhadaranyaka Upanisad*, I.5.21.

Besides identifying the self with the source and principle of unity, the *Upanisads* often connect it with the essence of the world, or the aim of desire. Instead of seeking objects because one wants *them*, or needs to idealize or be mirrored by them, one seeks them only because they are a part or aspect of the 'self,' which is alone *truly* desirable. The 'self' side of the self-object seems to have become dominant, and to have totally assimilated the 'object' side.

The sage Yajnavalkya said to his wife Maitreyi, 'Not for the sake of the husband is the husband dear (to the wife); he is dear for the sake of the self.' Similarly for all other things humans hold dear. By knowing the self, one knows everything.

In the end, then, a position of absolute monism is reached, where there is no other. No more is the husband 'dear' only *because of* the self; he like everything, 'has *become* the self.' *Brhadaranyaka Upanisad*, II.4.14.

DISCUSSION OF THE PRAJAPATI/ATMAN/MATERIAL

The Cosmic man image in the Vedic Purusa and Prajapati represents an attempt to bring about a unit of man and world in fantasy. It is a grandiose fantasy which alternates with moments of disillusion and despair. The later Upanishadic *atman* doctrine just discussed seems in a way even more grandiose, since selfhood, in this theory, is freed from all the vicissitudes of life in the human and cosmic worlds and offers a kind of conceptual solution to the eternal cycle of grandiosity and despair, by transcending both phases of the cycle.

It seems clear that one motive for the grandiosity of the cosmic Man image was the need to preserve a sense of self cohesiveness and continuity in the face of the threat of fragmentation. These Kohutian ideas are expressed quite literally in the language of the Brahmanas, where the whole point of the sacrifice was to bring about cohesiveness for the sacrificer, a state of fused unity which could withstand all environmental shocks, including death. When, inevitably, the sense of self shifted from secure (if defensive) cohesion to the generativity of fatherhood and incipient fragmentation, tactics had to be devised to overcome the threat. The primary way this was accomplished, as recorded in the Upanisads, and to some extent earlier, involved a regression in fantasy to the mother, or more exactly to the stage of empathic merger with her, so that the fragmented self ('ashes') could be renewed and reborn whole. Gradually, the *parent* half of this primitive union became also identified with the self and was referred to as the 'immortal' part of Prajapati, or his 'unimanifested' part. This maternal *source of the self* was reinterpreted in a concept of the *self as source*. The historical antecedent of this move is the 'three-fourths' of the Cosmic Man which is 'immortal life in heaven' in the Purusasukta of the *Rig Veda* (X.90). It is as if one part of the self gave birth to the other part. The self became the origin of everything in an absolute denial of dependency on anything, including *its own* source. Like Kipling's Kim when he finds himself alone, the *atman* is afraid because he has no second; although he talks himself out of it, it is clear that aloneness makes him afraid of falling apart, of losing his sense of self.

The situation has the appearance of Kohut's 'vertical split,' a defensive stance of denying need for a genuine other through unconscious merger with the parent image. (See the diagram in Kohut, 1977, p.213.) The person characterized by a vertical split is often overtly grandiose, isolated and self-sufficient. For Kohut there is an underlying mother image which confirms his sense of superiority provided that the person does not try to become independent of it. In the Vedic material the Waters are like the mother who mirrors, while father Prajapati or the Sacrificer resembles the continually emitting narcissistic self. On the other side of the vertical split, according to Kohut, is a sense of being empty and ineffective, depressed and isolated, i.e., cut off from the affirming maternal mirror. The person presumes to a merger on one side of the split which he 'really' knows (on the other side) to be disastrously absent. Prajapati's state of chaotic disarray after creation, when he becomes disarticulated and 'emptied out,' resembles the depressed, empty side of Kohut's vertical split; in Prajapati's life it periodically alternates with the state of inflated greatness and completion.

When the Upanisads interiorized the source of goods in the absolute *atman* which put an end to alternation, there must have been a sense of tremendous psychic victory. It would have seemed as if nothing was needed from outside, and the danger of falling periodically away from the state of inner fullness was obviated for one and all. 'I-ness' could be experienced free from the constant need for repair and renewal. As the Hindu philosopher Sankara is supposed to have said a thousand years later, 'Behold I! Obeisance to Me who need nothing.'

CONCLUSION

The Indian vision of personality is one that finds the self embedded essentially in a world of self-objects, towards which it turns constantly and eagerly, but which it introjects or incorporates when necessary to preserve a threatened sense of self-world mutuality. At times in Indian thought much of what modern western psychology thinks of as the 'inner' personality structure is conceived as outside the self, while at other times more or less of the 'outer' world is understood as within the self. 'Inside' and 'outside' are defined in terms of appropriateness, not physical ('real') location. That which is more alike, homogeneous or fitting is treated as nearer while that which is less homogeneous and fitting and more unlike is seen as farther out. Meissner's understanding of introjects as 'inner' structures which are felt as partially outside is parallel to the Indian view, as is his treatment of projections that are in a way felt to be within. When this process of self-world adjustment fails, the move towards an objectless inner *atman* may occur, at a philosophical level, and various forms of split-level consciousness at an experiential level.

Western, and in particular classical psychoanalytic ideals of stable, permanent individuality based on identifications with and respect for the unalterability of the environment are foreign to the Indian perspective. The Indian personality and world are more fluid, blending together at times, while at other times (or even at the same time) an interior core of the self is held aloof with practiced detachment. We are tempted to say that the two cultures provide contexts in which particular myths of the self are pursued. Western psychology has idealized a myth of autonomy, whereas Indian thought idealizes the myth of merger. While the *atman* ideal seems to contradict this, offering an image of absolute isolation and renunciation of the world, we have seen that the *atman*, too, can only be understood in the context of the *ahamkara*-self and its various sorts of appropriateness and cohesiveness; in particular in its failures to maintain these.

NOTES

1 As Hanly and Masson (1976) point out, the expression and concept derive from the Indian mystic Sri Ramakrishna, about whom Rolland wrote extensively.
2 Personal observation: Collins, 1968–71.
3 As Carl Rogers (1961) similarly writes, one's self-feeling becomes constrained by 'conditions of worth' laid down by others, and one may get locked into an unconsciously accepted role at variance with one's 'real self.' Optimally, the I-ness will become stably identified with a fairly broad sense of family and occupational identity, and will be flexible enough to include other aspects of I-feeling when required by a changing environment of the developmental process.
4 These include 'idealizing self-object relationships, where the child's sense of self participates in the idealized image of the parent, and which develop into internal ideals, and mirroring self-object relations,' where the child's sense of self is magnified and reflected back to itself by the parent; these become ambitions (Kohut, 1971).
5 Brhadaranyaka *Upanisad* I.5.17.
6 Freud's 1914 discussion of narcissism is relevant here.

REFERENCES

Aitareya Aranyaka. Text and Translation: A.B. Keith, ed. and tr. (1909). Oxford: Oxford University Press.
Atharvaveda. Text: R. Roth and W.D. Whitney, eds. *Atharvaveda Samhita*. Bonn Ferd. Dummlers Verlag. Translation: W.D. Whitney, tr., *Atharvaveda Samhita*. Cambridge: Harvard University Press.
Bhagavad Gita. Text and Translation: J.A.B. VanBuitenen, ed. and tr., *The Bhagavadgita in the Mahabharata* (1981). Chicago and London: University of Chicago Press.
Biardeau, M. (1965). '*Ahamkara*, the ego principle in the Upanisads.' *Contributions to Indian Sociology*, 8, 62–84.
Brhadaranyaka Upanisad. Text: S. Radhakrishnan, *The Principal Upanisads* (1969). London: Allen & Unwin. Translation: R.E. Hume, tr., *The Thirteen Principal Upanisads* (1971). New York: Oxford University Press.
Carstairs, G.M. (1957). *The Twice-Born: A Study of a Community of High Caste Hindus*. Bloomington: Indiana University Press.

Collins, A. (1976). *The Origins of the Brahman–King Relationship in Indian Social Thought*. Ph.D. Dissertation, University of Texas at Austin.

Dasgupta, S.N. (1965). *A History of Indian Philosophy*, vol. I. Cambridge: Cambridge University Press.

Desai, P. (1971). 'Western Science of Psychiatry and the Hindu Mind.' *India Digest* 1, 43–6.

Desai, P. (1980). 'Psychoanalysis and the Hindu Psyche.' Paper presented at the Institute for Psychoanalysis, Chicago, 22 October.

Desai, P. and Coelho, G. (1980). 'Indian immigrants in America: Some cultural aspects of psychological adaptation.' In *The New Ethics: Asian Indians in the United States*. P. Saran and E. Eames, eds., New York: Praeger.

Dumont, L. (1970). *Homo Hierarchicus: The Caste System and its Implications*. London: Weidenfeld & Nicolson.

Erikson, E.H. (1968). *Identity Youth and Crisis*.. New York: W.W. Norton.

Erikson, E.H. (1981). 'The Galilean sayings and the sense of "I," ' *The Yale Review*, 70, 321–62.

Fenichel, O. (1945). *The Psychoanalytic Theory of Neurosis*. New York: W.W. Norton.

Freud, S. (1914). 'On Narcissism: an introduction.' *S.E. 14*, 69.

Freud, S. (1915). 'Instincts and their vicissitudes.' *S.E. 14*, 111.

Freud, S. (1917). 'Mourning and Melancholia.' *S.E. 14,* 239.

Freud, S. (1930). 'Civilization and its Discontents.' *S.E. 21*, 59.

Gedo, J. (1979). *Beyond Interpretation*, New York: International Universities Press.

Gonda, J. (1975). *Vedic Literature (Samhitas and Brahmanas)*. Weisbaden: Harrassowitz.

Hanly, C.M. and Masson, J. (1976). A critical examination of the new narcissism. *International Journal of Psycho-Analysis*. 57, 49–66.

Hartmann, H. (1964). *Essays on Ego Psychology*. New York: International Universities Press.

Heesterman, J.C. (1957). *The Ancient Indian Royal Consecration*. The Hague: Mouton.

Heesterman, J.C. (1962). 'Vratya and Sacrifice.' *Indo-Iranian Journal*, 6, 1–37.

Heesterman, J.C. (1964). 'Brahman, Ritual and Renouncer.' *Wiener Zeitschrift fur Kunde Sud und Ost-asiens*, 8, 1–21.

Hulin, M. (1978). *Le Principe de L'Ego dans la Pensée Indienne Classique: La Notion d'Ahamkara*. Paris: Editions de Boccard.

Inden, R. and Marriott, M. (1977). 'Toward an Ethno-sociology of South Asian Caste Systems.' In K.A. David, ed., *The New Wind; Changing Identities in South Asia*. The Hague: Mouton.

James, W. (1980). *The Principles of Psychology*. New York: Holt, Rinehart & Winston.

Kakar, S. (1980). 'Observations on the "Oedipal alliance" in a patient with a narcissistic personality disorder.' *Samiksa*, 34, 47–53.

Selfhood in context

Kakar, S. (1981). *The Inner World: A Psycho-analytic Study of Childhood and Society in India* (second edition). Delhi: Oxford University Press.
Kane, P.V. (1973). *History of Dharmasastra*, vol. 4 (second edition). Poona: Bhandarkar Oriental Research Institute.
Kernberg, O. (1975). *Borderline Conditions and Pathological Narcissism*. New York: Jason Aronson.
Knipe, D.M. (1977). Sapindikarana: The Hindu rite of entry into heaven.' In F.E. Reynolds and E.H. Waugh, eds., *Religious Encounters with Death: Insights from the History and Anthropology of Religions*. University Park: University of Pennsylvania Press.
Kohut, H. (1971). *The Analysis of the Self*. New York: International University Press.
Kohut, H. (1977). 'The Restoration of the Self, Selected writings of Heinz Kohut: 1950–1978' (2 volumes), edited by Paul H. Ornstein New York: International Universities Press.
Kuiper, F.B.J. (1975). 'The basic concept of Vedic religion.' *History of Religions*, 15, 107–20.
Lacombe, Oliver (1939). *L'Absolu selon la Vendanta*. Paris: Gallimard.
Laplanche, J. and Ontalis, J.B. (1973). *The Language of Psycho-analysis*. New York: W.W. Norton.
Marriott, M. (1976). 'Hindu transactions: diversity without dualism'. In B. Kapferer, ed., *Transaction and Meaning: Directions in the Anthropology of Exchange and Symbolic Behavior*. Philadelphia: Institute for the Study of Human Issues.
Marriott, M. (1980). *The open Hindu person and interpersonal fluidity*. Unpublished manuscript.
Masson, J. and Patwardhan, M.V. (1969). *Santarasa and Abhinavagupta's Philosophy of Aesthetics*. Poona: Bhandarkar Oriental Research Institute.
Meissner, W.W. (1980). 'The problem of internationalization and structure formation'. *International Journal of Psycho-Analysis*, 61, 237–48.
Meissner, W.W. (1981). *Internalization in Psychoanalysis*. New York: International Universities Press.
Mus, P. (1956) 'La stance de la Plénitude', *Bull, de l'école Française d'External Orient* 44, 591–613.
Paraskara Grhya Sutra. Translation: H. Oldenberg, tr., *The Grhya-Sutras* (1964). Delhi: Motilal.
Ramanujam, B.K. (1980). *Odyssey of an Indian villager: mythic orientations in psychotherapy*. Paper presented at the First Workshop of the Person in South Asia project sponsored by the ACLS-SSRC Joint Committee on South Asia, Chicago, September 1977.
Ramanujan, A.K. (1972). The Indian Oedipus. In A. Podder, ed., *Indian Literature*, proceeding of a Seminar. Simla.
Ramanujan, A.K. (1980). 'Is there an Indian way of thinking? An informal essay.' Paper presented at the First Workshop of the ACLS-SSRCC Joint Committee on South Asia sponsored by Person in South Asia, project, Chicago, September 16.
Renou, L. (1951). 'On the word *atman*.' *Vak*, No. 1, 151–7.

Renou, L. (1953). *Religions of Ancient India*. New York: Schocken.

Renou, L. (1956). *Hymnes Spéculatifs du Veda*. Paris: Gallimard.

Reynolds, H.B. (1980). 'The auspicious married woman.' In S.S. Wadley (ed.) *The Powers of Tamil Women*.

Rig Veda. Text: T. Aufrecht, ed., *Die Hymnen des Rigveda*. (1968). Wiesbaden: Harrassowitz. Translation: K.F. Geldner, tr., *Der Rig-veda aus dem Sanskrit ins Deutsche Ubursertzt* (1951). Cambridge: Harvard University Press.

Rogers, C. (1961). *On Becoming a Person: A Therapist's View of Psychotherapy*. Boston: Houghton Mifflin.

Roland, A. (1980a). 'Psychoanalytic perspectives on personality development in India.' *International Review of Psychoanalysis*, 7, 73–88.

Roland, A. (1980b). *The Indian Family Self in its Social and Cultural Contexts*. Unpublished manuscript.

Roland, A. (1981). *Towards a Psychoanalytic Psychology of Hierarchical relationships in Hindu India*. Unpublished manuscript.

Roy, Manisha (1972). *Bengali Women*, Chicago: University of Chicago Press.

Satapatha Brahmana.Text: A. Weber, ed., *The Satapatha-Brahmana in the Madhyandina-Sakha* (1964). Varanasi: Chowkhamba Sanskrit Series. Translation: J. Eggeling, tr., *Satapatha-Brahmana, According to the Text of the Madhyandina School* (1966). Delhi: Motilal.

Segal, H. (1980). *Melanie Klein*. New York: Viking Press.

Simon, B. and Weiner, H. (1966). 'Models of mind and mental illness in ancient Greece: I. the Homeric model of mind.' *Journal of the History of the Behavioral Sciences*, 2, 303–14.

van Buitenen, J.A.B. (1957). Studies in Samkhya (II): Ahamkara. *Journal of the American Oriental Society*, 77.

Winnicott, D.W. (1971). *Playing and reality*. New York: Basic Books.

Zimmer, H. (1946). *Myths and Symbols in Indian Art and Civilization*. New York: Bollingen Foundation.

Zimmerman, F. (1975). 'Rtu-satmya: le cycle des saisons et le principe d'appropriation.' *Purusartha*. 2, 87–105.

Appendix

PROJECT ON HUMAN POTENTIAL

Harvard Graduate School of Education

ARCHIVE

Cross cultural research papers

Acha, Juan, 'Nuestro Potencial Cognoscitivo de la Realidad Artistica,' March 1983.

Anandalakshymy, S., 'Biographing a Grandfather: Family Reportage and Personal Documents,' June, 1982.

Anumonye, Amechi, 'West African Healing in Mental Health in Urban Areas,' January, 1983.

Arango, Marta and Nimnicht, Glen, 'Organizing Environments to Enhance the Development of Persons and Communities in Isolated Regions of Colombia: A Challenge to the Development of Human Potential,' March 1983.*

Ba, Cheikh, 'Pedagogy of Nature and Modernization Among the Pastoral Societies of the Peul in Senegal,' January 1983.

Bakare, Christopher C.M., 'The Development of African Children in Early Childhood: The Mother's Role,' January 1983.

Barry, Boubacar, 'The Foundations of Regional Unity in Senegambia During the 15th and 16th Centuries,' January 1983.

Das, Veena, 'The Work of Mourning: Death in a Punjabi Family,' to appear in *The Cultural Transition. . .* PHP, 1985.*

Davis-Friedmann, Deborah, 'Current Chinese Approaches to Issues in Human Development: A Preliminary Foray', December 1980 (working draft).

Desai, Prakash and Collins, Alfred, 'Selfhood in Context: Some Indian Solutions,' to appear in *The Cultural Transition . . .* PHP, 1986.*

Desai, Prakash, N., 'Indian Psychotherapist in Training,' June 1982.

Desai, Prakash, 'Learning Psychotherapy: A Cultural Perspective,' June 1982.

Ekejiuba, Felicia, 'At the Frontiers of Change: Patterns of Responses of Nigerian Women to Opportunities and Challenges of Social Change,' January 1983.

Fulton, Paul, R., 'Indigenous Psychologies of Self and its Development,' May 1983.*

291

Appendix

Garcia Rivera, Carlos H., 'Analisis Comparativo de Los Perfiles de Los Ejecutivos,' March 1983.

Gordon, Leonie, Strauss, Claudia, Taniuchi, Lois and White, Merry; 'Workshop on Healing, Personal Transformation and the Life Course in India,' June 1982.

Gordon, Leonie and White, Merry I., 'China Workshop,' May 1982.

Gordon Leonie and White, Merry I., 'Japan Workshop,' May 1982.

Gordon, Leonie and Staff of Project on Human Potential, 'Workshop on African Models of Human Development,' January 1983.

Gordon, Leonie, 'Education in China: Traditional and Modern'.

Hoch, Erna, M., 'Attitudes and Expectations with Regard to Health and Healing of Illiterate Mountain Peasants in India,' June 1982.

Iwao, Sumiko, 'Skills and Life Strategies of Japanese Business Women,' to appear in *The Cultural Transition* . . . PHP, 1986.*

Kadja Mianno, Daniel, 'Une Problématique Sociologique du sens des mouvements religieux en Afrique de l'Oest (L'Exemple de la Côte d'Ivoire),' November 1982.

Kadja Mianno, Daniel, 'Les Mouvements Religieux en Afrique de l'Ouest,' January 1983.

Kakar, Sudhir, 'Person and Personal Transformation in Tantra,' June 1982.

Kakar, Sudhir, 'Psychotherapy and Culture: Healing in the Indian Tradition,' to appear in *The Cultural Transition* . . . PHP, 1986.*

Katz, Richard, 'Healing and Transformation Perspectives on Education, Development and Community,' to appear in *The Cultural Transition*. . . PHP, 1986.*

LeVine, Robert A., 'The Self in Culture I: Person-Centered Ethnography and Psychoanalytic Anthropology,' October 1980.*

LeVine, Robert A., 'The Social Conditions of Child Development: An Historical and Comparative Perspective,' December 1980.

LeVine, Robert A., 'Cultural Variations in Ethnography,' January 1981 (preliminary notes).

LeVine, Robert A., 'Statement for Workshop on the Anthropology of Human Fertility,' February 1981.

Lutz, Catherine and LeVine, Robert A., 'Culture and Intelligence in Infancy: An Ethnopsychological View,' January 1982.

Magana, Paul and Pliego, Jose, 'Percepcion del Entorno y Participacion de La Comunidad Como Un Enfoque Al Dessarrollo Humano,' March 1983.

Miklos, Tomas, 'Anticipando el Futuro,' March 1983.

Miklos, Tomas, 'Potencial Humano,' March 1983.

Nieto-Cardoso, Ezequiel, 'La Investigacion Cientifica y sus Condicionamientos Sociales, Una Introduccion Critica,' March 1983.

Pollak, Susan, 'Traditional Jewish Learning Philosophy and Practice,' December 1981 (working draft).*

Pollak, Susan, 'Traditional Islamic Education,' March 1982 (working draft).*

Pollak, Susan, 'Traditional Indian Education,' April 1982.*

Pollak, Susan, 'Of Monks and Men: Sacred and Secular Education in the Middle Ages,' December 1982.*

Pollak, Susan, 'Ancient Buddhist Education,' April 1983.*

Pollak, Susan, 'Quranic Schooling: Setting, Context and Process,' May 1983.*

Pria, Maria Teresa, 'Taller Sobre Potencial Humano,' March 1983.

Quintanilla C., Josefina, I., 'Hacia Una Madurez Permanente Un Modelo Mexicano de Preparacion a la Jubilacion,' March 1983.

Ramanujam, B.K., 'The Indian Family: Patterns and Process,' March 1980.

Ramanujam, B.K., 'Response to Social Change in India,' June 1982.

Ramanujam, B.K., 'Social Change and Personal Crisis: A View from an Indian Practice,' to appear in *The Cultural Transition* . . . PHP, 1986.*

Ramanujam, B.K., 'Technical Issues of Psychotherapy in India'.

Ramanujam, B.K., 'India: A Case Study'.

Ramanujam, B.K., 'Odyssey of an Indian Villager: Mythic Orientations in Psychotherapy.'

Sanneh, Lamin, 'Source and Influence: A Comparative Approach to Religion and Culture,' April 1983 to appear in *The Cultural Transition* . . . PHP, 1986.*

Sanneh, Lamin, 'Healing and Conversion in New Religious Movements in Africa: Elements of an Indigenous Epistemology,' January 1983.*

Shiang, Julia, 'Heart' and Self in Old Age: A Chinese Model,' to appear in *The Cultural Transition*. . . PHP, 1985.*

Sidibe, B.K. and Galloway, Winifred, F., 'Senegambian Traditional Families,' January 1983.

Sidibe, B.K. and Galloway, Winifred, F., 'Women in Traditional Gambian Society – Past, Present and Future,' January 1983.

Spratt, Jennifer and Wagner, Daniel, 'The Making of a Fqih,' to appear in *The Cultural Transition*. . . PHP, 1985.*

Taniuchi, Lois K., 'The Creation of Prodigies Through Special Education: Three Case Studies,' March 1980.

Taniuchi, Lois K., 'Psychological Themes in Japanese Mother–Child Socialization and Their Influences on Other Indigenous Learning Situations,' April 1981 (working draft).

Taniuchi, Lois K., 'Talent Education: A Case Study of Cultural Adaptation,' to appear in *The Cultural Transition*. . . PHP, 1985.*

Taniuchi, Lois, White, Merry and Pollak, Susan, 'Draft Summary Bernard van Leer Project on Human Potential Workshop on United States and Japanese Perspectives on Potential,' July 15–21, 1981.

Vasco, Carlos E., 'Learning Elementary School Mathematics as a Culturally Conditioned Process,' to appear in *The Cultural Transition*. . . PHP, 1986.*

Vasco, Carlos E., 'Tagging Along with the Urban Poor in Colombia 1973–1983,' March 1983.*

White, Merry I. and Taniuchi, Lois K., 'The Anatomy of the Hara: Japanese Self in Society,' May 1980 (working draft).*

Appendix

White, Merry I., 'Workshop on Human Potential,' Cairo, Egypt, January 1982.

INDEX

297